ANTIRACIST MEDIEVALISMS

ARC MEDIEVALIST

Series Editors

Nadia Altschul, *University of Glasgow*
Josh Davies, *King's College London*

Further Information and Publications

www.arc-humanities.org/our-series/arc/am/

ANTIRACIST MEDIEVALISMS

FROM "YELLOW PERIL" TO BLACK LIVES MATTER

by
JONATHAN HSY

British Library Cataloguing in Publication Data

A catalogue record for this book is available from the British Library.

© 2021, Arc Humanities Press, Leeds

ISBN (print): 9781641893145
e-ISBN (PDF): 9781641893152

www.arc-humanities.org
Printed and bound in the UK (by CPI Group [UK] Ltd), USA (by Bookmasters),
and elsewhere using print-on-demand technology.

For Dad, Viv, and Colin
and to family,
in all senses of the word

CONTENTS

LIST OF ILLUSTRATIONS

Preface

COALITIONS, SOLIDARITIES, AND ACKNOWLEDGMENTS

THIS BOOK TELLS stories of collective struggle against racism, from campaigns against xenophobia during the global era of anti-Asian "Yellow Peril" in the late nineteenth century to the transnational Black Lives Matter movement today. In this study, I use medievalism—which I define as a critical analysis of the Middle Ages, as well as the artistic reinvention of medieval pasts in literature and culture—to trace efforts by communities of color to critique longstanding systems of white supremacy and to advance new forms of social justice.

As I discuss in this book's introduction, the coopting of medieval imagery and rhetoric by modern extremist groups for racist, antisemitic, and Islamophobic aims has been carefully contextualized and resoundingly denounced by scholars of color in recent years.[1] *Antiracist Medievalisms* shows that people of color have been addressing the relationship between white supremacy and the historical or imagined Middle Ages for a very long time, and nuanced intellectual and artistic forms of antiracist critique by people of color date as far back as the very emergence of medieval studies as a discipline.

When I first set out to write this book, I had assumed that academics in the predominantly white field of medieval studies would comprise my primary audience. I did, after all, write this book in English, the *lingua franca* of my disciplinary training in medieval British literature and the cultural reception of medieval traditions—and the conventional centers of power and prestige in medieval studies are still located within predominantly white anglophone countries. Over time, my sense of the book's audience began to shift. What would happen if I wrote a book about antiracism in my discipline that directly addressed people of color and racialized communities more broadly, wherever such readers are situated? Could I bring my academic and cultural background as a queer Asian American not only to the professional field of medieval studies in which I happen to work, but also to the concurrent marginalized communities in which I belong? This book, which draws upon the writings of queer scholars of color and intersectional feminist scholarship, has become an effort to reshape the field of medieval studies from how it is conventionally configured by bringing academic and activist communities together.[2] My work tells a range of stories of communities of color working collectively to advance racial justice.

---

1 See this book's introduction.

2 For first-person reflections by medievalists from intersecting marginalized communities, see: Arvas, McCannon, and Trujillo, ed., "Critical Confessions Now"; Rambaran-Olm, Leake, and Goodrich, ed., "Race, Revulsion, and Revolution."

My research related to this project and my writing of this book was completed prior to two significant geopolitical events in the first half of the year 2020: the global spread of the COVID-19 (coronavirus) pandemic, and the transnational resurgence of the Black Lives Matter movement with protests against anti-Black racism and police violence that were set in motion after the killing of George Floyd. As I write this preface (in July 2020), these conjoined worldwide events continue to impact communities of color in complex and divergent ways. As the COVID-19 pandemic began to spread internationally beyond its first reported cases in the city of Wuhan in China, the wide circulation of xenophobic and anti-Asian phrases such as "Chinese Virus" and "Kung Flu" throughout the UK, Canada, the US, Australia, and European countries have contributed to an atmosphere of racist scapegoating and hostility toward people perceived to be of East Asian ancestry.[3] Those of us living in predominantly white countries who identify as Asian in some way (or who could be perceived as such) can find our fears of racist violence confirmed not only by our own lived experiences,[4] but also by quantitative studies documenting a rise in anti-Asian hate incidents including acts of physical harm.[5] Within these same predominantly white countries, Black communities remain vulnerable not only to police violence on a daily basis but also to disproportionately high rates of death (relative to white peers) due to the coronavirus pandemic. Black, Indigenous, and Latinx communities are especially harmed by both the medical and socioeconomic impacts of the crisis in the US,[6] while Black, Asian, and Minority Ethnic (BAME) groups in the UK have been found to be, according to an analysis of data by the University College London, "two to three times more likely to die from COVID-19 compared to the general population."[7]

In the midst of these ongoing crises, I find myself encouraged by how communities of color are supporting one another locally and globally in collective struggles—even if the particular combination of harms that each group faces is not identical. In my own neighborhood of Capitol Hill in Washington, DC, leaders of cultural institutions representing Black communities and histories have expressed solidarity with Asian Americans by publicly denouncing anti-Asian hate. Lonnie G. Bunch III, Secretary of the Smithsonian Institution and the founding director of the Smithsonian National Museum of African American History and Culture (NMAAHC), stated in the context of commemorating Asian American and Pacific Islander Heritage Month in May 2020 that "Asian Americans are facing increased racism and hate crimes while also serving on the front lines in this [pandemic] crisis."[8] In the context of promoting NMAAHC's new online resources

---

3 Zhang, "Racism Hinders the Fight against COVID-19"; Wong, "Sinophobia Won't Save you from the Coronavirus"; Chao-Fong, "Anti-Chinese Abuse"; Yu Danico, "Anti-Asian Racism During COVID-19."

4 Chao-Fong, "Anti-Chinese Abuse"; Kambhampaty and Sakaguchi, "I Will Not Stand Silent"; Lau, "On Virality."

5 Raukko and Poon, "Asian American Outlook"; ong and Zhang, *Anti-Asian Racism*.

6 APM [American Public Media] Research Lab Staff, "Color of Coronavirus"; Oppel et al., "Racial Inequity of Coronavirus"; Taylor, "Black Plague."

7 Godin, "Black and Asian People," referring to England specifically.

8 Lonnie G. Bunch III, Twitter post, May 19, 2020, 10:06 a.m., https://twitter.com/SmithsonianSec/status/1262746438204657666.

for national conversations about race and racism since the George Floyd protests began, Bunch remarked: "We find ourselves in a period of profound social change, grappling with the dual pandemics of COVID-19 and deep-rooted racism" (the words "we" and "ourselves" in this instance inviting a range of potential racial and social positionings inclusive of Black Americans as well as allied communities).[1]

During local Black Lives Matter marches and community rallies since the George Floyd protests began here in Washington, DC, I have witnessed fellow Asian Americans among varied non-Black protestors from disparate racial, ethnic, and religious backgrounds coming together to take a collective stance against anti-Black violence, and Asian Americans are seeking to address anti-Blackness within our own communities and act in solidarity with Black communities against systemic racism.[2] Meanwhile, webinars and crowdsourced reading lists on Black/Asian solidarities such as those organized by Black Women Radicals and the Asian American Feminist Collective foreground multiple genealogies of Black/Asian coalitions within the US and across the globe,[3] and scholarship on such solidarity movements among people of color more broadly is vital for understanding how communities can work together against the combined harms of systemic racism, socioeconomic and gender injustice, and global white supremacy.[4]

The dynamism of solidarity endeavors in the current geopolitical and cultural landscape has made me think very carefully about the seeming incompatibility of my professional identity as a medieval literary and cultural historian with my personal identity as an activist committed to antiracist movements today. In a time of global pandemic and ongoing struggles against systemic racism (literally urgent issues of life and death), why should I—or anyone—make a "retreat" into the past, or engage in the apparent luxury of researching historical phenomena so distant from the here and now? My hope is that this book, which explores divergent forms of medievalism from the late nineteenth century to the present day, demonstrates that thinking about the Middle Ages need not entail a nostalgic escape from modernity into an allegedly simpler time (with all the racial, gendered, and classed implications thereof). Rather, this book promotes a deeper understanding of the medieval past as heterogeneous and complex in its own right, and my work centers a long and underacknowledged history of literary and cultural reimaginations of medieval pasts—crafted by people of color—in pursuit of racial justice.

It remains to be seen where the international Black Lives Matter movement will head from this point, and how the longstanding systems of socioeconomic and racial inequality and so-called "health disparities" that disproportionately impact Black communities and other communities of color will be addressed on a global scale.[5] It is my hope that this book's focus on Black and non-Black communities of color, among other

---

1 Bunch, "Recovery and Resilience."

2 Ebrahimji and Lee, "Asian Americans Uproot Racism"; Basu, "Asian Americans Explain Racism."

3 Black Women Radicals and the Asian American Feminist Collective, "A Reading List" (see "Further Readings and Resources" at the end of this book).

4 Bae and Tseng-Putterman, "Black-Asian Internationalism"; Blain, "Roots of Afro-Asia"; Itagaki, *Civil Racism*; Onishi, *Transpacific Antiracism*; Wu, *Radicals on the Road*.

5 Brooks, "African Americans Struggle"; Randall, "Asian Americans Suffer."

vulnerable racialized groups, can offer readers a fuller appreciation for the vitality of solidarity movements across time and also serve as a reminder of the transformative potentials of navigating past and present.

Some of my initial research and writing related to this book has been presented at academic conferences, such as the MLA (Modern Language Association) International Symposium on "Remembering Voices Lost" in Lisbon, Portugal (July 2019), "Race in the Middle Ages: A Symposium," hosted by Saint Joseph's University in Philadelphia, PA (March 2019), and the conference entitled "Celebrating Belle da Costa Greene: An Examination of Medievalists of Color within the Field," organized by Tarrell Campbell and held at Saint Louis University, in Saint Louis, MO (November 2018). My research was partially supported by grants from The George Washington University, including a Columbian College Facilitating Fund Award and an Enhanced Faculty Travel Award from the Columbian College of Arts & Sciences.

Additional research for this book was conducted at the Angel Island Immigration Station (San Francisco), Chinese Historical Society of America Museum (San Francisco), Migration Museum (London), Chinese American Museum of Chicago, Le Musée de f.p.c. (New Orleans), Museum of Chinese Australian History (Melbourne), Museum of Chinese in America (New York), and Wing Luke Museum of the Asian Pacific American Experience (Seattle).

I would like to acknowledge and thank scholars of color whose in-person and virtual conversations related to this project—in addition to considerable intellectual, institutional, and emotional support in "doing the work" of antiracist activism—have proven invaluable as I wrote this book: Seeta Chaganti and Cord J. Whitaker especially. I also thank Patricia Akhimie, Tarren Andrews, Daniel Atherton, Manu Samriti Chander, Jennifer Chang (and students in our team-taught "ABCs of Poetry" course in Fall 2015), Patricia P. Chu, Kavita Daiya, Amrita Dhar, Marisa Galvez, Kim F. Hall, Carissa M. Harris, Geraldine Heng, Lynn Mie Itagaki, Jennifer C. James, Wan-Chuan Kao, Dorothy Kim, Travis Chi Wing Lau, Erika T. Lin, Sierra Lomuto, Myra Lotto, Afrodesia McCannon, Kimberly D. McKee, Adam Miyashiro, Erin O'Malley, Lisa Page, Atiba K. Pertilla, Shokoofeh Rajabzadeh, Shyama Rajendran, Ayanna Thompson, and Sydnee Wagner—and many more who will find themselves cited throughout this book.

I give thanks not only to individuals but also to communities working to support academic and activist endeavors concurrently: the Medievalists of Color, the Society for Medieval Feminist Scholarship, and the Queerdievalists; the #RaceB4Race, #MedievalTwitter, #ShakeRace, #Bigger6, and #LitPOC communities on Twitter; the translators, poets, artists, and scholars throughout the *Global Chaucers* network; my fellow co-bloggers at *In the Middle* and its online network; the Crip/Queer Reading Group at The George Washington University; and the Association for Asian American Studies Feminisms Workshop.

Thanks also to Gabriel García Román for permission to use a work from the luminous "Queer Icons" series on the cover of this book. To find out more about the artist, this series, and the subject depicted in this particular work, see "About the Cover."

I am grateful to Arc Humanities Press for the careful and attentive reader reports that I received for this book, which all helped me to improve its overall structure and arguments. The press's support for this book reflects a generous and open-minded intellectual mindset, particularly in contrast to other responses to this project that found its medievalist orientation too restricted for a general study or perceived lesser-known Chinese diaspora authors and anonymous migrants as insufficiently canonical by Eurocentric standards to merit close attention. I am hopeful that this book will introduce readers to a wide range of authors, and critical conversations, that they have not yet previously considered.

Washington, DC, July 2020

About the Cover

The image on this book's cover is used with the permission of queer "left-handed Mexican-Amaricón artist" Gabriel García Román,[6] whose "Queer Icons" series portrays contemporary people of color "drawn from many facets of the gender and queer spectrum" in a visual style that incorporates influences from premodern religious iconography.[7] "From the queer Latina fighting for immigration rights to the non-binary disabled Trans Filipino, the artist perceived these figures as heroes in their own right,"[8] and just as "traditional religious paintings conferred a sense of safety and meditative calm on a home," so does this series "aspire to provide a similar sense of refuge that's drawn from the inner grace of the subjects and projected outwards onto a world that might not be safe."[9] For more, visit http://www.gabrielgarciaroman.com/queer-icons-home.

The subject of this artwork and creator of the text incorporated into the image, Alán Pelaez Lopez,[10] is a queer Black Zapotec poet and multimedia artist from the Coastal Zapotec community of what is now known as Oaxaca, México.[11] Their writings include *Intergalactic Travels: poems from a fugitive alien* (The Operating System, 2020) and *to love and mourn in the age of displacement* (Nomadic Press, 2020). They are on Instagram and Twitter as @MigrantScribble.[12] For more, visit http://www.alanpelaez.com.

A Note on Citations

This book foregrounds the intellectual labor, cultural perspectives, and sociopolitical investments of communities of color. Authorities and authors named in the body of the text are all people of color, with the exception of a few individuals (such as nineteenth-century authors or politicians) who are quoted as background context. As queer theorist and critical race scholar Sara Ahmed states in her book that exclusively cites feminists of

---

6 García Román, "About."

7 García Román, "Queer Icons."

8 Ibid.

9 Ibid. See also Singh, "Not Your Mother's Catholic Frescoes"; Glasgow, "Q&A."

10 García Román, "ALAN: Alán Pelaez Lopez."

11 Pelaez Lopez, "About Me." See also Twitter post by @MigrantScribble, July 23, 2020. https://twitter.com/MigrantScribble/status/1286398717105340416

12 On the art and activism of Pelaez Lopez, see Noel, "Queer Migrant Poemics."

color: "Citation is how we acknowledge our debt to those who came before; those who helped us find our way when the way was obscured because we deviated from the paths we were told to follow." Sara Ahmed, *Living a Feminist Life* (Durham: Duke University Press, 2017), 15–16.

A Note on Hyphens

In this book, I use hyphenated identity terms only in quotations or if I refer to historical terms with significance for communities of color (e.g., "Afro-Caribbean," "Anglo-African," etc.). In order to acknowledge the flexibility of identities that cannot be constrained by national borders nor reduced to subcategories of a mainstream culture, I never hyphenize compound identity phrases in my own prose (e.g., "African American," "Chinese American," "Arab American," etc., in all instances).

Introduction

PERFORMING MEDIEVALISM, CRAFTING IDENTITIES

ONE OF THE most rewarding aspects of being an educator is learning from students and collectively creating new kinds of knowledge in the classroom. I teach medieval literature among other topics in an urban campus in Washington, DC, with a student body that includes a significant share of international students as well as American students from varied racial, religious, and ethnic backgrounds. Such a campus environment can generate animated conversations—particularly on the topics of race and social justice.

In a recent iteration of my course on the poetry of Geoffrey Chaucer and modern-day adaptations of his works, one of our required texts was *Telling Tales*, a literary anthology by Nigerian British poet and spoken-word performance artist Patience Agbabi.[1] In Chaucer's *The Canterbury Tales*, a group of pilgrims varied in gender, age, social rank, geographical origins, and occupations engage in a storytelling contest, and Agbabi transforms Chaucer's medieval pilgrimage into a multiracial cast of storytellers in present-day London. "Sharps an Flats,"[2] Agbabi's spoken-word counterpoint to Chaucer's antisemitic "Prioress's Tale," sparked a wide-ranging class discussion about modern racial violence and harmful legacies of the medieval past.

By this point in the semester, our class had already read Chaucer's "Prioress's Tale" in the original Middle English, and we had discussed our various uneasy reactions to his antisemitic story of violence set in an unspecified multiethnic Asian city inhabited by Christians and Jews.[3] The Prioress recounts the martyrdom of a young Christian boy, and she presents her entire versified performance as if it were an extended song of prayer to the Virgin Mary; all the while, she circulates disturbing medieval stereotypes that vilify her story's Jewish characters and the narrative concludes with a state-sanctioned killing of Jews en masse.[4] Agbabi, by contrast, assigns her spoken-word poem "Sharps an Flats" to a fictive Afro-Caribbean social justice activist in Britain who relates a story that gives posthumous voice to an individual Black victim of unprovoked violence in modern London.[5]

Agbabi's choice to transport Chaucer's story into a radically new sociopolitical context generated a range of responses in the classroom. Some of the students who identified as African American and as Afro-Caribbean, and who were familiar with the conventions of spoken-word poetry in the US, welcomed Agbabi's engagements with social jus-

---

1 Agbabi, *Telling Tales*.

2 Ibid., 81–82.

3 Chaucer, *Canterbury Tales*, "Prioress's Tale," lines 488–94.

4 Ibid., lines 453–87 and 864–90. See Heng, *England and Jews*, 76.

5 Agbabi, *Telling Tales*, 116.

tice activism and her transformation of a medieval antisemitic narrator into a contemporary Black British performance artist committed to social justice.[6] At the same time, some students—whether or not they happened to self-identify as Jewish—expressed concerns that Agbabi's adaptation could obscure the specific history of antisemitism that we had been discussing as a crucial background for Chaucer's poem. Does a story that centers a modern Black victim of violence, and foregrounds contemporary racial and socioeconomic injustices, risk displacing what was originally a conversation about medieval English forms of antisemitism?

One student of color, who self-identified in this particular context as Jewish, remarked that she didn't actually think about Agbabi's adaptation in terms of "replacing" one particular history for another, but rather she interpreted the modern work as a reminder of how vulnerable groups separated by time and space (Jewish and Black diaspora communities, in this case) can share certain experiences of violence. From this point onward, our discussion turned to the question of how distinct forms of xenophobia and violence in the medieval past—made evident through the texts and artworks that we examine in a classroom setting—can inform careful considerations of racial injustice in our present.

At this point in the class discussion, I felt it was appropriate to acknowledge the heterogeneous perspectives and identities we had in the classroom. I never expect anyone in class to act as the "spokesperson" for some identity category they might happen to embody, but in this particular context I observed that Agbabi's poem did resonate with me individually as a queer Asian American, and a son of immigrants, who does not identify as Jewish nor as Black. I pointed to one line of "Sharps an Flats" where the posthumous Black British narrator refers to "my spar [i.e., pal, buddy, mate] Damilola,"[7] an allusion to the high-profile murder of ten-year-old Nigerian immigrant Damilola Taylor who was stabbed in southeast London on November 27, 2000, while he was walking home from a library; he had been mocked for his African accent and taunted with homophobic epithets before his killing.[8] Agbabi's modern Chaucerian poem with its vivid portrayal of the complex conditions of modern-day violence helped me to carefully consider how simultaneous forms of oppression are interrelated. It was through our classroom discussion that I had come to recognize Damilola Taylor as a target of violence not only due to anti-immigrant xenophobia but also the homophobia of his assailants.[9]

Our discussion of Agbabi's poem alluding to xenophobic and homophobic violence against a young Black immigrant in contemporary Britain, along with Chaucer's own story of medieval English antisemitism displaced to a city in Asia, opened up a nuanced conversation about forms of violence and injustice across time and space. What does it mean to read medieval literature, or adaptations of medieval stories, not only to understand their historical contexts but also to read in a pursuit of racial justice? How can

---

6 For a videorecording of Agbabi performing this piece, see Agbabi, "The Prioress' Tale."

7 Agbabi, *Telling Tales*, 82.

8 Peachey, "Damilola African Accent"; Bright, "Damilola 'gay link.'"

9 I discuss "Sharps an Flats" further in the "Pilgrimage" chapter of this book.

people of divergent backgrounds come together to address past and ongoing harms of racism and related oppressions?

Claiming Collective Identities

This book, *Antiracist Medievalisms*, starts with my own account of a classroom experience to indicate that conversations about medieval and modern forms of xenophobia, racism, and oppression never occur in a vacuum.[10] In recent years, public and academic discussions about antiracism in medieval studies have addressed egregious acts of racist violence and overt manifestations of white supremacy. Cord J. Whitaker's *Black Metaphors: How Modern Racism Emerged from Medieval Race-Thinking* demonstrates how the so-called "alt-right" or ethnonationalist groups throughout predominantly white countries exploit fantasies of a European medieval past in order to vilify blackness (and Muslims) and to nostalgically valorize Christian whiteness,[11] and a longstanding rhetorical and conceptual alignment of blackness and criminality in Western culture has deep implications for anti-Black violence and the global Black Lives Matter movement today.[12] Years before antiracist protests after the killing of George Floyd contributed to a resurgence of grassroots efforts to remove symbols of the Confederacy from public spaces throughout the US, Seeta Chaganti suggested how medievalists can intervene in critiquing the ongoing violence wrought by white nostalgia and Confederate monuments.[13]

The urgency to address racism in the field of medieval studies encompasses not only histories of anti-Black violence but also an interconnected set of social issues worldwide. Dorothy Kim's work names the harms of white supremacy in online medievalist communities and contemporary geopolitics,[14] and Adam Miyashiro reveals how appropriations of Knights Templar iconography in deadly acts of Islamophobic violence in Australasia participate in a long history of white settler colonialism whose origins can be traced back to militant European ideologies of Christian supremacy during what we now commonly call the Crusades.[15] Shokoofeh Rajabzadeh situates contemporary Islamophobic hate crimes in North America and Europe in the context of a harmful history of glamorizing anti-Muslim violence in Western culture (especially in medieval romances), and she connects "the historical representation of Muslims in the Middle Ages" and "violent and painful Islamophobia and racism" evident in medieval "objects of study" to her own "sense of the ever-present threat of attack" on individual Muslims and Muslim communities within predominantly white countries today.[16]

---

10 See also Hsy, "Racial Dynamics"; Kao, "White Attunement"; Kao, "#palefacesmatter?"

11 Whitaker, *Black Metaphors*, 187–97.

12 Ibid., 1–3.

13 Chaganti, "B-Sides"; Chaganti, "Confederate Monuments."

14 Kim, *Alt-Medieval*; Kim, "White Supremacists."

15 Miyashiro, "Our Deeper Past."

16 Rajabzadeh, "Muslim Erasure," 2.

The harms of white supremacy and racist violence that were on display at the "Unite the Right" rally in Charlottesville, VA, in August 2017, where white supremacists and neo-Nazis marching to uphold the symbolism of a Confederate statue chanted anti-semitic slogans and held shields featuring modified Knights Templar iconography,[17] marked a watershed moment in galvanizing predominantly white medievalist communities to denounce racism through public statements.[18] Although the events at Charlottesville offered a vital sociopolitical "awakening" for white medievalists who had not publicly taken action against racism before, a deep understanding of the historical and ongoing violence of white Christian supremacy was nothing "new" to Jews, Muslims, or people of color with experience working in medievalist spaces.[19]

For racialized minority groups and for people of color, interpreting the Middle Ages or transforming modern understandings of the medieval past (usually framed as a European Christian past specifically) requires a careful deployment of expertise as well as a complex form of disidentification with the field of study itself.[20] My use of the term "disidentification" refers to a phenomenon named by José Esteban Muñoz, whose analysis of cultural productions by queer people of color attends to "the survival strategies the minority subject practices in order to negotiate" environments that are hostile, exclusionary, or alienating to people who are deemed to be in the minority relative to a mainstream or dominant culture,[21] and to "disidentify" means "to read oneself and one's own life narrative in a moment, object, or subject that is not culturally coded to 'connect' with the disidentifying subject."[22] People of color who choose to disidentify with a medieval past can work to transform existing norms in order to create new worlds, or in the words of Muñoz, "perpetuate disidentification ... not only as a hermeneutic" (i.e., mode of analysis and interpretation) but also as "a possibility for freedom."[23]

For scholars of color across all kinds of genders and orientations, acts of disidentification with the Middle Ages, as well as with the academic field of medieval studies, challenge persistent social messaging that we are perpetual "outsiders" to all things medieval. Whitaker, for instance, interprets a fellow person of color's incredulous response to his own academic self-identification as a medievalist as suggesting that Whitaker had "apparently turned my back on African-American literature and culture."[24] Even if Whitaker had learned from an early age that "black boys from Philadelphia are not supposed to concern themselves with knights and ladies," his scholarship on race in European medieval culture refutes the idea that blackness marks him as "out of time and

17 Whitaker, *Black Metaphors*, 187–97.

18 Medieval Academy of America, "Medievalists Respond to Charlottesville."

19 Medievalists of Color, "Solidarity With Our Jewish Colleagues."

20 See forthcoming publications: Arvas, McCannon, and Trujillo, eds., "Critical Confessions Now"; Rambaran-Olm, Leake, and Goodrich, eds., "Race, Revulsion, and Revolution."

21 Muñoz, *Disidentifications*, 4.

22 Ibid., 12.

23 Ibid., 179.

24 Whitaker, "Race-ing the Dragon," 3.

out of place" in the Middle Ages.[25] In *The Dark Fantastic: Race and the Imagination from Harry Potter to the Hunger Games*, Ebony Elizabeth Thomas remembers being told as a child that the "real world held trouble enough for young Black girls, so there was no need for me to go off on a quest to seek [the] Neverlands, Middle-Earths, or Fantasias" of medieval and fantasy worlds.[26] Even if Thomas enjoyed medieval and fantasy fiction as a Black girl and as an adult, her scholarship on fictional worlds centering Black female characters confronts how often people of color are made to feel we "do not belong either in magical medieval settings or in the spaceships of the future."[27]

These pervasive feelings of being "out of time and out of place" in the Middle Ages, and the desire to transform understandings of the medieval past accordingly, also affect non-Black people of color. In *Re-Enchanted: The Rise of Children's Fantasy Literature in the Twentieth Century*, Maria Sachiko Cecire, an American of Japanese-Italian descent, notes a formative moment of "racialized self-alienation" as a young girl seeing her own dark hair and eyes in a mirror and realizing she would never "be a blonde-haired, blue-eyed fairy-tale princess."[28] Cecire's study of anglophone American and British children's literature addresses the "role that actual medieval literature plays in the rise and shape of medievalist children's fantasy" and idealizing a particular transnational vision of racialized whiteness and social privilege that coldly excludes more people than it includes.[29] Rajabzadeh, self-identifying as an Iranian American and as a Muslim, notes the pains and fears that reading medieval romances glorifying violence against Muslims can create for her even in the process of conducting her own research and scholarship.[30]

Whitaker, Thomas, Cecire, and Rajabzadeh each write from divergently gendered racial and ethnic backgrounds—and they each work within the particular disciplinary conventions of their respective academic fields and intended audiences—but they all perform strategies of disidentifying with the Middle Ages. Each offers a distinct recognition of being (to adapt an idea from Cecire) racially "exiled" from medieval pasts that are constructed as exclusively white, European, and Christian.[31] Such a pervasive feeling of racial exile informs an intellectual drive to understand, and to transform, a profoundly alienating sense of the medieval past.

This book explores how people of color who do not (exclusively) trace their ancestry to Europe can claim and transform divergent racial, social, and intellectual relationships to the Middle Ages—not only in the space of the classroom, but also through scholarship or artistic creations. White medievalists trained in reflective modes of analyzing medieval European literature and culture have produced informative books on the complexities of affect and medieval studies, as well as thoughtful assessments of medieval-

---

25 Ibid.

26 Thomas, *Dark Fantastic*, 1.

27 Ibid., 73.

28 Cecire, *Re-Enchanted*, vii.

29 Ibid., viii.

30 Rajabzadeh, "Muslim Erasure," 1–2.

31 Cecire, *Re-Enchanted*, vii.

ism and fantasy through the academic field of critical whiteness studies,[32] but this book is not interested in developing approaches to affect and medievalism that rely upon marked or unmarked structures of white feeling. I explore how public understandings of the past can change if a global medievalist community situates the scholarly expertise and lived experiences of people of color at the center of our ongoing discussions about what the Middle Ages can mean today.

Thomas has identified a systemic "imagination gap" in medieval and fantasy genres that craft magical and historically distant worlds by means of excluding or marginalizing characters of color within them, and she observes that the global industries of publishing and popular media have long failed to envision communities of color as their audiences.[33] Thomas calls for a proliferation of "stories [narrated] from the perspectives of readers, writers, fans, and audiences who are racialized" as people of color to counter this longstanding imagination gap,[34] and she emphasizes the importance of "restorying the imagination itself" by centering people of color as protagonists within fictive worlds and also as the creators and audiences of such stories.[35] My account of a classroom discussion of Agbabi's "Sharps an Flats" offers one example of how the "restorying" of one medieval tale, through a work composed by a contemporary poet of color, can resonate with a racially heterogeneous audience. One of my objectives in this book is "restorying" the past of medievalism itself, showing how people of color have always been part of the history or the stories that can be told about medievalism—even if such contributions have not been widely recognized by the academy nor by a general public.

This book tells stories of people of color engaging in varied forms of medievalism, a phenomenon that I expansively define as drawing inspiration from a medieval past through cultural productions such as visual art, literature, political writings, scholarship, storytelling, or performance.[36] In approaching medievalism in this capacious way to encompass forms of cultural critique as well as works of art, I address the academic study of a historicized medieval past as well as non-academic receptions of the Middle Ages—including interpretations of things understood or "felt" to have medieval origins. *Antiracist Medievalisms* argues that people of color are vital figures in shaping meanings of the medieval past for modern audiences. I examine how medievalism operates at different points in time, from the age of anti-Asian "Yellow Peril" in the late nineteenth century to our current era of Black Lives Matter and related racial justice movements. Whether I address historical contexts or present-day concerns, I situate people of color as political agents, thinkers, and creators in their own right. By tracing medievalism through literature and cultural productions created by people of color, I demonstrate transformative possibilities of decentering whiteness in medieval studies.

---

32 Burger and Crocker, eds., *Medieval Affect*; Prendergast and Trigg, *Affective Medievalism*; Young, *Habits of Whiteness*.

33 Thomas, *Dark Fantastic*, 6.

34 Ibid., 11.

35 Ibid., 163.

36 Hsy, "Co-disciplinarity," 43. See D'Arcens, ed., *Medievalism*, for many current approaches.

This book grows out of my longstanding interests in the multilingual and multicultural heterogeneity of the Middle Ages as well as a commitment to addressing race and racism in the present-day field of medieval studies,[37] and it is my hope that the global medievalist community can shift how it addresses racism and cultural appropriation in the public sphere. As Sierra Lomuto has stated on the medieval studies website *In the Middle*, "public medievalist scholarship" that opposes racism must "not only center people of color in their discussions (a bare minimum expectation)," but it must also "identify white supremacy as a power structure" that does not solely "reside in the hearts and minds of individuals, but within oppressive institutions."[38] Denouncing the "abuse" of the medieval past by extremist groups, as the title of one recent book co-authored by white medievalists conspicuously does,[39] can make it too easy for a global medievalist community to ignore how the overwhelming whiteness of our own institutions and professional structures quietly continue to exclude, alienate, and harm people of color.[40]

Critical race scholar and cultural theorist Sara Ahmed has observed that the "reduction of racism to the [externalized] figure of 'the racist' allows structural or institutional forms of racism" such as the longstanding whiteness of academic publishing itself to remain unchallenged, and by "projecting racism onto a figure that is easily discarded ... as someone who is 'not us'" (such as the open racist or modern-day extremist),[41] white medievalists can create a falsely reassuring sense of progressive collective identity that leaves longstanding racial power structures unchanged. Moreover, earnest calls by white medievalists to defend an "abused" Middle Ages can misleadingly send a message to the public that medieval Europe was somehow "innocent" of historical forms of racism, xenophobia, or prejudice in its own right.[42]

Rather than trying to "rescue" a medieval European past from unsavory connections to present-day racism and violence, I trace how people of color have long confronted racist legacies of the European Middle Ages and have powerfully rejected medievalizing endorsements of white supremacy. Just as importantly, I take up Thomas's call for "restorying" medievalism itself, attending to how people of color and racialized minority communities have long repurposed medieval pasts in order to build new forms of solidarity and to create a more just world.

This book, in other words, attends to the sophisticated strategies that people of color employ in order to disidentify with the Middle Ages and to disprove the notion

---

37 Hsy, *Trading Tongues*; Barrington and Hsy, "Chaucer's Global Orbits"; Hsy, "Antiracist Medievalisms"; Hsy, "Language-Networks"; Hsy and Orlemanski, "Race and Medieval Studies"; Hsy, Pearman, and Eyler, "Disabilities in Motion"; Hurley, Hsy, and Kraebel, "Thinking Across Tongues."

38 Lomuto, "Public Medievalism."

39 Kaufman and Sturtevant, *Extremists Abuse the Medieval Past.*

40 Medievalists of Color, "Race and Medieval Studies"; Chaganti, "Statement Regarding ICMS"; Chan, "White Supremacy"; Coles, Hall, and Thompson, "BlacKKKShakespearean"; Otaño-Gracia, "Lost in Our Field"; Otaño-Gracia and Armenti, "Constructing Prejudice"; RaceB4Race Executive Board, "End Publishing Gatekeeping"; Rambaran-Olm, "Misnaming the Medieval."

41 Ahmed, *On Being Included*, 150.

42 Whitaker, *Black Metaphors*, 191 and 193. See also Wekker, *White Innocence*, 139–67.

that the medieval past is exclusively white property. In an essay foundational in critical race theory entitled "Whiteness as Property," Cheryl I. Harris demonstrates how (in societies structured by white supremacy) whiteness is not only inextricably tied to and invested in property rights, but whiteness itself is also a form of property; that is, "the set of assumptions, privileges, and benefits that accompany the status of being white have become a valuable asset," and whiteness is a property to be claimed, cherished, possessed, and defended.[43] In her analysis of race in the context of Shakespeare studies, Kim F. Hall has observed that race in the premodern past, as well as the present, is "a social construct that is fundamentally more about power and culture than about biological difference," and white anglophone discourses of race have "been used invariably to rationalize property interests, either in the use of humans as property, as in slavery, or the appropriation of land or resources, as in colonization."[44]

In the context of academic Shakespeare studies, Arthur L. Little, Jr., asks if there's an unspoken "working assumption in the field" that the entire Renaissance or early modern period itself is, "as a field, white property."[45] My own approach to medieval literary and cultural analysis seeks to dislodge a pervasive felt understanding, or deeply entrenched social encoding, of the entire time and place of the European Middle Ages as white property. I'm interested in how the critical project of "restorying" medieval pasts by people of color can help everyone—especially but not exclusively people of color—to interrogate our own identities and to deeply self-reflect on our sociopolitical positions. Just as importantly, I recognize that academic medievalists are never dispassionate interpreters of historical phenomena.

Although my professional training is in literary and cultural analysis and most of the materials discussed in this book are literature or related texts, I maintain that medievalism always constructs cultural understandings of a medieval past regardless of the media it uses: visual art, historical narrative, architecture, political discourse, scholarship, or performance. As I have stated elsewhere, "academic studies of medievalism span a number of established disciplines and modes of inquiry," including "literary criticism, art history, and [media and performance] studies, to name just a few."[46] The academic field of medieval studies and the creative practices of adapting medieval materials are all "about" constructing (or reconstructing) a medieval past—so I don't draw a rigid distinction between academic medievalism and so-called amateur, non-academic, or popular medievalism. Instead, I suggest that professional academic scholarship about the Middle Ages and the cultural reception of the medieval past are two sides of the same coin. I attend to what medievalist and queer theorist Carolyn Dinshaw calls a "shared desire in both amateurs and professionals" to re-create a medieval past, and in sympathy with Dinshaw, I explore the racially heterogeneous and "complex interplay of

---

43 Harris, "Whiteness as Property," 1713.

44 Hall, *Things of Darkness*, 6.

45 Little, "Re-Historicizing Race," 88.

46 Hsy, "Co-disciplinarity," 43.

nonacademic and academic agents" that drives intellectual, artistic, and public forms of medievalism.[47]

In a foundational essay on race, affect, and religion in medieval studies, Dinshaw asks "[what] the medieval European past [might] have to do with my Asian American present," and she situates a contextually rich reading of "India" in the Middle English *Travels of Sir John Mandeville* within long histories of Western colonialism and first-person reflections on her own "pale and fair" Indian background.[48] Dinshaw notes that the "paleness of my face" not only creates a complex "affect" within predominantly white medievalist professional spaces but her paleness is also "a racial/religious mark that affords me a feel for the sedimentation of times in the present, the medieval in the modern," and this "'feel' is constitutive of me as … a queer medievalist" who hopes that "'the pale' of our disciplines can be expanded, redefined, to engage with the challenging heterogeneity of our times."[49] Dinshaw elsewhere expresses a feeling of "kinship with the amateur [medievalist] that I can only call queer," and not just because "I am a queer—a dyke and only sort of white," but also because "I am a medievalist" and "studying the Middle Ages is, finally, about desire—for another time, for meaning, for life."[50]

My own thinking about the past as a queer Asian American medievalist also grapples with the heterogeneity of our present, but my approach diverges from Dinshaw's in a few respects. As a person who does not share Dinshaw's paleness and who is typically recognized as "Asian" in some way due to my facial features and seemingly unpronounceable monosyllabic surname, my presence in medievalist professional spaces doesn't produce the particular kinds of affect that Dinshaw so thoughtfully explores.[51] Moreover, my interest lies not so much in the question of what the medieval past might mean to me as a particular queer Asian American medievalist but rather the significance of medieval pasts for racialized communities more broadly. *Antiracist Medievalisms* asks what is at stake when communities of color create things (texts, stories, objects) that "feel" medieval, and I examine how people from heterogeneous racial positionings create urgent feelings of pastness or reinvent a distant past for present-day concerns.

Affective bonds with the past are never innocent nor neutral; they can be fraught and perpetuate harmful ideas and practices—or they can set the stage for transformative futures. This book explores divergent strategies of claiming or disidentifying with a medieval past (whatever "medieval" means in any given context) to question received notions of history and to pursue racial justice. I hope this book opens up space for new stories of medievalism and what it achieves—in the past and the present.

---

47 Dinshaw, *How Soon Is Now?*, 38–39.

48 Dinshaw, "Pale Faces," 20.

49 Ibid., 40–41.

50 Dinshaw, *How Soon Is Now?*, 32.

51 Hsy, "Racial Dynamics." See also Kao, "White Attunement"; Kao, "#palefacesmatter?"

The Knights Templar Go to Chinatown

I start with some stories of medievalism in a seemingly unlikely space of interracial encounter and racialized identity performance: Chinatown theaters. In 1883 local chapters of the Knights Templar, a "social brotherhood" with a mission to "defend the Christian faith," made "pilgrimages" from various points across the United States to gather in San Francisco, CA.[52] These white Knights were welcomed with pomp and pageantry at various sites along the way, and commemorative programs hawked a range of souvenirs and gilded chivalric artifacts.[53] After converging from their various points of origin, the Knights marched in San Francisco under Gothic and Norman arches with the cross and motto "in hoc signo vinces" [the imperial Latin phrase meaning "in this sign you shall conquer"] in a celebration of co-called "Anglo-Saxon" Christian identity.[54] In one speech, Grand Master Benjamin Dean declares there was "nothing" significant in California, Indigenous nor Hispanic, "before the Anglo-Saxon came."[55]

The grand ball held in Boston on January 31, 1883, to announce and raise funds for the pilgrimage itself had taken place in an elaborate building decorated with a "large painting in heroic style of the warrior who, in the days of early knighthood, clove through the Saracens—Richard the Lion-hearted."[56] It is worth noting that these modern-day Knights Templar traveling across the country didn't openly present themselves as violent; they rhetorically distanced themselves from the anti-Muslim warfare of the medieval past by claiming a well-intentioned mission of "peace and good-will among all men" and presented their transcontinental journey as one "undertaken for pleasure, profit, and friendship."[57] Nonetheless, writings produced by the Knights—and contemporary accounts of their travels—assert the perceived superiority of white Christian masculinity over everything (and everyone) else.[58]

Fusing medieval themes of crusade, pilgrimage, and adventure, *The California Pilgrimage of Boston Commandery Knights Templars, August 4–September 4, 1883* reads as much as a travel account and record of medievalizing performances as an ethnographic study affirming the inferiority of non-white and non-Christian communities. Its chapter

---

52 Roberts, *California Pilgrimage*, 6.

53 *Salt Lake Daily Herald*, August 18, 1883, 8. The front page of *The Seattle Daily Post–Intelligencer*, August 12, 1883, describes the Centennial exhibition display of "magnificent bronzes" including "Mounted Knight on a Pedestal" in bronze, silver, and gold, "Knights Templar armor in silver and bronze, with a shield bearing a cross, and the other the coat-of-arms of California," and a globe of silver and gold with a "knight in armor with drawn sword" (information attributed to *S.F. News Letter*).

54 Roberts, *California Pilgrimage*, 169.

55 Ibid., 249.

56 Ibid., 22.

57 Ibid., 6.

58 Upon the departure from Boston, four Knights, "dressed in women's clothes, gave a minstrel show on the cars as the 'colored quartet,'" and even if they were all "prominent business men" they "cracked original jokes and make the excursionists roar." Ibid., 163. Such performances assert a collective white identity by exploiting racial and gendered stereotyping.

on San Francisco's Chinatown describes the neighborhood's physical layout and demographics (including race, gender, and professions of its inhabitants) and a white "Sir Tristam Burges, a notable guide in Chinatown" leads the Knights through the "'Celestial' quarter" on a festival day to witness a "dark-visaged pagan" burning "cheap paper" and offered up as "golden prayers," and the gutters produced a "pungent odor and lighted up the scenes of barbaric peculiarity."[59]

The Knights' ethnographic "pilgrimage" not only exoticizes Chinatown; it also exhibits an unwitting irony rivaling Mark Twain's travel narrative *Innocents Abroad*.[60] The account of the Knights' visit to the Chinese opera on August 17, 1883, at the Grand Chinese Theatre on Washington Street reveals more about the entitlement of the white audience members than it does about the Chinese performance itself. The Knights fill the entire space (angering Chinese who have been waiting to enter) and applaud its "acts ... from military dramas," stories of "heroes [and] strong men," and acrobatically "stag[ed] fights between ... warriors" via "whirling," "tumbling," and "gymnastics."[61] The Knights enjoy the masculine athleticism on display but find it "all strange, unintelligible, and queer."[62] Moreover, they laugh at inappropriate moments, disconcerting the Chinese actors.[63]

However curious these Knights might be in observing this performance, they show little appreciation for the conventions of Chinese theater or appropriate forms of audience behavior within such a cultural space (even if an official program could have prepared them better).[64] The Knights arrayed in "Templar jewels and badges" with "ladies [in] opera hats and diamonds"[65] made their own presence conspicuous, asserting their entitlement to a Chinese social space and displaying ignorance of an alien performance tradition, enacted in this context exclusively by Chinese men and boys, which they dismiss as "queer." Popular news coverage of the "pilgrimage" transformed the Knights themselves into a strange spectacle and an unnerving occupation of Chinese space. One newspaper reported that Chinatown was "uncomfortably full of white people" during the Knights' visit, with "special performances given at the theaters" from which Chinese "were excluded."[66]

---

59 Ibid., 157. Sir Tristam Burges is elsewhere identified as the Grand Senior Warden of the Grand Commandery of California, viii et passim.

60 Twain, *Innocents Abroad*.

61 Ibid., 154–55.

62 Ibid., 154.

63 Ibid.

64 Ira G. Hott's *Pacific Coast Guide and Programme of the Knights Templar Triennial Conclave* (San Francisco, CA, 1883) describes "Chinese Theatre" (89–91), comparing its minimalist staging to historical Shakespearean practices (89). For an account of performances in this particular theater on Washington Street, see Arthur Inkersley, "The Chinese Drama in California," *The Strand Magazine*, May 1898, 402–9.

65 Roberts, *California Pilgrimage*, 154.

66 *Japan Weekly Mail* (citing *St. Louis Globe Diplomat*), 77.

Stylized battle and Chinese exclusion weren't innocent play in the day's political climate.[67] At the height of restrictive and discriminatory Chinese Exclusion laws in the United States and Canada, the casual racism of the Knights in the theater embodies a performance of toxic medievalism.[68] San Francisco experienced anti-Chinese violence in 1877 when white men rallied under the cry "The Chinamen Must Go!" and supported agitators embarking on a "crusade" against Chinese laborers and their employers.[69] Inflammatory rhetorics of the Knights of Labor and militant white brotherhoods, at times supported by police, incited anti-Chinese massacres and expulsions in 1885 (Rock Springs, WY; Tacoma, WA), and 1886 (Seattle, WA; Vancouver, BC).[70] In the lead-up to one of the notorious incidents of anti-Chinese violence (in Tacoma), an opera house served as the staging ground for incendiary rhetoric.[71]

In the geopolitical climate of 1883, white Knights entering a Chinatown theater—and forcing the Chinese to be "excluded"—are not innocent tourists. The Knights and ladies "occup[ied] the whole auditorium," according to the *California Pilgrimage*, and "the unobstructed entrance of 'white folks' and their ladies enraged the Chinese theatre-goers, whose violence called the police."[72] The written account of the white Knights' occupation of Chinese space and reliance upon police force attributes the idea of "violence" to the Chinese, but not to the white intruders themselves. In their disruptive "medieval" self-presentation and calling of police in order to clear the space for their own exclusive use, these Knights perform an assertion of white supremacy and pose a threat to Chinese safety.

Spectacular Solidarity: Fighting Antisemitism and Sinophobia

I move to New York City's Chinatown for another instance of white audiences filling a Chinese theater—but this time, they were invited. On May 11, 1903, a Chinese theater in Doyers Street hosted a performance fundraiser for Jewish victims of the recent Kishinev pogrom (a massacre of Jews, enabled by local authorities, in what is now Chișinău, Moldova, and at the time part of the Russian Empire).[73] The atrocity attracted international outrage, and the Chinese community joined American Jews in response. Joseph H. Singleton, the Chinese American manager of the theater, said to the Jewish relief society: "We want to help you. We believe in liberty and want to aid those who suffer from bigotry."[74]

---

67 "Next the President of the United States, decked out more fantastically than ever chief of the various tribes of redskins in war paint, partook of a supper with the Emperor of China, this scene, too, ending up with fire and bloodshed" (Roberts, *California Pilgrimage,* 155).

68 I expand on my term "toxic medievalism" and its relationship to sinophobia in particular in the "Plague" chapter of this book.

69 Perlman, "Anti-Chinese Agitation," 254–55. See also Lew-Williams, *Chinese Must Go.*

70 Gomez et al., "Mapping Anti-Chinese Violence."

71 Morgan, *Puget's Sound,* 294–97.

72 Roberts, *California Pilgrimage,* 154.

73 Seligman, "Chinese for Jews."

74 "Evidences Chinamen are Mentally Broadening," 5.

News reports confirmed the Kishinev massacre was provoked by "blood libel" narratives falsely blaming Jews for the death of a young Christian man,[75] and such propaganda has its origins in medieval "blood libel" traditions that instigated acts of antisemitic violence throughout Europe.[76] In raising funds and awareness for pogrom victims, this act of solidarity across communities confronted one of the most harmful legacies of the medieval past.

Even more remarkable than the act of solidarity itself is the historical context for the Chinese-language drama performed that night. Entitled *The Lost Ten Tribes* (seemingly evoking the biblical dispersal of Jews), the Chinese play staged a traumatic event for the Han Chinese: their subjugation by the Tartars, and the imposition of the queue (i.e., long braided hairstyle) with its origins in medieval Eurasia.[77] One journalist characterized the play as depicting "the times of the bloody Tartars, when the Chinese were first made to wear the queue by their savage conquerors as a token of subjection,"[78] with Manchu domination in the early Qing Dynasty resonating with histories of Jewish oppression by imperial rulers.[79]

Some (white) journalists at the time sneered at this alliance of Chinese and Jews: "As Shakespeare might have said, one touch of abuse makes the alien races kin."[80] For Chinese Americans, the global harms of urban antisemitism and sinophobia were undeniable, and this apparent "unholy alliance" (or kinship) of two diaspora communities grew out of shared experiences of prejudice and marginalization. Chinese American civil rights activist Wong Chin Foo (1847–1898) conjoined the legacies of medieval antisemitic "blood libel" to modern anti-Chinese violence when he critiqued "rat libel"— a term that Wong's primary biographer has coined to refer to the dehumanizing and ubiquitous "Yellow Peril" discourses and visual art of the Exclusion era equating Chinese with filth, infestation, disease, and barbarity.[81] A long history of "libel," discourses of contamination and plague, and experiences of urban violence conjoin the historical phenomena of antisemitism and this era's sinophobia. To modify a phrase from Edward W. Said, modern sinophobia—insofar as it is rooted in European modes of discursive "othering"—emerges as a "strange, secret sharer of Western anti-Semitism."[82]

Wong's repurposing of "blood libel" to critique "rat libel" speaks to some of his other forays into autoethnography and fictive forms of medievalism. Wong's autoethnographic writing, most pointedly, inverted white-authored tropes of Chinatown travel. In "The Chinese in New York" (1888), Wong assumes the position of a "native informant" while

75 Seligman, "Chinese for Jews."

76 Heng, *England and Jews*; Rubin, *Gentile Tales*.

77 Seligman, "Chinese for Jews."

78 "Evidences Chinamen are Mentally Broadening," 5.

79 Seligman, "Chinese for Jews."

80 Untitled, *The Indianapolis Journal,* evoking Shakespeare's *Troilus and Cressida*: "One touch of nature makes the whole world kin" (3.3.181).

81 Seligman, *First Chinese American*, 101. See also Tchen and Yeats, *Yellow Peril!*

82 Said, *Orientalism*, 27.

strategically employing an objective third-person voice; his text describes Chinese hygiene and grooming, religious worship, food preparation, and rich food traditions.[83] Wong's medievalism took shape through the historical romance "Poh Yuin Ko, The Serpent-Princess" (1888) and serial novel *Wu Chih Tien, The Celestial Empress* (1889), incorporating allusions to the fourteenth-century Chinese *Romance of the Three Kingdoms* (三國演義) and Tang Dynasty figures.[84] Wong's fictions were presented as if they were English "translations" of Chinese originals, with each narrative featuring a healthy dose of heroism.

As literary critic Hsuan L. Hsu observes, the novel *Wu Chih Tien* "[takes] as its protagonist the handsome, robust, intelligent, and sympathetic prince," and it "resists the equation of whiteness with imperial manhood" so pervasive in the era's historical romances.[85] Such works offered Asian-inspired alternatives to the historical romances of Sir Walter Scott and contemporaneous forms of medievalism such as Mark Twain's *Connecticut Yankee in King Arthur's Court*.[86] By using autoethnography to subvert a white gaze and to craft his own brand of medievalism, Wong created new spaces for Chinese Americans in lieu of imperial white Christian masculinity.

Perhaps anticipating the alliance of Chinese Americans and Jewish Americans in the Chinese theater on Doyers Street in 1903, Wong himself had sought to encourage cross-cultural understanding by using Chinese theater for social change. In 1883, Wong wrote a few articles promoting Chinese theater. One essay outlined how theatrical traditions of Chinese and Western cultures diverge, with Chinese productions using minimal staging and props without adhering to Eurocentric expectations of "realism."[87] Another of Wong's publications proposed taking a Chinese troupe "on the road" to encourage cross-cultural understanding: "I have an idea that will help each people to understand the other. I will establish the Chinese theatre in the United States for the presentation of the Chinese drama, the oldest in the world, going back to the first stages of recorded history."[88] Although Wong's vision went unrealized, his advocacy aimed to make a seemingly alien, "strange," or "queer" art form into something that could be appreciated on its own terms—and respected as a cultural tradition with a legacy predating foundational works of medieval Europe.

These concurrent medievalisms in Chinatown theaters suggest divergent deployments of the medieval past. Toxic medievalisms can exoticize, intimidate, and incite violence, but antiracist medievalisms can confront prejudice, increase understanding, and build solidarity. The complex duality of medievalism is made clear by the actions of the white Knights Templar and contemporaneous Chinese Americans.

---

83 Wong, "Chinese in New York."

84 Wong, "Serpent-Princess"; Wong, *Celestial Empress*. *Wu Chih Tien* takes place in the time of Tang Dynasty figure Wu Zetian (武則天), China's only female ruler.

85 Hsu, *Comparative Racialization*, 132.

86 Ibid., 109–38.

87 Wong, "Chinese Stage."

88 Wong, "Chinese Drama," September 2, 1883.

Scope and Focus of this Book

In my discussion of medievalism and Chinatown theaters, I have shown how white Knights Templar and contemporaneous Chinese Americans aimed to reinvent the medieval past. In *The Black Middle Ages: Race and the Construction of the Middle Ages*, Matthew X. Vernon has argued that the "adoption of medieval texts" by nineteenth-century African Americans created a "surrogated kinship," a feeling of connectedness with the past that is not based on notions of lineal descent nor direct ties to European cultural heritage.[89] I have described how early Chinese Americans crafted their own kinds of surrogated kinship via medievalism—through the space of the Chinatown theater and genres of historical romance. The surrogated kinship that Chinese Americans expressed with Jewish Americans challenges the idea that the medieval past is the exclusive property of white Christians. At the same time, this collective act of communities coming together in the performance space of a Chinatown theater produces what Muñoz might call transformative disidentifications across race, religion, language, and culture.

Within academia, an appreciation for the complexity of medievalism around the globe is expanding, including foundational work on the appropriation of Western medieval materials in contexts beyond Europe,[90] as well as beyond a privileged predominantly white "inner circle" of anglophone societies.[91] Cultural studies of global medievalism, racial representation, and the sociopolitical engagements of fan communities inform the scholarship of Kavita Mudan Finn and Rohit K. Dasgupta, to name a few.[92] This book focuses on people of color and racialized minority groups within predominantly white anglophone societies. African American and Afro-Caribbean scholars such as Maghan Keita, Barbara Lalla, Kofi Omoniyi Sylvanus Campbell, Ebony Elizabeth Thomas, Matthew X. Vernon, and Cord J. Whitaker,[93] as well as non-Black medievalists,[94] have explored how European medieval artistic traditions inform anglophone Black contexts. *Antiracist Medievalisms* expands on this body of scholarship on medievalism by people of color by putting Black and non-Black communities in conversation with one another. Divergent critical and historical perspectives operate in solidarity to illuminate shared struggles.

---

89 Vernon, *Black Middle Ages*, 29.

90 Davis and Altschul, eds., *Medievalisms in Postcolonial World*; Momma, "Medievalism—Colonialism—Orientalism"; Kabir and Williams, eds., *Postcolonial Approaches*; Warren, *Creole Medievalism*.

91 Barrington and Hsy, "Chaucer's Global Orbits"; Kearney and Medrano, *Mexican American Borderlands*.

92 Finn, "Decolonizing Popular Medievalism"; Finn, "Queen of Sad Mischance," 30–31; Finn, "Introduction," 11–12; Dasgupta, "Queer Intimacies."

93 Keita, "Race"; Lalla, *Postcolonialisms*; Campbell, *Black Atlantic*; Thomas, *Dark Fantastic*; Vernon, *Black Middle Ages*; Whitaker, ed., "Making Race Matter"; Whitaker, "B(l)ack in the Middle Ages"; Whitaker, *Harlem Middle Ages*.

94 Barrington, "Dark Whiteness"; Forni, *Chaucer's Afterlife*; Wallace, "New Chaucer Topographies"; Warren, "Chaucer in Caribbean."

Most of this book discusses the later nineteenth century through early twentieth century, with its "center of gravity" in the anglophone United States and Canada. This period coincided with the era of Chinese Exclusion in North America as well as anti-Chinese sentiment globally, and much of this book is indebted to Edlie L. Wong's nuanced account of how American polemics of Black inclusion in civic life after Reconstruction were inextricably tied to discourses of Chinese exclusion.[95] This historical period was also, of course, an age of proliferating forms of medievalism throughout anglophone societies—across literature, visual art, and architecture. As Whitaker elegantly states: "Medievalism and the idea of the idyllic Middle Ages has continued to permeate popular ideas of the period since at least the eighteenth century," and white nineteenth-century figures such as "Thomas Carlyle or Sir Walter Scott, especially in his *Ivanhoe*—took up the charge in the so-called medieval revival ... fictionaliz[ing] medieval historical events [and] emphasizing chivalric heroism."[96] Non-Black scholars have noted how medievalism intricately shaped predominantly white expressions of national belonging before and after the Civil War.[97]

Acknowledging these broader contexts, this book centers manifold forms of medievalism crafted by people of color. Much of this book addresses the Chinese diaspora throughout North America, and I put Chinese Americans in dialogue with contemporaneous groups: African Americans, self-identified Eurasians (multiracial people of European and Asian ancestry), free black Creoles in Louisiana (*gens de couleur libres* or free people of color), as well as Arab and Jewish diaspora communities. The terminology used to refer to particular racial and ethnic identities will vary depending on context, as I aim to respect how people self-identify in their own time and place (in the historical past or today).[98]

As a general term I refer to "people of color" or "communities of color" not to erase the distinct histories of racialized ethnic groups but rather to foreground the power of coalitions, and to honor the multiracial solidarity movements through which the term "people of color" first arose.[99] In this context, the term "people of color" expresses racial identities in positive and affirming terms, rather than as a mere negation or "absence" of whiteness (as the term "nonwhite" can imply). I also respect the validity of BIPOC (Black, Indigenous, and People of Color) and BAME (Black, Asian, and Minority Ethnic) as formulations used throughout anglophone North America and in the UK respectively. My use of the descriptor "minority" only signals how communities of color are outnumbered by white people within certain environments, and it does not imply that people of color are inherently "minor" or "lesser than" white people in any given multiracial context. My terminologies for particular communities of color vary throughout this book,

---

95 Wong, *Racial Reconstruction*.

96 Whitaker, *Black Metaphors*, 194. See also Whitaker and Gabriele, "Ghosts of Nineteenth Century."

97 Barrington, *American Chaucers*; Moreland, *Medievalist Impulse*.

98 I capitalize Black to signal contemporary sociopolitical identities shaped by African diaspora experiences, but the adjective "black" is not always capitalized in earlier historical instances or in quotations.

99 Grady, "Why 'BIPOC.'"

but what remains constant is an awareness of global white supremacy as a power structure that disadvantages and harms racialized minority groups.

Due to my disciplinary training in medieval British literature, my focus is communities of color within anglophone societies, but I seek to disrupt a pervasive form of white anglocentrism in medieval literary and cultural studies more broadly. This book pluralizes English across race and space by attending to heterogeneous racialized varieties of English such as Jamaican Patois (Patwa or Patwah), Black English, Spanglish (code-switching mixture of Spanish and English), Singlish (Singaporean English), Chinglish (English language influenced by Chinese), and poetic reinventions of Old English and Middle English—alongside poetry composed entirely in Chinese, as well as works by francophone and polyglot authors of color. Challenging what Shyama Rajendran calls "English raciolinguistic supremacist structures,"[100] the heterogeneous contents of this book invite readers to question the privileged or normative status of forms of English literary expression that are culturally coded as white.

I hope this book, in all its variety, can appeal to readers beyond academic medievalists. For readers with interests in the field of Ethnic Studies, these chapters trace how a received (or imposed) cultural repository of medieval materials shaped the formation of early minority literatures. My comparative approach to reception history puts communities of color in conversation, but I do not assume that all the authors I discuss directly knew each other's work (even if they draw from similar influences). Some of my readings are exploratory, leaving room for future study. I hope this work models a mindful engagement across fields and creates dialogue across communities that are too often segregated.

Aims of this Book

This book, simply put, makes three arguments.

First, academic medievalists who oppose racism must move beyond merely critiquing the most spectacularly violent forms of white medievalism and avoid casting the European Middle Ages themselves as somehow in need of defending. To talk of an "abused" medieval past implies that medieval Europe was somehow innocent of racism, and critiques of "bad" medievalism often emphasize white feelings and white audiences rather than the historical (and present) targets of racism. I am profoundly uninterested in whether the self-identified Knights Templar who occupied San Francisco's Chinatown had any access to "accurate" information about the phenomena commonly called the Crusades nor how they got facts "wrong" in discussing the past. I focus on how these modern Knights Templar used the memory and fantasy of an illustrious past in order to assert and enforce Christian white supremacy—and I attend to the effects of these actions once they entered Chinese spaces.

Second, academics must value rich forms of medievalism practiced by and for people of color. The European medieval past in particular has complex meanings for racialized minority groups traditionally excluded from—and harmed by—forms of medieval-

---

100 Rajendran, "Raciolinguistic Supremacy," 2.

ism prevalent in predominantly white cultural environments, and medievalism can be deployed for liberatory aims such as critiquing racism or combating exclusion and discrimination. My objective is not merely to make medieval studies more "inclusive" by incorporating more people of color into existing frameworks of study but rather to ask how the whole field transforms once people of color drive the conversations.

Third, medievalism by and for communities of color helps to tell a fuller story of multiracial solidarity and social justice activism from the late nineteenth century to today. In the spirit of Yuichiro Onishi's scholarship on antiracism and Afro-Asian solidarity movements, I trace how medievalism has played a role in developing strategies for communities of color to work together toward ending the global "theory and practice of white supremacy."[101] My discussions of nineteenth-century struggles against white supremacy are mindful of what Lisa Lowe calls the "intimacies" of four continents: Africa, Asia, the Americas, and Europe.[102]

My research methods and approach to opposing racism follow Tania Das Gupta, who notes that antiracism "names, analyzes, and provides the frameworks to engage in a process of ending racism and with it a multiplicity of other oppressions."[103] My mode of antiracist analysis honors the methods of intersectional Black feminist and critical race theorist Kimberlé Crenshaw as well as queer and feminist scholars of color who examine how interrelated systems of oppression operate on the basis of race, gender, class, and disability (to name a few such phenomena).[104] If you need to educate yourself regarding antiracist work more broadly, *Dismantling Racism Works* defines concepts grounded in critical race theory in terms applicable to the US and predominantly white countries (see also the bibliography of readings at the end of this book).[105] The ensuing chapters in this book recognize medievalism as a productive means for racialized minority groups to engage with one another and address shared struggles.

The overall message of this book is that medievalism is always polemical. When anyone invokes the Middle Ages, they are making an argument about the past or its meanings for the present. This book is not about critiquing the "abuse" of the Middle Ages but rather understanding the social consequences of medievalizing rhetoric and imagery. For communities of color and racialized minority groups so often excluded from, and damaged by, predominantly white power structures, embracing medievalism can enable acts of resistance to oppression and help to dismantle systems of racial injustice.

---

101 Onishi, *Transpacific Antiracism,* 13 and 30. Afro-Asian alliance in the era of W. E. B. Du Bois and Black/Asian solidarity in the Civil Rights era are richly documented elsewhere. Bae and Tseng-Putterman, "Black-Asian Internationalism"; Blain, "Roots of Afro-Asia"; Itagaki, *Civil Racism*; Ossa and Lee-DiStefano, eds., *Afro-Asian Connections*; Wu, *Radicals on the Road.*

102 Lowe, *Intimacies of Four Continents.*

103 Das Gupta, "Teaching Anti-Racist Research," 456.

104 Crenshaw, "Intersectionality"; James and Wu, "Race, Ethnicity, Disability"; Kafer and Kim, "Edges of Intersectionality." See also Hall, *Things of Darkness,* 258; Betancourt, *Byzantine Intersectionality.*

105 "Racism Defined." *Dismantling Racism Works* (dRworks) Web Workbook.

What's Medieval? Time, Space, Genre, Worldbuilding

This book sometimes uses "medieval" and "medievalism" in reference to cultural and literary contexts beyond Europe. By disassociating the term "medieval" from an exclusively European framework, I signal the interconnectedness of peoples, ideas, and cultures across Afro-Eurasia throughout the time period broadly recognized as coinciding with a European Middle Ages (generally the years ca. 500 to 1500 in the Common Era). This recognition of a mobile and networked medieval world acts in conjunction with literary and cultural historian Geraldine Heng's capacious approach to the "early globalities" of medieval trade, travel, and exchange.[106]

My use of "medieval" does not merely impose a European framework onto non-European cultures, since people who do not identify as European have their own modes of expressing relationships to some idea of a medieval past.[107] Within conventions of Chinese literary historiography in East Asia, for instance, the English word "medieval" as a translation of the Chinese characters 中世 for "Middle Period/Era" can designate a dynamic time after a classical age of antiquity and before the emergence of modernity (regardless of how that modernity is defined).[108] Historians of Africa such as Michael A. Gomez use the term "medieval" in order to acknowledge African cultures and peoples as active participants in world history and to recognize Africa as profoundly interconnected with Asia and Europe throughout what Heng would call a global Middle Ages.[109] This approach to medieval Africa in history counters racist deployments of the "medieval" (in the pejorative sense of backwardness or barbarity) that Simon Gikandi in an African postcolonial context observes were "imposed on Africa by the agents of European modernization."[110] In a recent collaborative essay addressing art history and literature, Andrea Myers Achi and Seeta Chaganti explore the function of medieval Africa in shaping the intellectual thought of W. E. B. Du Bois and the early foundations of Black Studies.[111]

When I discuss the heterogeneous claiming of medieval pasts by individuals of (for instance) African or Asian descent in predominantly white anglophone environments, I will be careful to signal when they are deliberately rethinking some idea of the European Middle Ages, or a medieval past beyond Europe, or some combination of the two. I maintain throughout this book the strategic flexibility of the "medieval" as a geotemporal construct, an idea that situates a person or audience in space as well as time. In sympathy with Sharon Kinoshita's reflections on varied instantiations of medievalism as theorized around the globe, my discussions of antiracist forms of medievalism stress the "capital importance of attention to *context* [emphasis in original], whether chronologi-

106 Heng, "Early Globalities"; Heng, "Early Globalism." See also Ganim and Legassie, eds., *Cosmopolitanism.*

107 Heng, "Early Globalities"; Altschul and Davis, eds., *Medievalisms in the Postcolonial World.*

108 Tanigawa and Xiong, "Medieval China." See also the "Place" chapter of this book.

109 Gomez, *African Dominion*; Fauvelle, *Golden Rhinoceros*, 11–12.

110 Gikandi, "Africa and Medievalism," 371.

111 Achi and Chaganti, "Medieval African Art."

cal, geographical, social, cultural, or even generic" (i.e., genre-based).[112] As such, chapters in this book use genre-specific methods to discuss novels, short stories, journalism, theatrical performance traditions, and particular forms of poetry. I respect the divergent strategies that people of color employ to disidentify with some notion of a medieval past, whether or not such a past is coded as European.

By disassociating the "medieval" from an essentialized connection to Europe and its associations with white Christian identity, I avoid what Vernon calls the disciplinary practice of framing "questions of medievalism and the Middle Ages" as if they were "the province of whiteness"[113] or using medievalism to enact "a uniform and clearly-defined means of consolidating white identity."[114] That is, I discuss medievalism through questions posed by and for people of color, and as such this book furthers an ongoing strategy of what Thomas calls "restorying time and place."[115] The chapters in this book explore medievalisms by communities of color concurrently, shifting focus even within a chapter to explore flexible alignments in thought and divergent affective relationships to medieval pasts.

My use of scholarship by queer people of color such as Muñoz and Dinshaw in "restorying time and place" is not solely due to my positioning as a person of color who happens to be queer. One benefit of queer theory for everyone—beyond any particular identity category—is offering frameworks for questioning linear and progressive models of time. As I have written previously in reference to Dinshaw and Muñoz among others, "contemporary queer theory amply demonstrates that time need not be conceived as entirely straight—in all senses of the word,"[116] and "[t]hinking critically about medievalism invites us to reassess the boundaries of modern academic disciplines and explore manifold conceptual approaches to the past."[117] Queer people of color are well situated to critique white supremacy and Eurocentric norms of history and desire through asynchronous modes of cultural analysis, and such scholarship enacts a mode of thinking that I have characterized elsewhere as a "channel-flipping orientation toward time" that moves across historical periods.[118]

Queer medievalist Wan-Chuan Kao, also developing upon Dinshaw's scholarship, observes that maintaining a sense of "[t]emporal heterogeneity" in analyzing the medieval past offers a "more intimate and queer understanding of the interconnections among objects, persons, and events,"[119] and Kao advocates for thinking critically beyond notions of time, space, and affect that assume Eurocentric racialized forms of white-

---

112 Kinoshita, "Deprovincializing Middle Ages," 74.

113 Vernon, *Black Middle Ages*, 23.

114 Ibid., 29.

115 Thomas, *Dark Fantastic*, 159.

116 Hsy, "Co-disciplinarity," 44. Note also Dinshaw, *How Soon Is Now?*

117 Ibid., 43.

118 Ibid. See also Hsy, "Distemporality."

119 Kao, "#palefacesmatter?"

ness as their point of orientation.[120] It is this geospatial plurality and flexibility of affect across time, as expressed through medievalisms, that informs the writing of this book.

Outline of Chapters

Each chapter in this book is structured by a theme pertaining to literary and artistic forms of medievalism. Four chapters are "historical" (focusing on the later nineteenth or early twentieth century), and two are "contemporary" (exploring works by present-day poets of color).

The first chapter, on the theme of "Progress," shows how the *Bildungsroman* (narrative of intellectual and personal growth), informed by the genre of historical romance, structures early ethnic minority writing on national belonging and citizenship in the United States and global struggles against white supremacy. I focus on the racialization of masculinity in works by the formerly enslaved African American abolitionist and author Frederick Douglass (ca. 1818–1895), the Chinese American journalist and public speaker Wong Chin Foo (1847–1898), and the foundational Arab American writer Ameen Rihani (1876–1940), who published books in Arabic and in English. Each author composes a narrative about a masculine hero's development while also critiquing gendered discourses of "progress" and "civilization" that underlie ideologies of white settler colonialism and imperialism.

The second chapter, on the theme of "Plague," examines how medievalizing discourses of public health and contagion harm racialized immigrant communities. I situate discourses of toxicity in the context of the global fears of "Yellow Peril" at the turn of the twentieth century, especially through xenophobic and homophobic responses to the emergence of bubonic plague in Chinatowns around the world. I show how two writers of Chinese ancestry, Wong Chin Foo and Sui Sin Far (1865–1914), address anti-Chinese discourses of contagion in North America—and I reveal how modern sinophobia disturbingly revives medieval antisemitic traditions that arose after the so-called Black Death. The intricate relationships between Jewish and Chinese diaspora communities in urban spaces create novel forms of homosocial intimacy and queer domesticity.

The third chapter, on the theme of "Place," considers the mostly anonymous poetry that Chinese detainees composed and inscribed into the wooden walls of the men's barracks of Angel Island Immigration Station, located on an island in San Francisco Bay, between 1910 and 1940. This repository of poetry composed by incarcerated migrants attests to the pains of indefinite detention and the injustices of racial discrimination, and these poets collectively adapted the gendered and formal conventions of medieval Chinese lyric forms that were originally associated with literati scholars in exile in order to suit their harsh new American geopolitical environment. I trace how the Angel Island barracks themselves have become a locus for cross-racial activist movements and now serve as an enduring reminder of the harms of racist immigration policies and indefinite detention.

---

120 Ibid. See also Kao, *White Before Whiteness.*

The fourth chapter, on the theme of "Passing," shows how two multiracial female authors at the turn of the twentieth century experiment with flexible forms of racial positioning, in particular through stories about women of color who deliberately or ambiguously pass (present themselves and live in the world) as white. I examine medieval-themed stories and "local color" sketches by free black Creole journalist and author Alice Dunbar-Nelson (1875–1935), whose fictive protagonists include racially ambiguous characters in Louisiana; and Sui Sin Far, whose fictive first-person narrators (male, female, white American, Chinese, Chinese American, and "Eurasian") manifest complexities of the author's biracial ancestry. Both authors use Marian imagery and the figure of Joan of Arc to embody nuanced performances of disidentification with medieval archetypes and unsettle dominant social codes of gender, sexuality, and race.

The final two chapters center present-day authors of color and show how poets can disidentify with medieval European poetic traditions through strategic disclosures of racial subjectivity. The fifth chapter, on the theme of "Play," attends to humor and irony across Native, Black, Latinx, and Asian American adaptations of Old English alliterative poetry and Middle English poetic forms. Poets in this chapter include Carter Revard (Osage and European American), Yusef Komunyakaa (African American), Timothy Yu (Chinese American), Natalie Diaz (Latina and Mojave), Karenne Wood (Monacan Indian), Cedar Sigo (Suquamish), and Julian Talamantez Brolaski (Latinx, Apache, and European ancestry).

The sixth chapter, on the theme of "Pilgrimage," explores how Geoffrey Chaucer's *The Canterbury Tales* is adapted in multicultural environments throughout the Americas, Australasia, Europe, and African diaspora contexts. Chaucerian poets of color experiment with flexible first-person racial positionings and move Chaucer's pilgrimage structure into new hemispheric, transatlantic, and transpacific orbits. Poets in this chapter include Jean "Binta" Breeze (Jamaican), Marilyn Nelson (African American), Patience Agbabi (Nigerian British), Frank Mundo (Mexican American), and Ouyang Yu (Chinese-born Australian). These chapters demonstrate how "new" forms of Old English and Middle English poetry exploit the unfixed potential of medieval language as a vehicle to express racial and cultural hybridity today.

The book ends with a list of further readings that suggests future areas of study. Taken as a whole, *Antiracist Medievalisms* explores what it means for people of color and racialized minority groups to disorient or disrupt preexisting notions of the medieval past—no matter how that past might be situated in terms of time, space, or desire. Divergent medievalisms crafted by people of color can work to transform some idea of the European past that is typically coded as white and Christian—but at other times people of color can be indifferent to Eurocentric frameworks altogether. The sociopolitical project of "restorying" medievalism will never be complete. It is my hope that medievalist communities will maintain the centrality of people of color in our reassessments of what the Middle Ages can mean in our ever-changing present.

Chapter One

PROGRESS: RACIAL BELONGING, MEDIEVAL MASCULINITIES, AND THE ETHNIC MINORITY *BILDUNGSROMAN*

THIS CHAPTER EXPLORES how the genre of the ethnic minority *Bildungsroman*, or story of intellectual growth, was crafted in the nineteenth-century United States in conjunction with traditions of travel narrative and contemporaneous forms of medievalism (especially historical romance). If the phrase "medieval romance" usually conjures visions of chivalric knights in armor and fair damsels in distress, what space could people of color create for themselves within such expectations? This book's explorations of medievalism by people of color starts by tracing how medieval romance and conversion narratives offered a vital scaffolding for accounts of intellectual development. African American abolitionist and orator Frederick Douglass (ca. 1818–1895), Chinese American journalist and public speaker Wong Chin Foo (1847–1898), and Arab American author Ameen Rihani (1876–1940) repurposed the masculine *Bildungsroman* to reject medievalizing white fantasies of the past and to critique gendered Western imperial ideologies of progress and expansion. In their writings, they challenged stereotypes portraying Africans as "savage" and Asians as stagnant "Orientals." Conversations among African American and Asian American thinkers generated nuanced forms of racial belonging in lieu of white Eurocentric models.

As discussed in the introduction to this book, my analysis of early ethnic minority writing explores what José Esteban Muñoz calls strategies of disidentification.[1] The authors discussed in this chapter who find themselves positioned in the "minority" (in respect to white Christian masculinity) devise varied methods for disidentifying with European medieval pasts, and they seek to transform gendered notions of racial belonging through references to a Western Middle Ages that is not typically coded as properly "belonging" to them. Such gendered and politicized acts of disidentifying with the European medieval past—or openly refusing to engage with such a past—shape these authors' arguments for new forms of cultural and national belonging.

Frederick Douglass: Disenchanting Medieval Pasts

In the final chapter of *The Narrative of Frederick Douglass, an American Slave, Written By Himself* (1845), internationally renowned African American orator and abolitionist Frederick Douglass (ca. 1818–1895), originally named Frederick Augustus Washington Bailey, has achieved freedom and chooses a new surname (retaining his first name "Frederick," which he has held from birth). His white benefactor Nathan Johnson, who

---

1 Muñoz, *Disidentifications*; see also this book's introduction.

has just been reading Sir Walter Scott's historical romance *The Lady of the Lake*, suggests "Douglass" (derived from a character in Scott's narrative), a name which Frederick adopts.[2] In this episode, Douglass takes ownership of a name derived from a historical romance alluding to Arthurian legends—but it is only one moment in an extended life story where Douglass claims and repurposes medievalizing frameworks.

Douglass first published his story of intellectual growth and journey to political freedom in his *Narrative* (1845), and he revised his own life story in different iterations over time, including *My Bondage and My Freedom* (1855) and *Life and Times of Frederick Douglass* (1881, revised 1892).[3] In my discussion of Douglass's work, I focus on the first iteration of his *Narrative* and how his use of medievalizing discourse adapts over his lifetime in conjunction with his international travels and shifting political investments.

Douglass opens his *Narrative* with his birth into slavery in Maryland, noting his biracial "parentage." His mother, Harriet Bailey, was "colored" and "of a darker complexion" than both of her parents, while his father, who remains unnamed, "was a white man."[4] Even if it is "whispered that my master was my father," the law held that Frederick would be enslaved following his mother's legal "condition."[5] The text relates horrors of slavery including the cruelty of family separation and effects of dehumanizing violence. In the process, the *Narrative* dismantles medievalizing discourses that idealize white supremacy in the American South.

A formative moment in the author's intellectual life is his entry into literacy. His new white slaveholder in Baltimore, Mrs. Sophia Auld, "very kindly commenced to teach me the A, B, C." and he "learn[s] to spell words of three to four letters" before his current "master," Mr. Hugh Auld, expresses his disapproval of her teaching him how to read.[6] Mrs. Auld is initially presented as a gracious lady worthy of admiration: "My new mistress proved to be all she appeared when I first met her ... a woman of the kindest heart and finest feelings"; she was "by trade a weaver" and "a good degree preserved from the blighting and dehumanizing effects of slavery."[7] Initially "unlike any other white woman" he had encountered before, she "seemed to be disturbed" by displays of "crouching servility" and "[h]er face was made of heavenly smiles, and her voice of tranquil music."[8] Through such imagery, the text constructs a vision of white innocence prior to the corrupting experience of power that slavery as an institution would bring.

This image of a "heavenly" fair woman instilling a youthful eagerness to read connects to long history of alphabetic literacy and Marian devotion in medieval European literature. One of the foundational literary works in English tradition deploying such motifs is Geoffrey Chaucer's *ABC*, translated from a French source, which offers

---

2 Douglass, *Narrative*, chap. 11, 112.

3 Douglass, *Bondage and Freedom*; Douglass, *Life and Times*.

4 Douglass, *Narrative*, chap. 1, 2.

5 Ibid., chap. 1, 2–3.

6 Ibid., chap. 4, 33.

7 Ibid., chap. 6, 32.

8 Ibid.

a sequence of prayers to the Virgin with each stanza starting with a sequential letter of the alphabet; Chaucer's "Prioress's Tale," presented by "Madame Eglentine" in *The Canterbury Tales* as if it were a prayer to the Virgin, upholds violent Christian supremacy through a story of a "litel clergeoun" (schoolboy) of "Cristen blood" who exhibits eagerness to read as well as intense Marian devotion.[9] The *Narrative* transforms a medievalizing discourse that conflates the slaveholding "mistress" and the courtly maiden. In the context of later African American medievalism, Charles E. Wilson observes how nineteenth-century American idealizations of white womanhood and *noblesse oblige* are constructed through such medievalizing notions.[10]

The *Narrative* furthermore activates contemporaneous imagery aligning idealized white Christian domesticity with industrious household activities, including instruction of children and proper management of textile goods and related labor.[11] As a "weaver" with the "finest feelings" and a "face made of heavenly smiles" associated with the virtues of reading, Mrs. Auld is multiply inscribed by the *Narrative*'s fusion of medieval courtly and Marian discourses of idealized womanhood: a weaver and lady who adopts the role of the Virgin Mary in medieval imagery and acts as a mother, saint, and mediator.[12] When Mr. Auld "at once forbade Mrs. Auld to instruct me further," characterizing it as "unlawful, as well as unsafe, to teach a slave to read,"[13] the slaveholder's opposition "inspire[d] me with a desire and determination to learn."[14] Enabled by the kind assistance of Mrs. Auld acting as his benevolent intercessor, the author finds in alphabetic literacy "the pathway from slavery to freedom."[15]

The *Narrative* does not sustain its idealized Marian imagery for very long, as the medievalizing discourse of white womanhood is soon revealed to enable a cruel system of violence, and the text enacts a structural critique of slavery's toxic effects on white people as well as illustrating the harms of the institution against black women and men who are enslaved. For Mrs. Auld, the "fatal poison of irresponsible power" that she accesses through the institution of slavery in the domestic sphere transforms her into a strange inversion of a lady in a medieval courtly blazon: "under the influence of slavery" her "cheerful eye … became red with rage,"[16] and "that voice, made all of sweet accord, changed to one of harsh and horrid discord" and "that angelic face gave place to that of a demon."[17] Douglass's disenchanted portrayal of the "poison of irresponsible power" as embodied by Mrs. Auld suggests Toni Morrison's observation that nineteenth-century

---

9 Brogan and Colón, "Abecedarius (abecedarian)"; Chaucer, *Canterbury Tales*, "Prioress's Tale," lines 503 and 497.

10 Wilson, "Medievalism, Race, and Social Order," 76.

11 Smith, "Domesticity and Race," 345.

12 Manuel Cuenca, "Angel in Plantation," 98.

13 Douglass, *Narrative*, chap. 6, 33.

14 Ibid., chap. 6, 34.

15 Ibid., chap. 6, 33.

16 Ibid., chap. 6, 32.

17 Ibid., chap. 6, 32–33.

American literature can reveal "it is the white racial ideology that is savage" in upholding slavery, and it is not just "racist institutions or their laws, but the very concept of whiteness" as a violent power structure that comprises "an inhuman idea."[18]

Douglass describes the verbal and physical abuse that a neighboring white woman, Mrs. Hamilton, enacts against Mary, an enslaved black woman in her household, as particularly abhorrent: "The head, neck and shoulders of Mary were literally cut to pieces" and her head is "covered with festering sores, caused by the lash of her cruel mistress."[19] By dwelling on the notable brutality of violence directed upon an enslaved black woman, Douglass anticipates what later Black feminist theorists Moya Bailey and Trudy would identify as misogynoir, a term they use to describe the harms that contemporary Black women experience due to the combined forces of anti-Black racism and misogyny.[20] By associating Marian discourse and courtly imagery not with idealized white womanhood nor maternal pity but instead with the corrupting influence of slavery upon white slaveholders,[21] as well as the dehumanizing horrors of antiblack and misogynist violence that the institution enables, Douglass in his own time offers a disenchanted inversion of gendered medievalizing imagery.

Douglass's Appendix to the *Narrative* ironically names the hypocrisy of systemic oppressions including racism and misogyny upheld in the name of "Christianity" by claiming it all as a distortion of "Christianity proper."[22] Douglass states: "What I have said respecting and against religion, I mean strictly to apply to the *slaveholding religion* [emphasis in the original text] of this land ... I love the pure, peaceable, and impartial Christianity of Christ," and "I therefore hate the corrupt, slaveholding, women-whipping, cradle-plundering, partial and hypocritical Christianity of this land."[23] Due to the deep associations between slavery and violent white supremacy, it is not surprising that the Christian and European medieval past was anything but idealized for African Americans with experience of plantation life. African American educator Edward L. Blackshear (1862–1919), born into slavery in Alabama, aligns the Southern plantation and the medieval European past: "The plantation," with "cultivated acres," "forest lands," and "hunting grounds," offers an idealized "theatre" of "home-life and ... beautiful and lavish hospitality," but enslaved black laborers "were like the feudatories of Middle Age Chivalry," with the legal and social conditions of slavery producing a "master class by the constant, daily, personal exercise of domination over the enslaved class" analogous to "the feudal system of Europe."[24] As Matthew X. Vernon notes, Blackshear exposes how "the Middle Ages can be deployed as a seductive illusion that disguises historical fact."[25]

---

18 Morrison, "Unspeakable Things," 178.

19 Douglass, *Narrative*, chap. 6, 35.

20 Bailey and Trudy, "On Misogynoir."

21 On Marian imagery and racialized motherhood more broadly, see Tapia, *American Pietàs.*

22 Douglass, *Narrative*, Appendix, 118.

23 Ibid.

24 Blackshear, "Negro in American History"; quoted in Vernon, *Black Middle Ages*, 75.

25 Vernon, *Black Middle Ages*, 76.

Douglass's formative account of entry into literacy in the *Narrative*—crucial to the author's intellectual growth—marks a key moment in his structural analysis of how the "master class" asserts dominance, with knowledge and power as intertwining racialized and gendered systems of control.

Whenever he is left in the house unsupervised, Frederick practices how to write: "after a long, tedious effort for years, I finally succeeded in learning how to write."[26] Literacy is a mechanism for advancement and growth. Frederick notes that he has changed names many times throughout his travels out of practical necessity, but it is now an appropriate time for him to assume a new (and final) name.[27] The concluding chapter marks this pivot in identity, and the selection of a final new name is expressly framed in terms of reading itself as well as a racialized power play between men:

> I gave Mr. Johnson the privilege of choosing me a name, but told him he must not take from me the name of "Frederick." I must hold on to that, to preserve a sense of my identity. Mr. Johnson had just been reading the "Lady of the Lake," and at once suggested that my name be "Douglass." From that time until now I have been called "Frederick Douglass;" and as I am more widely known by that name than by either of the others, I shall continue to use it as my own.[28]

The *Narrative*'s account of the name selection marks the act of becoming a "changed man" through an intellectual journey, and it also conveys the paradox of retaining a core original identity while marking a transformation in status. In 1846, Douglass notes that "Frederick Douglass, the freeman, is a very different person from Frederick Bailey (my former name), the slave," and "I feel myself almost a new man—freedom has given me new life."[29] Douglass's reference to a "new life" and becoming a "new man" signal an implicit allusion to the *Vita Nova* of medieval poet Dante Alighieri, whose courtly love poetry and retroactive gloss on his own younger self states "ond'io mi cangio in figura d'altrui" [I am changed into something new—another man].[30] Douglass's drive toward racial equality and freedom suggests a faith in "the inexorable movement from chaos to order and from violence to peace," akin to what Vernon in a related context refers to as a "progression of Dante's pilgrim from the Inferno to Paradise."[31]

The *Narrative*'s account of the selection of a new name is portrayed as a negotiation process between two men, or a nuanced navigation of what is, and is not, white property.[32] Mr. Johnson is granted the "privilege" of choosing a name (a "privilege" only Frederick can bestow), and Frederick sets the limiting terms. The name "Douglass" (after a

---

26 Douglass, *Narrative*, chap. 7, 44.

27 Ibid., chap. 11, 111–12.

28 Ibid., chap. 11, 112.

29 Douglass, "Letter to William Lloyd Garrison, Jan 27, 1846," 133.

30 Dante Alighieri, *Vita Nova*, trans. Frisardi, 7.12 [XIV.12], lines 12–13, page 18. On African American poet Henrietta Cordelia Ray's appropriation of Dante's sonnets, see Vernon, *Black Middle Ages*, 70–73 and 95–96. On Douglass and Dante, see Looney, *Freedom Readers*, 58–61.

31 Vernon, *Black Middle Ages*, 73.

32 On Cheryl I. Harris and white property, see the introduction to this book.

Figure 1: Writing desk of Frederick Douglass in his Gothic Revival residence at Cedar Hill in the Anacostia neighborhood of Washington, DC. His library, preserved much as it was upon his death, includes editions of the works of Sir Walter Scott, historical romances, and slave narratives. Frederick Douglass National Historic Site. December 2019. Photo by the author.

Scottish character in Scott's poem) might seem incidental as it's not clear how *The Lady of the Lake* relates to Frederick's life, but the importance of this literary name proved meaningful to Douglass in later years. In his library at Cedar Hill, the Late Gothic Revival style home in Washington, DC, where Douglass spent the final years of his life, the book collection that remains largely preserved as it was upon his death contains multiple editions of *The Complete Works of Sir Walter Scott*, among other works of nineteenth-century medievalism and historical romances.[33] In Douglass's later transatlantic travels on the lecture circuit as an abolitionist and civil rights advocate, the name "Douglass" would gain great significance—and the relationship of this name to a politicized inter-pretation of the medieval past would become more apparent.[34]

I will discuss the meanings of "Douglass" soon, but one African American contempo-rary who provides a useful literary contrast to Douglass is Albery Allson Whitman (1851–1901), born into slavery in Kentucky and later an accomplished poet.[35] Whitman engages directly with nineteenth-century poetic medievalism and the historical romances of Scott. While attending Wilberforce University, at the time owned by the African Method-ist Episcopal (AME) Church, Whitman composed a versified historical romance *Not a Man, and Yet a Man* (1877) about a mixed-race hero Rodney (of African and European descent) who is born enslaved and becomes a Union officer during the Civil War, and his journey from bondage to freedom recalls narrative tropes of heroic romances such as *Ivanhoe* and also Douglass's own *Narrative* of becoming a "changed man."[36] The narrative reaches its climax when Rodney encounters his injured former "master" Aylor on the battlefield who asks for (and is granted) forgiveness for his wrongdoings.

Whitman's epic poem, produced in "that spirit of 'self-development'" associated with Wilberforce,[37] abounds with medievalizing imagery. In the final scene, Rodney with his "old heroic heart" raises with "sable hands" his "country's banner, soiled and battle-torn" streaming in the sun's "deep golden light" and the flag "rival[s] Heaven in her bla-zon bright."[38] The Union's victory marks "the day when Southern chivalry / Beheld black manhood clothed in liberty."[39] The poem concludes with a vision of national reconcili-ation (of North and South, black and white) emphasizing the righteous cause of black soldiers or "our sable comrades" fighting under "America's escutcheon [shield or coat of arms] bright" who fought against the social ill or "seething gangrene [of] Slavery" with the patriotism of "knightly Norman[s]" and Crusaders.[40] Claiming African American

---

33 US National Parks Service, "Collections," *Frederick Douglass National Historic Site.*

34 Pettinger, *Douglass and Scotland.* On Douglass and Macbeth, see Briggs, "Exorcism of Macbeth."

35 Wilson, *Dusk of Dawn*, "Introduction," 1–18.

36 Whitman, *Yet a Man.* On Douglass's writings on "black male military valor" and contem-poraneous racialized discourses of national progress and citizenship, see James, *Freedom Bought with Blood*, 12–13 et passim.

37 Whitman, *Yet a Man*, 7.

38 Ibid., 201.

39 Ibid., 202.

40 Ibid., 206.

heroism in chivalric terms recognizable to contemporary white peers, Whitman lever-ages the transformative power of medievalism.

Whitman's poetry reclaims some of the heroism traditionally associated with Euro-pean chivalry (Norman knights and Crusaders) for a mixed-race hero and for African American soldiers, but Douglass's own imaginings of the medieval European past cri-tique pervasive myths of "Anglo-Saxon" racial purity and their implications for global white supremacy in anglophone societies. Douglass and writers within the African American intellectual milieu of the AME Church used the coinage "Anglo-African" to dis-lodge myths of white "Anglo-Saxon" racial purity defined as direct ancestry from Britain and Northern Europe. In the "Apology" to *The Anglo-African Magazine* (1858–1862), a publication providing a venue for black thought, the editors characterized the unreal-ized intellectual and political might of African Americans as a "*noir fainéant* [or] black sluggard" that would eventually agitate to "[s]hake the pillars of the commonweal!";[41] this term *noir fainéant* alludes to an epithet for the disguised King Richard I in Scott's *Ivanhoe* referring to the king as one who springs Britain into action once he reveals him-self.[42] The glories of medieval Britain jut up against the editors' rebuke of white Ameri-cans who idealize "unbroken lineal descent" from early medieval Britain, and the editors emphasize how "Anglo-Saxon" itself implies hybridity: "[t]he inhabitants of Africa, like the Anglo-Saxons, are a mixed people."[43] Vernon notes that the coinage "Anglo-African" asserts a "double emphasis on origins ... while it also [holds] out the possibility for a novel reading of identity" that not only debunks myths of racial purity but also inter-twines black and white anglophones in a narrative of collective advancement.[44]

In the years immediately after the first publication of his *Narrative*, Douglass further developed his own analogies between the modern US and medieval Europe, compar-ing medieval conflicts in the English/Scottish border zones of Britain to the recent war between the US and Mexico (1846–1848). In an 1848 article in the *North Star* (abolition-ist newspaper that Douglass founded in Rochester, NY), Douglass references the mythos of medieval Britain to critique US imperialism and ideologies of westward expansion: "Mexico seems a doomed victim to Anglo Saxon cupidity and love of dominion."[45] In this case, "Anglo Saxon cupidity" names the ongoing harms of white American settler colo-nialism and imperialism along the US/Mexico border zone. During his time in Scotland, Douglass expressed his support for ongoing struggles for Scottish independence and the Scottishness of the name "Douglass" accrues layered meanings.[46] Invoking the "free hills of old Scotland," Douglass refers to an "ancient 'black Douglass'" who might stand

---

41 Vernon, *Black Middle Ages*, 61.

42 Ibid.

43 Ibid., 61–62.

44 Ibid., 62.

45 Ibid., 75.

46 Douglass writes from "Scotland, [where] almost every hill, river, mountain and lake ... has been made classic by the heroic deeds of her noble sons" and streams "poured into song" and many a hill "associated with some fierce and bloody conflict between liberty and slavery" ("Letter to Francis Jackson").

Figure 2: Metropolitan African Methodist Episcopal (AME) Church, featuring grand Gothic arches and stained glass. Frederick Douglass attended this church throughout his residence in the city and his funeral was held here in 1895. Washington, DC. December 2019. Photo by the author.

up to any foe who seeks to "make a slave" of him,[47] and Douglass's own fight for freedom is aligned with historical struggles for independence in different border zones in Britain. This expressed analogy between Scottish independence struggles and the current US/Mexico border conflict reflects what Vernon calls a "crucial ... understanding [of] hemispheric solidarities caused by American expressions of force" and its "evocation of mythical self-exceptions" that "Anglo-Saxon" alignments support.[48]

Douglass's use of geopolitical analogies to express solidarity with liberation struggles globally contextualizes his famous lecture on "Our Composite Nationality" (1869), delivered a few years after the Civil War ended, positing a new form of multiracial American collectivity. In this speech, Douglass expresses principles of universal "human rights" or "rights of humanity" that are "eternal, universal and indestructible," including equal citizenship laws, the right to vote, and unrestricted mobility defined as the "right of locomotion" and "right of migration."[49] In response to what Edlie L. Wong has characterized as an increasing late nineteenth-century "exclusionary discourse of Christian civilization" that "refashioned Native American and Chinese racial differences" through a rhetoric of "heathenism" that presented these communities of color as "morally unfit for citizenship,"[50] Douglass makes clear that the nation must live up to the "principle of perfect civil equality to the people of all races and of all creeds."[51]

Douglass observes that "a new race is making its appearance within our borders" (i.e., Chinese),[52] and that the Chinese in America should have the right to be "naturalized [and] invested with all the rights of American citizenship" and not be subject to exclusionary immigration laws.[53] Moreover, people "from Asia, Africa, or the Isles of the Sea" can find a home in the nation,[54] and Douglass "want[s] a home here not only for the negro, mulatto, and the Latin races,"[55] but also for the "Indian and Celt, negro and Saxon, Latin and Teuton, Mongolian and Caucasian, Jew and gentile"—all of whom claim belonging in a composite nationality, a microcosm of the globe, enhanced by immigration and heterogeneity.[56] By invoking "a liberal and brotherly welcome to all likely to come to the United States,"[57] Douglass revises contemporaneous claims to "Anglo-Saxon" purity and "Anglo-African" identities by stating the equality of the "negro and Saxon" among many other configurations of racial and ethnic groups, and he makes clear his

---

47 Vernon, *Black Middle Ages*, 46.

48 Ibid., 75. See also Abrams, "Douglass and Mexican War."

49 Douglass, "Composite Nationality," 294. On his support of women's suffrage, see Douglass, "Radical Woman Suffrage Man."

50 Wong, *Racial Reconstruction*, 98.

51 Douglass, "Composite Nationality," 295.

52 Ibid., 286.

53 Ibid., 293.

54 Ibid., 302.

55 Ibid., 294.

56 Ibid., 303.

57 Ibid., 295.

own investments in expressing solidarity with communities of color against white supremacy.

Throughout the *Narrative* and his career, Douglass repurposes medievalizing discourse for three important ends: exposing the brutality and harms of white supremacy in the US; using racialized analogies across Britain and America to dismantle notions of "Anglo-Saxon" purity; and envisioning a progressive "composite" model of collective identity. Douglass's antiracist polemic expresses support for the rights of aspiring Chinese Americans and solidarity with communities of color and minority groups including Jews and immigrants of Asian and Latin ancestry. Douglass and other African Americans set the stage for Chinese Americans who would soon, from their own vantage points, join the struggle to dismantle medievalizing claims to white supremacy and to oppose racial exclusion.

Wong Chin Foo and Chinese American Medievalisms

Early Chinese Americans didn't share with African Americans a collective experience of slavery, but the legal institutions and barriers that Chinese Americans faced during the second half of the nineteenth century through the era of Chinese Exclusion (1882–1943) were a set of policies severely restricting immigration and denying citizenship on the basis of race, as well as broader perceptions of Chinese immigration as a threat to white labor and stereotypes of Chinese as "heathens" and "perpetual aliens" who could never assimilate into white anglophone society. Edlie L. Wong's careful work of literary and cultural analysis *Racial Reconstruction* (2015) reveals how polemics of Black inclusion in the later nineteenth century coincided with, or even depended upon, discourses of Chinese exclusion. Early Chinese Americans (and Chinese unsuccessfully seeking to obtain US citizenship) found themselves confronting harms of the era's medievalizing discourses of "heathenism" and they developed strategies for arguing against racial exclusion and critiquing white missionary ideologies of assimilation.

In contrast to Douglass who distinguishes between a peaceful "Christianity proper" and a white supremacist perversion of religious ethics, Wong Chin Foo (1847–1898), likely one of the first people to use the term "Chinese American" in reference to a sociopolitical identity, unapologetically rejects the alignment of white supremacy and Christian progress. Composed after he was naturalized as a citizen in 1874 in Michigan (which took place before the implementation of the Chinese Exclusion Act of 1882), he penned a scathing essay "Why Am I a Heathen?" (1887).[58] Wong notes he was "[b]orn and raised a heathen," and although he had in early life "seriously contemplated becoming the bearer of heavenly tidings to my 'benighted' heathen people" upon exposure to Christian missionaries,[59] he found no form of Christianity satisfying and he critiques the sinophobia of white Christians. He imagines entering heaven to meet Denis Kearney, Irish American instigator of violent anti-Chinese labor riots in California and the American West, and see him "forget his heavenly songs, and howl once more: 'The Chinese

---

58 Wong, "Why Am I a Heathen?"

59 Ibid., 169.

must go!' and organize a heavenly crusade to have me and others immediately cast out to the other place."[60] Wong exposes the bigotry of white self-proclaimed Christians and rebukes their greed and imperialism abroad, sarcastically concluding by saying he "earnestly invite[s] the Christians of America to come to Confucius."[61] Thwarting the developmental trajectory of a spiritual journey or assimilation narrative, Wong maintains an ethical "heathen" status.

In the summer of 1887 one of Wong's most ostentatious performances of chivalric masculinity took place: he challenged Kearney to a duel. Wong's challenge to his opponent was this: "I would give him his choice of chopsticks, Irish potatoes or Krupp guns."[62] Kearney's disdainful retort to Wong deployed medievalizing and sinophobic discourses: "I'm not to be deterred ... by the low blackguard vaporings of Chin Foo ... or any other representative of Asia's almond-eyed lepers."[63] Wong's offer to have Kearney choose among "Irish potatoes" or "Krupp guns" as weapon options not only implicates Kearney's own immigrant status and socioeconomic status; Wong also references Kearney's career of enabling armed violence through racist appeals to aggrieved white masculinity. In his speech on "composite nationality," Douglass had noted the hypocrisy of Irish American racism against the Chinese, deploying his own discourse of chivalric brotherhood to make his point: "Already have our Celtic brothers" (i.e., Irish Americans), started to "[form] associations ... in avowed hostility to the Chinese," eager to "execute the behests of popular prejudice against the weak and defenseless."[64] As Tania Nicole Jabour demonstrates, Wong's performances of chivalric masculinity in 1887 and onwards displayed to the public both the rhetorical and physical violence of anti-Chinese rhetoric itself.[65]

Douglass's thinking about racial mixture (given his own "parentage") and contemporaneous African American efforts to claim an "Anglo-African" or "composite" identity can be set in contrast with Wong's public medievalism. One of Wong's most overt literary strategies for resisting white norms was to embrace historical and mythological Chinese traditions and to use medieval genres to create spaces for Asian heroism in lieu of European models. *Wu Chih Tien, The Celestial Empress* (1889), Wong's serial novel and alleged English "translation" of a Chinese romance, is set during the time of China's only female ruler Wu Zetian (武則天) who lived in the Tang Dynasty, a historical period contemporaneous with the Western Middle Ages. The novel alludes to classics of Chinese literature such as the fourteenth-century *The Romance of the Three Kingdoms* (三國演義), repurposing a familiar set of narrative and visual conventions from European historical novels and challenging readers to accept Asian protagonists.[66] Wong's

60 Ibid., 171.

61 Ibid., 179.

62 "Denis Kearney," *Chicago Tribune*; Seligman, *First Chinese American*, 116.

63 Ibid.

64 Douglass, "Composite Nationality," 291.

65 Jabour, "Spectacular Subjects," 127–73.

66 I discuss this work further in the introduction to this book.

embrace of non-European historical influences marks a divergence from African American strategies of reclaiming historical romances set in medieval Britain.

Wong was not the only early Chinese American thinker to create space for national belonging through first-person writing and literary historical narratives. Yan Phou Lee (1861–1938), one of the first Chinese students to earn a degree in the US (at Yale, aided by the Chinese Educational Mission), published a memoir *When I Was a Boy in China* (1887) with his surname "last" just like white Americans.[67] Although he submitted paperwork around 1887, an amendment to the exclusion law prevented him from ever claiming citizenship. Lee's "Why I am Not a Heathen: A Rejoinder to Wong Chin Foo" (1887) distinguishes between "religion" (or as Douglass calls it, "Christianity proper") and "ethics" as practiced in real life, and Lee emphasizes the benevolence of white Christians who supported his integration into American society.[68]

Lee's childhood memoir offers a narrative of education, assimilation, and progress palatable to white audiences while subtly critiquing Western adventure stories.[69] In a chapter describing his education in China, Lee notes the appeal of Chinese legends and narratives that are "historical or romantic" relating stories "of war, of love, of magic and enchantment" that are "really beautiful ... and as interesting as an English novel,"[70] including the *Romance of the Three Kingdoms*, which Lee calls a "historical novel" with such "delineation of characters and elegance of diction" that he finds "few books in English its equal."[71] Yung Wing (1828–1912), another key figure in the Chinese Educational Mission, became a citizen of the US only to have his citizenship revoked years after the Chinese Exclusion Act. Yung's *My Life in China and America* (1909) fondly recalls reading Sir Walter Scott and English authors at the Monson Academy in Massachusetts.[72] In contrast to the unapologetically "heathen" Wong, assimilationists such as Lee and Yung posit Chinese historical romance traditions as structural equivalents to the medieval-themed "English novel."

Yung interweaves conventions of travel narrative and missionary accounts of progress to craft what Asian American literary historian Patricia P. Chu calls a "Chinese sequel to the slave narrative."[73] Just as Douglass and other formerly enslaved male narrators "spoke as global citizens for the concerns of enslaved Africans everywhere," so does Yung address "liberal white readers as both a global citizen" and as an "elite American-educated Chinese" who also seeks to "improve the fates of less fortunate Chinese."[74] In this global social context it is "unsurprising that Yung shared with Douglass ... the

---

67 Lee, *Boy in China*.

68 Lee, "Not a Heathen."

69 Cheung, "Early Chinese American Autobiography," 50–51.

70 Lee, *Boy in China*, 81.

71 Ibid., 82.

72 Yung, *China and America*, 31.

73 Chu, *Where I Have Never Been*, 40; also 145–49 and 165–76.

74 Ibid., 165.

imperative to demonstrate cultural mastery and Western masculinity."[75] The historical construction of a European "global subject" has its earliest antecedents, as Chu suggests, in the thirteenth-century *Travels of Marco Polo* and famous medieval adventurers.[76] Medieval literary historians Geraldine Heng and Shirin A. Khanmohamadi have shown how medieval European forms of ethnographic writing (narratives about "self" and "other") establish modes of elite masculine self-fashioning through travel; both secular romance narratives and writings by medieval missionaries participate in a historical process of constructing the masculine Western European writer as the "omniscient" narrator and "universal" subject of discourse.[77]

As a counterpart to Wong's resistant "heathen" identity and rejection of medieval European models in favor of Chinese traditions, Yung's construction of a masculine subject aligns Chinese historical romances with literary traditions established by the European Middle Ages. Due to his affinity for Eurocentric masculinity, Yung has been characterized as a white supremacist and assimilationist, with Asian American literary critic Frank Chin describing Yung's work as "mission-schoolboy-makes-good Gunga Din licking up white fantasy."[78] Yung's invocations of medieval narrative traditions (Chinese and European) are not expressly antiracist, but his rhetorical positionings and desire to assimilate as a person whose citizenship had been revoked can be useful for theorizing what would later be called "honorary whiteness."[79]

Wong's public performance of chivalry bespeaks an ambivalent relationship to white Eurocentric models of masculinity and exposes his own implication in systemic anti-blackness. A circular published on behalf of the Chinese Equal Rights League in Chicago as the "First Voice of the Americanized Chinese in the United States to the Public" (1897), and signed by Wong as the League's president,[80] invokes a restoration of full rights of citizenship for "Americanized and American-born Chinese of the United States" and the "glories and responsibilities" of the "home and country in which we live" and "cherish in our hearts" but "cannot legally call ... our own."[81] In making this appeal, Wong invokes "Americanized Chinese" feelings of injustice in beholding "our colored brethren, even from the wilds of African jungles" who "sit and eat at the National family table, while we, the descendants of the oldest race on earth, are not even allowed to pick up the crumbs."[82]

Wong's statement on behalf of the League indulges in its own forms of ethnocentrism (the claim that the Chinese are the "oldest race" on earth with all the associations of civilization and cultural superiority that the term implies), and the text problemati-

---

75 Ibid., 166.

76 Ibid., 147.

77 Heng, *Empire of Magic*, 239–306; Khanmohamadi, *Light of Another's Word*.

78 Chin, "Ye Asian American Writers," 11.

79 López, *White by Law*; Sen, *Not Quite Not White*; Valdez Young, "Honorary Whiteness."

80 "A Chinese League," *The San Francisco Call*, May 27, 1897, 6.

81 Ibid. See also Chinese Equal Rights League, *Appeal for Equality of Manhood*, 2–3.

82 Ibid.

cally invokes tropes of primitive blackness for rhetorical effect. By using such tropes of antiblackness within a document ascribed to a Chinese American community, and seeking to address a white audience in particular, the document anticipates what would later be called the "model minority" myth that positions Asian Americans as responsible subjects worthy of full rights of citizenship in an implicit or overt contrast to allegedly undeserving African Americans.[83]

However problematic Wong's document on behalf of the League reads in retrospect, it importantly allows for early Chinese Americans to claim African Americans as "our colored brethren," casting legally enfranchised African Americans and disenfranchised Chinese Americans as fellow people of color. As literary historian Edlie L. Wong observes, "Wong [Chin Foo], like Douglass ... before him," names "Reconstruction's failed vision of racial egalitarianism" while also challenging "the Orientalizing discourse of heathenism" that upholds the binary of "black inclusion / Chinese exclusion."[84] The statement on behalf of the League reveals how the power structures upholding white supremacy can set communities of color against one another as if in a competition for resources (e.g., seeking a limited number of seats at the table or fighting for "crumbs"), as if white supremacy itself were not the real problem. Even with its flaws, the League's appeal at least exposes to white audiences the very arbitrariness of racial exclusions enacted by unequal citizenship laws.

The "national family table" metaphor used in the Chinese Equal Rights League's appeal at the end of the nineteenth century anticipates discourses of national belonging adopted by African American writers in the decades to come. In the iconic poem "I, Too" (1926) by Langston Hughes, the speaker states that he is "the darker brother" excluded from the national table and yet "I, too, am America" and will "be at the table / When company comes" in the near future.[85] A reconfigured "table" through the Arthurian knights of the Round Table informs Benjamin Brawley's sonnets published in 1922 to "Chaucer" and "My Hero" (Colonel Robert Gould Shaw of the African American Civil War regiment),[86] and a poem (ca. 1907) composed in heroic couplets by Hallie E. Queen addressed to James Weldon Johnson invokes the latter as a "gallant knight" and invites him to partake in "choicest viands, rich and mete for all."[87] These later African American writers experiment with medievalizing metaphors in a vision of "arriving at a court in which all are equal."[88]

Early African American and Chinese American thinkers divergently employ medieval motifs and medievalizing discourses to participate in public discussions of racism, citizenship, and collective national belongings. Douglass offers an ethnic model of a

---

83 Chou and Feagin, *Model Minority*, 23 and 175 et passim.

84 Wong, *Racial Reconstruction*, 118.

85 Rampersad and Roessel, eds., *Poems of Langston Hughes*, 46.

86 Vernon, *Black Middle Ages*, 93.

87 Ibid., 94.

88 Ibid., 95. On medievalism and Harlem Renaissance writers, see Whitaker, "B(l)ack in the Middle Ages"; Whitaker, *Harlem Middle Ages*.

masculine *Bildungsroman* that later Chinese American authors would engage, and both Douglass's "composite nationality" discourse and Wong's "national family table" metaphor create more racially expansive visions of belonging and new forms of solidarity across communities of color.

Ameen Rihani: Medievalism and Auto-Orientalism

I have put early African American and early Chinese American authors in conversation to explore how they adopt, or reject, white Eurocentric medievalizing models of masculinity. I end by discussing Arab American writer Ameen Rihani (1876–1940), who was not only the author of the first Arab American poetry collection in English, *Myrtle and Myrrh* (1905), but also wrote in Arabic and English and was an accomplished English translator of medieval Arabic poetry.[89] Born in Lebanon to a Maronite Christian family and naturalized as a US citizen in 1901, his spiritual and philosophical novel *The Book of Khalid* (1911) claims dual status not only as a foundational Arab American immigration narrative but also a fusion of medieval Arabic traditions and medieval Western intertexts (including hagiography and chivalric romance).

Literary critics such as Waïl S. Hassan have noted how Rihani's work disrupts contemporaneous forms of Orientalism, a dominant "colonialist hierarchy of values that defines the East as primitive, childish, superstitious and the West as advanced, mature, rational."[90] This "inaugural text of Arab American fiction" by a first-person narrator "fuse[s] Arabic and Western literature thematically, linguistically, formally, and structurally,"[91] and Rihani was fully capable of "[writing] against the grain of Orientalism."[92] The book broadly evokes the structures of an ethnic immigrant *Bildungsroman* with its protagonist, Khalid, who is born in Lebanon, moves to New York, and navigates influences of "Eastern" spirituality and "Western" materialism. Nonetheless, as literary historian Layla Al Maleh observes, the narrative is not only loosely based on Rihani's life recounting an "intellectual development" but also "a philosophical dissertation and a work of ... mystical imagination, and satirical and political understatement"[93] with "myriad allusions to stories from such diverse sources [as] the Qur'an to *Arabian Nights*."[94] The book is consequently "the offspring of more than one culture and one literary genre, a unique hybrid."[95]

The book jacket advertisement for the original 1911 edition of *The Book of Khalid* presents it as "a frank, free and striking criticism of the Occident by the Orient," i.e., "the Immigrant" conjured as a "dark-eyed, swarthy gentleman who presides over a

---

89 Al Maleh, "Literary Parentage," 313.

90 Hassan, "Orientalism and Cultural Translation," 378.

91 Ibid., 385.

92 Ibid., 400.

93 Al Maleh, "Literary Parentage," 315.

94 Ibid., 321.

95 Ibid., 337.

pushcart" who now "break[s] forth into excellent English [to] give a clear, spirited, care-fully considered and telling criticism of America, Americans, our manners, habits [and] institutions."[96] This trope of an "Oriental" figure disarmingly critiquing the "Occident" and "our" habits evokes longstanding tropes of "othering," as medieval literary historian John M. Ganim notes in his work on orientalism and medievalism and the uncanny Asian or "Oriental" origins underlying founding myths of white European identity.[97] One vivid instance of this from European medieval travel writing is the English knight-narrator of the *Travels of Sir John Mandeville* whose journeys throughout the Middle East and Asia include encounters with a French-speaking Sultan who offers a forceful critique of the moral failings of European Christians, a "dis-orienting" process that Khanmohamadi describes as being "othered" and "worlded" through travel across the globe.[98]

The distinctly cross-cultural and mystical medieval "aura" of Rihani's book is estab-lished in its opening, with its vivid trope of the miraculous "found book." "The Editor" states that in the "Khedivial Library of Cairo, among the Papyri of the Scribe of Amen-Ra and the beautifully illuminated copies of the Korân," was found the "modern Arabic Manuscript which forms the subject of this Book" now entitled in English *The Book of Khalid*.[99] An "amanuensis" is hired to make a copy, and its "weaving" is composed of "material ... of such a mixture that here and there the raw silk of Syria is often spun with the cotton and wool of America."[100] This richly textured opening synthesizes mate-rial associated with Asia (silk) and America (cotton, wool), and the Khedivial Library itself was known for its fusions of neo-Islamic architecture and collection of illuminated medieval Qur'an manuscripts.[101]

In *The Book of Khalid*, two young boys, Khalid and Shakib, arrive in New York's "Little Syria" in Lower Manhattan after embarking on the "Via Dolorosa," or arduous journey from Beirut to Europe to New York, characterized as "the suffering and misery which emigrants must undergo, before they reach that Western Paradise of the Oriental imagination."[102] They initially make a living by selling trinkets they claim are from the Holy Land, "a common occupation for impoverished Lebanese immigrants at that time."[103] The irony of selling fake Holy Land souvenirs upon arriving from the real Levant is not lost on literary critics, who find an affinity with Chaucer's knowingly corrupt pilgrim the Pardoner in *The Canterbury Tales* who sells fake holy objects for profit. As Suheil B. Bushrui states: "Like Chaucer's Pardoner, Khalid is sufficiently clear-sighted to feel disgust for his own deceptive practices in convincing a credulous public to buy spurious

---

96 Rihani, *Book of Khalid*, ed. Fine, "Introduction," 9.

97 Ganim, *Medievalism and Orientalism*; see also Akbari, *Idols in the East.*

98 Khanmohamadi, *Light of Another's Word*, 113–44, at 140.

99 Rihani, *Book of Khalid*, 17.

100 Ibid.

101 Ibid., 472–73.

102 Ibid., 36.

103 Hassan, "Orientalism and Cultural Translation," 393.

relics and 'sacred' wares."[104] The author reconfigures an immigrant journey along the lines of the "Via Dolorosa" of Christ in the Holy Land, and the capitalist replication of the "Holy Land" for Western consumption upon arrival enacts a satire of human foibles and a disorienting inversion of space and place.

Khalid is more free-spirited and bohemian, while Shakib is more pragmatic—and by the time they both return to Lebanon they find themselves transformed by their experiences. Khalid imparts his philosophical knowledge and calls for religious transcendence. Rihani's appropriations of the medieval past don't fully conform to "Western" (Eurocentric) or "Eastern" (in this case Muslim) conventions. In one scene reflecting contemporary forms of regionalized Arab nationalism, Khalid sees "antique colour prints" from a bazaar in Damascus with "heroes of Arabia" including Saladin and states: "We need another Saladin" in the present day, "a Saladin of the Idea" who will "wage a crusade" not against any religion ("Christianity [nor] Mohammedanism," i.e., Islam),[105] but instead against the political sovereignty of the Ottomans, who controlled much of the Mashriq (eastern part of the Arab world) in Rihani's day. Rihani transforms Saladin from an exemplary medieval Muslim leader standing against Christian European crusaders to a figure for Arab resistance to Turks, abstracting "Saladin of the Idea" into a figure for local sociopolitical struggles for self-determination.

Rihani's enigmatic *Bildungsroman* not only avoids monolithic constructions of "Western" and "Oriental" cultural identities but also experiments with racial positionings that sidestep white hegemony. Swati Rana has explored the sociopolitical notion of "brownness" as a literary construction that creates "mixed identifications" in the writings of Rihani and twentieth-century minority immigrant American authors, and *The Book of Khalid* opens up space for complex forms of American racial and national subjectivity that elude narrowly defined norms of white Christian identity.[106] When Khalid meets "a certain American lady, a Mrs. Goodfree, or Gotfry," who is of the Bahá'í faith and evades clear racial categorization, the narrator describes her as "an Oriental gem in an American setting," or a "strange Southern beauty in an exotic frame," or a woman of Mexican or "of Andalusian, and consequently of Arabian, origin" due to her brownish "complexion, neither white nor olive, but partak[ing] of both," and she happens to be dressed in both black and white, "like myself."[107] Such a multifaceted and racially ambiguous description of an American whose non-Black cultural identity cannot be reduced to whiteness suggests the author's own mobile "Oriental," "Arabian," "swarthy," or "brown" positionings across time and space, an unfixed form of racial belonging that might potentially "partake" in whiteness only under certain circumstances.

The Book of Khalid ultimately does not idealize Lebanon or America, and the text demonstrates the protagonist's detachment from both of his "homelands." Disillusioned by his experiences with a monastic community upon his return to Lebanon, Khalid's

---

104 Bushrui, "First Arab Novel in English," 31.

105 Rihani, *Book of Khalid*, 220–21.

106 Rana, "Brownness," 19–44.

107 Rihani, *Book of Khalid*, 207–8.

concluding exile into the desert (where he mysteriously vanishes at the end of the text) evokes Saint Anthony's temptation in the desert and "read[ing] in the *sinksar* (hagiography) the Life of the Saint of the day" in a monastic community recalls medieval Christian monks in Egypt or North Africa.[108] At the same time, the book's pervasive references to "Oriental" cultural contexts evoke the Arabic genre of *rihla,* or an intellectual narrative of travel and search for knowledge, so often associated with medieval Muslim authors, that recounts movement across expansive spaces.[109] Christian and Muslim analogies circulate throughout *The Book of Khalid,* as "Al-Gazzali," the medieval philosopher whom Muslims "so much prize and quote," is likened to "St. Augustine of the Christians,"[110] the North African and Father of the Latin Church who converted after reading Saint Anthony's life in the desert.[111] A broad synthesis of "Oriental" (Arab and Islamic) influences, Rahini's text reframes through its Mediterranean settings some of the foundational Asian and African contexts of "Western" Christianity. By traversing America, Europe, Asia, and Africa, this "Oriental" narrator suggests how ideas and cultures circulate to construct any given intellectual or textual tradition, and the travels of peoples throughout medieval Afro-Eurasia are profoundly implicated in the very foundations of Western religious and literary traditions.

Building Solidarity Movements

This chapter has focused on three Americans of divergent ethnic and religious backgrounds: African American (Frederick Douglass), Chinese American (Wong Chin Foo), and Arab American (Ameen Rihani), writing respectively from Christian, "heathen," and a philosophical hybrid of Islamic and "Western" Christian perspectives. I have shown how motifs of medieval romance shape their divergent narratives of national belonging. Each author creates new venues for representation beyond Eurocentric models of masculinity, repurposing medieval influences to claim full citizenship, resist narrow forms of assimilation, and hybridize cultural and intellectual influences. These authors critique gendered white ideologies of progress and imperialism and offer transformative visions of social reform.

Medievalism offers a new appreciation of how "founding figures" of ethnic minority traditions transform dominant notions of race and masculinity by conspicuously disidentifying with a medieval European past, and by claiming a shared national identity that evades monolithic notions of "Anglo-Saxon" purity. This analysis moreover reveals early flows of Afro-Asian influence in public discourse and literary expression. Douglass, Wong, and their contemporaries enact antiracist dialogues across African American and Chinese American political frameworks. Rihani shares Wong's investments in dismantling Eurocentric forms of medievalism and critiquing nineteenth-century Orientalism,

---

108 Ibid., 166.
109 Touati, *Islam and Travel,* 2 et passim.
110 Rihani, *Book of Khalid,* 232–33.
111 Wilhite, "Augustine the African."

and his richly intertextual and syncretic thinking makes visible racial belongings beyond whiteness or blackness *per se*, as well as showcasing some of the pervasive North African influences within the very foundations of "Western" Christianity. It is this question of cross-racial solidarity, in response to converging histories of oppression, that I address in the next chapter.

Chapter Two

PLAGUE: TOXIC CHIVALRY, CHINATOWN CRUSADES, AND CHINESE/JEWISH SOLIDARITIES

THIS CHAPTER TRACES intertwined histories of sinophobia and antisemitism in the age of "Yellow Peril" and social anxieties about plague and public health at the turn of the twentieth century. I trace how Chinese and Jewish diaspora solidarity movements emerged and took action in response to a geopolitical environment that vilified racialized urban minorities as sources of physical contagion and moral corruption. The essays and ethnographic writings of Chinese American author Wong Chin Foo and the journalism and short stories of Sui Sin Far (born in England to a white English father and a Chinese mother) combat the dehumanization of Chinese communities throughout North America, and both authors critique the era's medievalizing discourses that support harmful forms of white Christian supremacy.

Bubonic Plague Returns: Sinophobia and Antisemitism

In the year 1900, the bubonic plague struck San Francisco's Chinatown. As the first modern outbreak of the epidemic approached the west coast of North America, news reports sparked widespread fears over public health and the corrupting forces of crowded urban environments. The Sunday edition of the *New York Journal* (March 18, 1900), owned by William Randolph Hearst, featured the headline "Black Plague Creeps Into America," accompanied by medieval iconography and biblical quotations.[1] Reports describing "bubonic plague" as "the dreaded 'black death' of the Orient" stoked public fears in the age of "Yellow Peril," a set of cultural discourses throughout Europe, North America, Australia, and New Zealand that associated Asians collectively with socioeconomic threat, disease, and contagion.[2] In one vivid example, the *Lincoln County Leader* (May 11, 1900) featured an illustrated map of the "Progress of the Plague Across the Pacific" from Australasia toward North America, stating that "[o]nce the plague gets a foothold among East Indians or Chinese coolies it is almost impossible to check it, except with the extermination of the population affected."[3] An illustration accompanying these headlines reveals "How Russia Cures the Bubonic Plague," depicting a group of

---

1 Risse, *Plague, Fear, and Politics*, 118.

2 "Chinatown Is a Menace to Health!," *The San Francisco Call*. Subheadings read "Physical Assimilation Impossible," "Grave Danger of Over-Production," "Crowding Out Americans," and "Question Involves Our Civilization." For an anthology of "Yellow Peril" texts and resources, see Tchen and Yeats, *Yellow Peril!*

3 "Scourge!," *Lincoln County Leader*.

soldiers with their guns aimed to execute a group of "[un]fortunate coolies" who carry the "terrible disease."[4]

When reporters and government officials used phrases along the lines of "Black Plague"—and envisioned the prospect of "extermination" of entire populations deemed a threat to public health—these "Yellow Peril" discourses recalled violent scapegoating rhetorics of the medieval European past. In Western Europe, disparate origin myths describing the fourteenth-century spread of the so-called Black Death had ascribed the source of what they called in their own time the great pestilence (*pestis*) or mortality (*mortalitas*) to somewhere in Asia, and accounts of disease transmission claimed that the plague entered into Western Europe through port cities, with European writers associating the disease itself with black rats and moral depravity.[5] In one notorious version of this origin myth, Sicilian chronicler Michele da Piazza ascribes the arrival of the pestilence "at the port city of Messina" in October 1347 to "Genoese galleys, fleeing our Lord's wrath which came down upon them for their misdeeds," who brought with them "a plague that they carried down to the very marrow of their bones."[6] Florentine chronicler Giovanni Villani (ca. 1348) ascribes the "pestilence" to Asian origins, stating that "God's justice fell harshly among the Tartars [Mongols], so much that it seemed incredible,"[7] and "at Silvas [in Anatolia], it rained an immeasurable quantity of vermin … all black and with tails, some alive and some dead," emitting a foul "stench" and all of those "who fought against the vermin fell victim to their venom."[8] French physician and medical authority Guy de Chauliac (1363) describes a great "mortality" that "overtook the whole world, or nearly all of it," which "began in the East, and like shooting arrows it passed through us on its way west."[9]

By ascribing the "pestilence" to foreign bodies and black vermin, and describing the disease as deeply ingrained in the bodies of those who transport it, Western European discourses of plague participate in what Geraldine Heng calls an essentializing process of biopolitical "race-making."[10] European writers circulated an array of discourses for describing "foreign" threats by associating plague with corpses, vermin, or "hordes," in addition to adopting racializing sensory discourses of smell,[11] in order to construct a dehumanizing and morally coded discourse of invasion and urban contagion (and interpreting the transmission or acquisition of the disease itself as a sign of divine

---

4 Ibid.

5 On the Black Death as a global pandemic via genetics and the history of medicine, see Green, "Making Black Death Global"; Green, "Learning How to Teach the Black Death."

6 Aberth, *Black Death*, 29. (Michele da Piazza, *Cronaca*, ed. Antonino Giuffrida (Palermo: ILA Palma, 1980), 82, 86.)

7 Ibid., 19. (Giovanni Villani, *Nuova cronica*, ed. Giuseppe Porta, 3 vols. (Parma: Bembo, 1990–1991), 3:486–88. Translated by Aubrey Threlkeld.)

8 Ibid., 20.

9 Ibid., 64. (Heinrich Haeser, *Lehrbuch der Geschichte der Medizin und der epidemischen Krankheiten*, 2 vols. (Jena: Mauke, 1853–1865), 2:175–76.)

10 Heng, *Invention of Race*, 3–4 et passim.

11 Heng, *England and Jews*, 71–72 et passim.

punishment). As the plague progressed throughout medieval Europe, scapegoating of vulnerable urban populations resulted in physical violence, most notoriously through massacres of Jews and segregation of "lepers" or people who exhibited symptoms of what we might now interpret as Hansen's Disease.[12] In a long view of histories of plague and dehumanization, the *Lincoln County Leader*'s reference to the "extermination of the population [of] Chinese coolies" who transmit the bubonic plague, supported by a chronology of "The Plague in History" that includes the "pestilence" in the fourteenth century moving "from Arabia" through "Asia Minor" before claiming "25,000,000 victims in Europe,"[13] exploits journalistic medievalism for alarmingly racist ends.[14]

In the age of "Yellow Peril," the resurrection of medievalizing origin myths for disease transmission presents white Europeans as the lamentable "victims" of a foreign threat, creating a fiction of what Cord J. Whitaker in a related context calls "a golden age of white racial homogeny ... a fantasy [medieval] era organized by the notion of white innocence" that cultivates "a prevailing sense of white victimhood" in which "all nonwhites are aggressors" or existential threats while "whites are blameless victims."[15] The vilification of "Chinese coolies" in the early twentieth century blaming Asian "hordes" for bringing disease upon "victims in Europe" revives medieval European forms of racial scapegoating. More recently, modern journalists writing during the outbreak of the global COVID-19 (coronavirus) pandemic in 2020 have used fourteenth-century European accounts of the bubonic plague's alleged origins to launch their own interpretations of the social consequences of the so-called Black Death, and academic medievalists such as Su Fang Ng and Mary Rambaran-Olm have exposed how such modern narratives of disease transmission can replicate the xenophobic propaganda that medieval writers promoted in their own day.[16]

In response to the bubonic plague outbreak at the turn of the twentieth century, public heath discourses regarding Chinatowns—in port cities around the globe—sought to scapegoat urban ethnic minorities and to quarantine the perceived threats (medical, social, and cultural) that these populations posed, and the era's discourses about Chinatowns have a long prehistory in the medieval ghetto itself.[17] In *Writing the Ghetto: Class, Authorship, and the Asian American Ethnic Enclave*, Yoonmee Chang frames the "China-

---

12 Nirenberg, *Communities of Violence*; on medieval leprosy, see Green and Hsy, "Disability, Disease, and a Global Middle Ages."

13 "Scourge!," *Lincoln County Leader*, May 11, 1900.

14 When the plague appeared in Honolulu's Chinatown, *The Hawaiian Star* featured the headline "Bubonic Plague, Breed of Filth, Here." It also notes that the rat is a "powerful medium for the propagation of the disease." *The Hawaiian Star* (Honolulu, Hawai'i), December 12, 1899. *Chronicling America: Historic American Newspapers*. Library of Congress; https://chroniclingamerica.loc.gov/lccn/sn82015415/1899-12-12/ed-1/seq-1/.

15 Whitaker, *Black Metaphors*, 3.

16 Ng, "Detention Islands"; Rambaran-Olm, "'Black Death' Matters." See also letters to the editor of the *New Yorker* by Carol Symes, July 15, 2020, https://twitter.com/medievalglobe/status/1283531803073171456; and Elly R. Truitt, July 16, 2020, https://twitter.com/medievalrobots/status/1283835800799649792.

17 Shah, *Contagious Divides*; Risse, *Plague, Politics, and Fear*; Echenberg, *Plague Ports*.

town" in predominantly white anglophone societies as a ghetto, challenging a persistent modern resistance to "naming Chinatown, and other Asian American ghettos more generally, as slums or ghettos."[18] The term "ghetto" first denotes an ethnic enclave or segregated community in reference to the Jewish quarter in Venice in 1516 but precursors to the term "ghetto" exist in other European languages, such as the ill-defined "Jewerye" situated amidst "Cristen folk" within a certain "greet cite [in] Asie" (a great city in Asia) as described in Chaucer's fourteenth-century Middle English "Prioress's Tale."[19] Over time the term "ghetto" has shifted targets among divergent ethnic and racial minority groups including European Jews and African Americans, and the idea of the "ghetto" is repeatedly deployed as a biopolitical tool to manage vulnerable groups through socioeconomic disenfranchisement, segregation, and urban violence.[20] The racial discourse and medievalism surrounding plague upon its modern emergence in Chinatowns suggest how global histories of sinophobia and antisemitism are intertwined, with Jewish and Chinese diaspora communities constructed as threatening contagious "others."[21]

Dehumanizing discourses of invasion and infestation did not only occur in the context of plague or disease; economics also played a key role in casting racialized minority groups as physically undesirable and socially corrupting. Mark Twain's "Concerning the Jews" (1899) observes that a long history of global antisemitism has "the business aspect of a Chinese cheap-labor crusade,"[22] and cultural historian Hsuan L. Hsu notes how Twain's observation "not only indicates parallels between the treatment of these ethnic groups but also avows that the racialization of Chinese and Jewish diasporas was rooted in anxieties about economic competition and falling wages."[23] As discussed in the previous chapter, Chinese American activist Wong Chin Foo publicly challenged the anti-Chinese labor organizer Denis Kearney to a duel, and Kearney's use of the epithets "low blackguard" and "almond-eyed leper" to reject Wong's challenge shows how readily xenophobia and racism exploit the rhetoric of disease. Aggrieved masculinity and white Christian supremacy combine to form a toxic chivalry—with whiteness itself as the harmful condition.

My term "toxic chivalry" refers to the particular resonance of toxicity in histories of anti-Chinese racism and white anxieties about illness, disability, and corruption that Chinatowns provoke, a set of cultural phenomena that critical race scholar and queer theorist Mel Y. Chen has richly explored.[24] I use terms such as "toxic medievalism" and

---

18 Chang, *Writing the Ghetto*, 25.

19 Chaucer, *Canterbury Tales*, "Prioress's Tale," lines 488–89.

20 Schwartz, *Ghetto: History of a Word.*

21 Renshaw, "Antisemitism and Sinophobia"; Sheshagiri, "Modernity's (Yellow) Perils." The "Fu Manchu" stereotype, invented by English novelist Sax Rohmer (pen name of Arthur Henry Ward), was famous globally by 1913. Rohmer's *Tales From Chinatown* (1922) opens with a wily Jew and demonic Chinaman as co-conspirators in the underbelly of London's Chinatown. See also Bae and Tseng-Putterman, "Black-Asian Internationalism."

22 Twain, "Concerning the Jews," 531.

23 Hsu, *Comparative Racialization*, 21.

24 Chen, *Animacies*, 159–88, esp. 169–71.

"toxic chivalry" along the lines of present-day intersectional feminist analysis of toxic masculinity, i.e., the critique of the pervasive harms of ideas of "manliness" that are associated with "oppressive, racist, misogynistic, homophobic, and transphobic" forms of violence, to name just a few.[25] Crucial to this chapter is an awareness of what Chang calls "the structural race, class, and gender inequities that materially and affectively aggrieve Chinatown life,"[26] and my analysis shows how systems of racial and gendered oppression interact within Chinatown spaces.

Racializing Urban Space

During the age of "Yellow Peril," urban space itself became racialized, and medievalizing discourses were one form of propaganda constructing Chinatowns as corrupting ghettos set apart from white Christian spaces. *The California Pilgrimage of Boston Commandery Knights Templars* (1884), an ethnographic narrative of modern-day white Knights Templar making a tourist visit to San Francisco in 1883, contrasts the Gothic and medieval beauty of Eurocentric architecture to Chinatown squalor. The Masonic Temple on Montgomery and Post looks "like an old castle of the Middle Ages,"[27] and a grand welcome arch on Market Street demarcates the parade route as white space: an "immense but beautiful specimen of Gothic architecture" bears an "inscription in gold on a black ground, '*In hoc signo vinces*'" [the imperial Latin phrase, meaning "in this sign you shall conquer"] beneath a red Maltese cross.[28] By contrast, Chinatown is a "labyrinth of passages" with "subterranean chambers and narrow alleys" where "Mongolians are packed in the sty-like dens, like herrings in a box" and along the curbs are "gutters ... which threw off a pungent odor and lighted up the scenes of barbaric peculiarity" full of "dark-visaged pagan[s]."[29] The crowded environments of Chinatown, created by racist legislation restricting Chinese inhabitants to a small section of the city, are described through dehumanizing representations of living space.

Such forms of racializing urban environments informed poetic medievalism as well. A travel account from 1883 reports that an organization associated with the anti-Chinese Knights of Labor in San Francisco disseminated engravings depicting a personified "America blowing a Chinaman from a gun" with the "following doggerel" underneath: "Blow loud your trumpets, / Beat well your drums, / And let the cannons roar; / The Mongolian Hordes / Shall never again / Invade our Golden Shore."[30] Such doggerel employs violent and militaristic imagery to endorse forced exclusion of Chinese, and later forms of medievalizing verse would further demarcate racialized urban spaces. *Lays of Chinatown* (1899), composed by physician George Macdonald Major, contrasts

---

25 Gilchrist, "What Is Toxic Masculinity?"

26 Chang, *Writing the Ghetto*, 113.

27 Roberts, *California Pilgrimage*, 167.

28 Ibid., 169.

29 Ibid., 157.

30 Adams, *Our American Cousins*, 309.

Figure 3: Old Saint Mary's Cathedral and Chinese Mission, San Francisco's
Chinatown. Built in Gothic Revival style ca. 1854 on stone foundations
from China, the church stands across from the Sing Chong Building built in
"Oriental" style just after the 1906 earthquake. July 2019. Photo by the author.

New York's Chinatown to an idealized medieval Britain. Major's "Westminster Abbey" casts the poetic speaker as a "pilgrim" who has come "far from my native land" in order "to worship at the shrine" of Poets' Corner which stands as an architectural-spatial monument to "Chaucer's golden morn" and glories of "the English tongue."[31] White anglophone peoples are collectively racialized throughout this poem, as the "Anglo-Saxon soul" and the "race of Alfred [the Great] and of [George] Washington"[32] spreads across continents and asserts dominion over all peoples including "China's millions walled [in] by custom."[33] The grand medieval architecture of Britain and Europe is a rhetorical cornerstone for the racial construction of Chinatown as a threatening ghetto, an alien presence within the modern city "walled in" by strange customs.

The opening poems within Major's collection, evoking medieval forms, juxtapose the fantasy of an exotic Chinatown—the "[g]olden legends of a place / Full of romance ... Chinatown, O Chinatown"[34]—with the disenchanted physical reality of experiencing the space: "Ramshackle houses, brick and wood, / Where hides Disease with shroud and hood ... mucky streets and garbage lanes ... pungent, sickening opium fumes ... this is Chinatown."[35] Major's dedicatory epistle blithely employs racial epithets for Jewish, Chinese, and Asian immigrants hurrying throughout the city: "[jostling in] that o'ercrowded place" are the "pig-tailed Chinaman, the Jew, / The Lascar [South Asian], Jap, and Arab, too."[36] This busy mix of ethnic minorities and "Oriental" communities of color fill a perceived space of urban blight. Through such representations across predominantly white anglophone cities (London, New York, and San Francisco), a crowded, filthy, dark, and "pagan" Chinatown populated by "heathens" and Jews marks a contrast with clean, spacious medieval spaces coded as white and Christian. Ethnographic writing and poetry conspire to racialize urban space.

Wong Chin Foo, a longtime resident of New York's Chinatown, offers a vision of his home environment countering accounts by white contemporaries—and he suggests how sinophobia and antisemitism intersect as systems of prejudice. Debunking "Yellow Peril" discourses aligning Chinese with filth, rats, and barbarism, Wong embarked on a quest in May 1883 to critique the anti-Chinese "libel" or ubiquitous false perception that Chinese ate rats, and the launch of his newspaper *The Chinese American* first published in New York in February 1883 propelled him into leadership against the "crusade against the men of Chinatown" by Mott Street's Catholic Church of the Transfigura-

---

31 Major, *Lays of Chinatown*, 114. Major's poem "Robert Burns" praises "my childhood's poet," noting "in my veins there runs some Highland blood" and it "grips my heart to hear a Scottish song" (Ibid., 201); he envisions the "blue-domed sky" of Scotland with a "Highland Mary, in the hawthorn bowers," hearing "some nightingale" singing "the bard's 'Mary in Heaven'" surrounded by the "white light" of "Religion" (Ibid., 202).

32 Ibid., 115.

33 Ibid., 119.

34 Ibid., 17.

35 Ibid., 18.

36 Ibid., 12.

Figure 4: Transfiguration School, Catholic parochial school associated with the Church of the Transfiguration on Mott Street in New York's Chinatown. Situated in a formerly Irish and Italian immigrant parish, the church now serves the largest Catholic Chinese-speaking congregation in the US. November 2019. Photo by the author.

tion accusing Chinese men of corrupting young white girls.[37] Throughout the European Middle Ages, "blood libel" traditions (false stories accusing Jews of murdering Christian children to use their blood in religious rituals) incited violence against Jews that continued for centuries, and in his own day Wong addresses how the so-called "rat libel" with its vilifying associations of social corruption contributes to violence against Chinese.[38]

In his aim to debunk "rat libel" and change how audiences think about Chinatown as a space and cultural community, Wong's "The Chinese in New York" (1888) depicts

---

37 Seligman, *First Chinese American*, 101.

38 Ibid. The term "rat libel" comes from Seligman.

Figure 5: Doyers Street (between Pell Street and Mott Street) in New York's Chinatown today. Wong Chin Foo lived near here and describes Mott Street vividly in "The Chinese in New York" (1888). April 2019. Photo by the author.

the environment in and around Mott Street, offering an autoethnographic corrective to white-authored accounts of Chinatown travel.[39] Assuming the position of a "native informant" while strategically employing an objective third-person voice, Wong discusses Chinese hygiene and grooming, religious worship, food preparation, and rich food traditions—dismantling myths of eating rats and opium consumption. "The hygienic functions of cooking elevate the kitchen director in China to high social status,"[40] Wong states, noting the quality of dining in New York's Chinatown: "There are eight thriving Chinese restaurants which can prepare a Chinese dinner in New York almost with the

---

39 Wong, "Chinese in New York."

40 Ibid., 305.

same skill as at the famous 'Dan quay Cha Yuen' (Delmonico's) of Shanghai or Canton."[41] Most importantly, Wong addresses ghettoization by implicating white Christians in self-segregation: "Chinatown is the most interesting corner of the 'Melican man's' metropolis—the little world composed of every variety of Christians, heathen, Irishmen, and other savages."[42] By listing "Irishmen" among "other savages," Wong signals the hypocrisy of anti-Chinese violence by Irish American men, including the "rat libel" campaign by the neighboring Church of the Transfiguration, and he ironizes white discourses of Chinatowns as "walled in" ghettos. By noting the "cosmopolitan tendency of New York" is "developing little foreign cities ... within our water-walls,"[43] Wong suggests how white Christians participate in ghettoization and "othering" of their own Chinese neighbors.

Wong's sketch of New York's Chinatown is consistent with his general strategy of rejecting white Christian supremacy. In the middle of his autoethnographic study, he states: "So long as a Chinaman continues a heathen he is generally honest," but he warns his audience to "look out for him once he becomes 'converted.' He is said then to have the 'devils' of two hemispheres," or the "shrewdness of both races, while his virtues are so confused that he finds it difficult to make use of them."[44] In contrast to the missionary discourses about "rescuing" Chinatown residents from vice, Wong suggests that converted Chinese inherit the bad qualities of white Americans. Wong enacts resistance to Christian white hegemony through his own authority as a "heathen," and the spaces that he calls "little foreign cities" in close proximity set the stage for forms of resistance to white Christian norms as well as opening up new kinds of intimacies among marginalized ethnic communities.

Shared Space: Chinese and Jewish Solidarity

The proximity of New York's Chinatown and its historically Jewish neighborhood on the Lower East Side set the ground for cultural exchange and acts of solidarity between these two ethnic communities. As discussed in the introduction to this book, the Chinese theater in Doyers Street managed by Joseph H. Singleton, a Chinese American and naturalized US citizen,[45] hosted a performance fundraiser in May 1903 for the benefit of Jewish victims of the recent Kishinev pogrom (massacre of Jews) in what is now Chișinău, Moldova.[46] Contemporary news reports widely confirmed that the Kishinev massacre had been incited by "blood libel" narratives,[47] and the Chinese-language historical drama staged that night entitled *The Lost Ten Tribes* not only depicts Chinese sub-

---

41 Ibid., 304.

42 Ibid., 297.

43 Ibid.

44 Ibid., 299.

45 "Evidences Chinamen are Mentally Broadening," 5.

46 Seligman, "Chinese for Jews."

47 Ibid. On "blood libel," see Heng, *England and Jews*; Rubin, *Gentile Tales*.

jugation by foreign rulers but also evokes the biblical dispersal of Jews.[48] This Chinese theater performance crafted in response to the violence of persistent "blood libel" traditions not only addressed harmful modern-day legacies of the medieval European past, but it also offered an urgent commentary on contemporary forms of oppression that Chinese and Jewish diaspora communities were experiencing around the globe.[49]

This fundraiser in the Chinese theater—followed by a not entirely kosher Chinese dinner nearby, most likely in the famous Chinese Delmonico's restaurant—provoked snide commentary by (white) journalists, who apparently didn't fully grasp nor appreciate this solidarity between Chinese and Jewish communities. One sentiment widely repeated in newspaper coverage of this event (unattributable to any named source) stated: "As Shakespeare might have said, one touch of abuse makes the alien races kin."[50] The surrogated kinship that the "alien races" of Chinese Americans and Jewish Americans expressed in this venue is a complex one, rooted in shared experiences of oppression, segregation, and urban violence yet also a complex reclaiming of medieval pasts. For American Jews in the audience, *The Ten Tribes* addressed persistent harms of "blood libel" on a global scale. For Chinese Americans (and converts to Christianity) such as Joseph H. Singleton, the fundraiser allowed for a conspicuous display of charity and status through political activism. The theater manager could publicize a maligned and misunderstood dramatic form with roots in medieval China, while also showing that Chinese Americans would stand up for Jews even if their white Christian peers would not.

Although Wong Chin Foo died years before this Chinese-Jewish solidarity event occurred, his essay "The Chinese in New York" praises the Chinese Delmonico's restaurant, and Wong expressed an earlier vision of taking a Chinese theater troupe on the road not only to popularize this particular performance tradition but also to encourage cross-cultural understanding.[51] In an article in the *New York Tribune* (1883), Wong expressed his hope that bringing a San Francisco Chinese theater troupe across the country would help "people to understand the other," and he aimed to "establish the Chinese theatre in the United States" as a venue for "Chinese drama," which is the "oldest in the world, going back to the first stages of recorded history."[52] Wong envisioned mobilizing the broad cross-cultural appeal of historical romance and the potential for Chinese theater to facilitate social change.

An informative literary commentary on acts of Chinese and Jewish solidarity in New York's Chinatown comes from the contemporaneous author, journalist, and essayist most commonly known as Sui Sin Far (1865–1914). Born as Edith Maude Eaton in Mac-

---

48 Ibid.

49 On medieval antisemitism and anti-immigrant rhetoric in the COVID-19 pandemic, see Ng, "Border Walls and Detention Islands."

50 Untitled, *Indianapolis Journal*, evoking Shakespeare's *Troilus and Cressida*: "One touch of nature makes the whole world kin" (3.3.181).

51 Wong, "Chinese Stage"; Wong, "Chinese Drama," August 28, 1883; Wong, "Produce Chinese Drama," September 2, 1883. Seligman, *First Chinese American*, 126–27.

52 Seligman, *First Chinese American*, 126.

clesfield, UK, to a white English father and a Chinese mother, she evades simple identity categories and unlike Wong she did not specifically claim an identity as a "Chinese American" (nor "Chinese Canadian"), as such a term could not fully encompass her shifting subject positions.[53] Although she was able to pass as white, she chose to write her most famous works under the Chinese pseudonym Sui Sin Far (a transcription of the Cantonese 水仙花 for "water lily")—among other pen names and fictive authorial personas.[54] Raised in a typically "English" manner, she moved at a young age to Montreal, then lived in Kingston, Jamaica, then locations throughout the US (San Francisco, Los Angeles, Seattle, and Boston) before relocating to Montreal. Her restless travel informs much of her works, which often explore Chinese immigrant communities throughout North America.

In a fictive work of journalistic travel writing published in the *Los Angeles Express* as "Wing Sing in New York City" (June 9, 1904), Sui Sin Far writes as a character named "Wing Sing" who is identified as an "American Chinaman."[55] The narrator describes a visit to "Mott street" in Chinatown within "the Country's Metropolis" and discusses a restaurant meeting where "Japanese, Chinese and Jews Affiliate in Common Cause."[56] Wing Sing's narrative, which takes shape as a stylized vernacular deviating from expected norms of standard American English, begins with an episode of sitting next to a "white man Jew" who feels a sociopolitical alignment of Japanese and Jews during the ongoing Russo-Japanese war (1904–1905): "he say he think the Japanese … are the avengers of the wrongs the Jews suffer at the hands of Russians."[57] Such a sentiment suggests that the eventual victory of the Japanese will constitute retroactive justice for antisemitism and anti-Jewish violence under the Russian Empire. Meanwhile, "Jews speak fine words to the Chinese" and the "Chinese merchants also contribute much to the aid of the poor Jews persecuted, as they say, by Russia."[58] Wing Sing continues: "I find Jew people like Chinese food, and many go to the Chinese restaurants," even if it all "seems strange, as the Chinese prefer the flavor of pork."[59] Such commentary constructs Chinatown restaurants as key venues for intercultural exchange as well as sociopolitical solidarity.[60]

In setting this Chinatown narrative in "the Country's Metropolis," Sui Sin Far retreads some of the same ground (literally) as Wong's "Chinese in New York," but through a reconfigured literary and geopolitical context. Sui Sin Far recognizes that Jewish Ameri-

---

53 Chu, *Assimilating Asians*, 100; Shih, "Seduction of Origins," 49; Chapman, *Becoming Sui Sin Far*, xxiv.

54 Her sister, Winnifred Eaton, styled herself as "Japanese," writing romances as Onoto Watanna (to commercial success). On the divergent trajectories of the sisters, see Ferens, *Chinatown Missions and Japanese Romances*; Chang, *Writing the Ghetto*, 61–66. On Watanna's medievalism and *The Tale of Genji*, see Ganz, *Eastern Encounters*, 37–38 and 142–159.

55 Chapman, ed., *Becoming Sui Sin Far*, 223–25, at 223. (Sui Sin Far [Wing Sing], "Wing Sing in New York City," *Los Angeles Express*, June 9, 1904, 6.)

56 Chapman, ed., *Becoming Sui Sin Far*, 225–27, at 225. (Sui Sin Far [Wing Sing], "Wing Sing in New York City," *Los Angeles Express*, June 14, 1904, 6.)

57 Ibid.

58 Ibid., 226.

59 Ibid., 225.

60 Liu, "Kung Pao Kosher."

cans have some claim to whiteness yet Jewish communities are also subject to prejudice and violence on a global scale. At the same time, the white Jewish man's praise for Japanese military power that rivals the might of Europeans hints at the idea that "honorary whiteness" could be extended to the Japanese in North America, a community who collectively enjoyed a more privileged status in the US and who were subjected to far less restrictive immigration laws than their Chinese counterparts.

This particular sketch follows within a week after "Wing Sing" recounts a Chinese Reform society meeting on Mott Street that names "Joe Singleton," praises a dinner at "the Chinese Delmonico," and discusses Chinese drama and white incursions into Chinatown spaces.[61] The narrator visits "one Chinese theater ... very much the same as in San Francisco," asking one Chinese actor, a "bright fellow," whether "he be the good princess in the play" and he responds: "I the villain."[62] All the "actors in Chinese theater of male persuasion," and he sees "plenty white men and two white women" inside the theater, as well as in the "joss house" where "plenty white people" are "much curious about things Chinese and sometimes their behaviour be not proper."[63] This literary version of the native informant critiques uninformed white intrusions into Chinese spaces (the theater and the space of worship), and this account offers some fuller context for appreciating the cultural conventions of Chinese drama on its own terms.

Although they both adopt autoethnographic postures, Wong and Sui Sin Far make strategically divergent choices in how they represent themselves and the predominantly male communities prevalent in Chinatowns. Wong uses an "objective" third-person voice that conforms to standard American English, while Sui Sin Far crafts for Wing Sing a "pidgin" or "accented" voice that oscillates between standard and nonstandard features. Although Chinese Americans such as Wong and Singleton aimed to recuperate Chinese drama and to promote its virtues, Sui Sin Far exposes some of the concerns that the homosocial spaces of "bachelor" societies and Chinatowns could provoke. The narrator states that all the Chinese actors are "of male persuasion" and a male actor could play the "good princess" or masculine "villain." Such a comment insinuates a potential for sexual deviancy or queer desire ("male persuasion"), confirming what social historian Nayan Shah calls "Chinatown's reputation for lascivious immorality" and "deviant" sexuality.[64] At the same time, the versatility of young male actors in this social context brings the conventions of the Chinese theater in alignment with historical English counterparts, such as Shakespearean and medieval performance practices.[65] Sui Sin Far's fictionalized visit to New York's Chinatown as "Wing Sing" creates new spaces for solidarity across ethnic groups, yet it also hints at white fears of the corrupting queer potentials of homosocial Chinatown spaces.

---

61 Chapman, ed., *Becoming Sui Sin Far*, 223–25, at 225. (Sui Sin Far [Wing Sing], "Wing Sing in New York City," June 9, 1904.)

62 Ibid., 224.

63 Ibid. On white audiences in Chinese theaters, see the introduction to this book.

64 Shah, *Contagious Divides*, 210; see also 77–104.

65 On cross-dressing in Sui Sin Far's fiction, see Chapman, ed., *Becoming Sui Sin Far*, xlviii.

Chinatown Missions and Queer Domesticity

This final section turns to Sui Sin Far's fictional narratives, particularly those partici-
pating in medievalizing conventions of sentimental romance. As many scholars have
observed, Sui Sin Far's fiction often seeks to use the genre of romance to humanize
the Chinese in North America, and to urge audiences to sympathize with experiences
of family separation, discrimination, poverty, and injustice. The author often engages
with the anglophone medievalism of her peers. "Sweet Sin" (1898) ends with its biracial (Chinese and white American) protagonist sending a deathbed letter, a trope dis-
tantly evoking "the lily maid" Elaine of Astolat's posthumous letter to Sir Lancelot of the
Lake in Arthurian narratives, including the versified retelling of this story in Tennyson's
Idylls of the King.[66] Sui Sin Far's *Mrs. Spring Fragrance and Other Writings* (1912) gath-
ers together tragic romances and stories of mixed-race protagonists and families. In the
story "Mrs. Spring Fragrance" set in Seattle's Chinatown, a young woman who is initially
forbidden to marry the man she loves has the "American name" of Laura (sharing the
name of the unattainable love object of Petrarch's sonnets) and a "Chinese name" of "Mai
Gwi Far (a rose)," evoking the medieval French *Roman de la Rose*, and the story's characters repeatedly recite the poetry of Tennyson.[67]

Sui Sin Far's Chinatown stories use medievalizing imagery and narrative structures
to respond to classed and gendered norms constructing Chinese as unfit for citizenship.
As Shah states: "The American system of cultural citizenship combined class discourses
of respectability and middle-class tastes with heteronormative discourses of adult male
responsibility, female domestic caretaking, and the biological reproduction legitimated
by marriage."[68] I place my reading of Sui Sin Far's work in the context of contemporaneous women's writing on public health and rescue narratives in Chinatown, showing how
the author addresses "Yellow Peril" discourses of disease, disability, and corruption that
seek to exclude Chinese from white norms of "respectability" and "cultural citizenship."

"The Chinese Lily" (1908), originally published in *Out West Magazine* and ascribed
to "Edith Eaton (Sui Sin Far)," is set in San Francisco's Chinatown with exclusively Chinese characters.[69] "The Chinese Lily" (reprinted with emendations in 1912) might seem
to conform to the genre of a sentimental romance (three characters, a romance plot,
and a tragic outcome), yet it inverts these expectations. Most conspicuously, the central
character is not a fair maiden but Mermei, a disabled and disfigured Chinese woman
whose story explores intimacy between women and affective relationships beyond het-

---

66 Chapman, ed., *Becoming Sui Sin Far*, 166–71. (Sui Sin Far [Sui Seen Far], "Sweet Sin: A Chinese-
American Story," *Land of Sunshine* 8, no. 5 (April 1898): 223–26.) On the deathbed letter of Elaine
of Astolat (or Ascolat), see Malory, *Le Morte Darthur*, bk. 18, chap. 20, p. 435; Tennyson, *Idylls of the
King*, "Elaine," 147–22, esp. 212–17.

67 Hsu, ed., *Mrs. Spring Fragrance*, 35–36. On this text's allusions to Tennyson and Dante among
other poets, see Howard, "American Words."

68 Shah, *Contagious Divides*, 204.

69 Eaton (Sui Sin Far), "The Chinese Lily," 508–10. In this first iteration of the text, the protagonist's name is "Tin-a" and the other woman is named "Sui Sin Far."

erosexual marriage.[70] The story bluntly introduces Mermei as a character unlike the others: "She was a cripple."[71] The narrator notes that a "fall had twisted her legs so that she moved with difficulty and scarred her face so terribly" that nobody except for her brother Lin John "cared to look upon it."[72] Mermei, restricted in mobility perhaps due to her injury or an undisclosed chronic condition, is enclosed in domestic space atop a building as if she were an imprisoned damsel: "Mermei lived in her little upstairs room [and] knew nothing of life save what [she] saw from an upstairs window" and she "could embroider all day in contented silence" if only she had company.[73] In "her mental portfolio" of thoughts,[74] it is clear Mermei desires companionship—but her company will not take the form of a male lover.

The story shifts upon the entry of "the most beautiful young girl that Mermei had ever seen," who stands at the door "extending to Mermei a blossom from a Chinese lily plant."[75] Mermei "understood the meaning of the offered flower, and accepting it, beckoned for her visitor to follow her into her room."[76] The narrator notes: "She forgot that she was scarred and crippled, and she and the young girl chatted out their little hearts to one another."[77] Such a moment reworks romance conventions in two ways. First, the beautiful maiden is subject to a woman's gaze. Secondly, the reference to momentarily "forgetting" Mermei's disability and deformity suggests that the audience might also almost forget that the fully humanized characters portrayed are Chinese, rather than the "universal" white subjects of anglophone literature.

The beautiful maiden intriguingly shares a variant of the author's name: "Sin Far—her new friend, and Sin Far, the meaning—of whose name was Pure Flower, or Chinese Lily."[78] When John Lin first "[beholds] Sin Far," the text presents her as the proper erotic object of the male gaze: "her sweet and gentle face, her pretty drooped eyelids and arched eyebrows" make him "think of apple and peach and plum trees showering their dainty blossoms in the country that Heaven loves."[79] The courtly blazon of medieval romance is eroticized and Orientalizing, associated now with an exotic beauty with her features implicitly racialized.

Lin John, the hardworking laundryman, fully emerges as a chivalric hero in the conclusion when Mermei's building catches fire and he seeks to rescue her: "The uprising tongues licked his face as he sprung up the ladder no other man dared ascend."[80] Both

---

70 Sui Sin Far, "The Chinese Lily," in *Mrs. Spring Fragrance*, ed. Hsu, 129–32.

71 Ibid., 129.

72 Ibid.

73 Ibid.

74 Ibid., 130.

75 Ibid.

76 Ibid.

77 Ibid.

78 Ibid.

79 Ibid., 131.

80 Ibid.

Sin Far and Mermei are inside but only one of them can fit on the ladder, and each offers to sacrifice herself for the other. "The ladder will not bear the weight of both of us," says Sin Far, and Mermei responds: "But he loves you best. You and he can be happy together. I am not fit to live."[81] Lin John hesitates for "one awful second" and "his eyes caught the eyes of his sister's friend"[82] who we infer has sent a signal for him to save Mermei. In the end, Lin John notes: "I—I did my duty with her approval, aye, at her bidding."[83] This tale of chivalric heroism and sacrifice demonstrates the nobility of familial duty over erotic love—and, curiously enough, the disabled woman is not sacrificed for the expected heterosexual pairing. Thwarting expectations that a disabled, deformed, or unwell Chinese woman is expendable and "not fit to live," Mermei has a potential future—and the author recuperates Chinese masculinity in the process.[84]

The author's decision to name a protagonist "Sin Far," along with Mermei's allusion to a "mental portfolio," marks an intertextual connection to Sui Sin Far's autobiographical essay published within a year entitled "Leaves from the Mental Portfolio of an Eurasian" (1909).[85] In this autobiographical text, Sui Sin Far reflects on the complexities of her biracial identity and notes that she has a chronic health condition, "prostrated at times with attacks of nervous sickness" with a "heart ... unusually large" and "the strength of my feelings [takes] from me the strength of my body."[86] Later she remarks that episodes of "rheumatic fever" exact a toll on her body, and "I still limp and bear traces of sickness."[87] Such a condition is not just physical, but psychic: "the cross of the Eurasian bore too heavily upon my childish shoulders."[88] Hsu argues that this "excessive sentimentalism contradicts stereotypes about the Chinese, who are 'said to be the most stolid and insensible to feeling of all races,'" and such "inordinate sensitivity to the suffering of others" makes the author "eminently qualified for her vocation as sentimental author."[89] The queer intimacy between women in "The Chinese Lily," one of whom bears the author's pen name, suggests possibilities for stigmatized Chinese women beyond dehumanization and death. Reading the "Mental Portfolio" alongside "The Chinese Lily" shows how Sui Sin Far's texts gloss one another. The proxy for the author is not just the beautiful maiden Sin Far but also the disabled Chinese Mermei who claims she is "not fit to live" and who can only be saved by a ladder that "cannot bear the weight" of both herself and her counterpart.

Sui Sin Far builds sympathy for Chinese characters within the medievalizing structures of sentimental romance, and her positioning of the Chinese laundryman Lin John

---

81 Ibid.

82 Ibid.

83 Ibid., 132.

84 See also Sibara, "Alien Body in Sui Sin Far."

85 Sui Sin Far, "Mental Portfolio of an Eurasian," in *Mrs. Spring Fragrance*, ed. Hsu, 221–33.

86 Ibid., 224.

87 Ibid., 229.

88 Ibid., 224.

89 Hsu, ed., *Mrs Spring Fragrance*, "Introduction," 19.

as a chivalric hero is particularly clear in contrast to Chinatown rescue narratives by contemporaneous white female authors. Mabel Craft Deering's "The Firebrand: A Short Story of Old San Francisco" (1907) offers a fictionalized account of Donaldina Cameron, a white Presbyterian missionary who helped immigrant Chinese girls and women to escape enforced sex work.[90] This fictionalized hagiography forms part of a genre of Chinatown rescue narratives glorifying "white saviors" who save Chinese women from Chinese men—and this story is fascinating for its exploration of cross-racial relationships between women.

It should be noted that Miss Mabel Craft (as she was known before marriage) was known locally as a crusader and white savior who "stood forth as the champion of the social equality of colored women,"[91] and a commitment to racial equality informs this narrative about Cameron. The story is narrated through the white missionary gaze. Situated within the safe house for women amidst the "motley background of the city's riff-raff," Miss Cameron sees a Chinese woman Jean Ho appearing at the doorbell and she thinks: "Is this a Chinese woman or a strapping boy masquerading in feminine dress?"[92] Jean Ho, described as "a figure of fury," and "so strange a figure,"[93] and "a queer 'un,"[94] does not fit the stereotype of the stoic, unexpressive Chinese woman. Cameron thinks: "She needed only the cross and coat of mail to look a Joan of Arc."[95] Cameron's inner thoughts align queerness with Joan of Arc, the French medieval martyr-saint renowned even in her own day for her extraordinary status as a maiden who assumes the trappings of elite masculinity (such as arms and armor) and leads troops to victory.[96] Through this momentary glimpse into Cameron's thoughts, the narrator marks the verbal correspondence of two names (Joan of Arc and Jean Ho) that anticipates the unconventionally queer crusading role that this particular Chinese woman will adopt later in the story.

The interracial intimacies in this story are complex. Jean Ho loves one teacher named Miss Evelyn who is "a beautiful, fragile, blonde girl, with indomitable spirit in a delicate sheath," and she "sang beautifully [while] Jean Ho, the long-armed, the sombrely dressed, never tired of hanging over the piano like a lover."[97] This idealized figure of feminine beauty is "beautiful, fragile, blonde" yet also strong, and the "sheath" (hidden sword) metaphor and simile "like a lover" disclose a potential for queer intimacy. The subversive prospect of homosocial desire between women is superficially resolved after Jean Ho's conversion and marriage, after which she exhibits a "Caucasian fury,"[98] rescues one of her biological children from abduction, and delivers the child to the Mission to

---

90 Deering, "The Firebrand."

91 "'Color Line,'" *San Francisco Examiner*, 1.

92 Deering, "Firebrand," 453.

93 Ibid., 453.

94 Ibid., 454.

95 Ibid.

96 Crane, *Performance of Self*, 73–106.

97 Ibid., 456.

98 Ibid., 460.

ensure her safety. This child, a daughter, becomes "one of the pets of the Mission" and "sings hymns for American visitors," as beautiful and "gay as a butterfly."[99] This white female missionary narrative of conversion, in broad terms, enacts a transformation of Jean Ho from a "heathen" stereotype ("figure of fury," "strange," "unexpressive," and "queer") into a "Caucasian fury" whose daughter helps to ensure the future of the Mission, and this progressive narrative of Chinese self-actualization relies upon a script of assimilation into heteronormative white Christian femininity.

The progressive impulse of white women's missionary narratives places "The Chinese Lily" within a broader context of "Yellow Peril" fears of homosocial intimacy. The disabled and disfigured Mermei in "The Chinese Lily" could also be a "queer 'un" due to her seeming desire for the company of women, and her weeping at the end of the story could disclose a mourning for her lost and impossible object of love (Sin Far). The fictive assimilation of Jean Ho into norms of white Christian heterosexuality and the persistence of Mermei's thwarted and undisclosed desires add a racial dimension to these characters. Writing from an Asian American perspective, literature scholar David L. Eng and psychoanalyst Shinhee Han theorize racial melancholia as unresolved grief.[100] Eng and Han "[configure] whiteness as contagion" through a reading of the novel *Caucasia* (1998) by biracial author Danzy Senna—who, like the protagonists in her book, have a white mother and African American father—noting that the novel "connects assimilation to illness and disease."[101] If the "ideals of whiteness for Asian Americans (and other groups of color) remain unattainable," then the perceived "processes of assimilation are suspended, conflicted, and unresolved."[102] In this situation, "melancholia" is an "unresolved process" in which "ideals of whiteness are continually estranged, [remaining] at an unattainable distance, at once a compelling fantasy and a lost ideal."[103]

In the context of racial melancholia and medievalizing romance, the biracial Sui Sin Far—who partially inserts an authorial namesake into her story "The Chinese Lily"—reveals how full belonging is impossible under the "condition" of white supremacy, and whiteness itself is revealed as the environmental harm. In "The Inferior Woman," Sui Sin Far implicitly thematizes "Yellow Peril" discourses along such lines: "Prejudices are prejudices. They are like diseases."[104] In "The Story of One White Woman Who Married a Chinese," the white first-person narrator recounts a friend's assessment of her sick (white) child: "There is no necessity for its being sick ... There must be an error somewhere."[105] Reflecting moralized understandings of illness as divine punishment, she states: "Sin, sorrow, and sickness all mean the same thing," and she claims that "[w]e have no disease

---

99 Ibid., 461.

100 Eng and Han, "Dialogue on Racial Melancholia."

101 Ibid., 668.

102 Ibid., 671.

103 Ibid.

104 Sui Sin Far, "The Inferior Woman," in *Mrs. Spring Fragrance*, ed. Hsu, 47–60, at 59.

105 Sui Sin Far, "White Woman Who Married a Chinese," in *Mrs. Spring Fragrance*, ed. Hsu, 94–104, at 96.

that we do not deserve, no trouble that we do not bring upon ourselves."[106] The narrator simply responds: "What had sin to do with [my child's] measles?"[107] This conversation among white women marks a distinct contrast to the humane reactions of the Chinese man Liu Kanghi, whom the narrator later marries, who immediately has sympathy for the "[p]oor little baby,"[108] and by witnessing her child "grow[ing] amongst the little Chinese children" the narrator learns that "the virtues do not all belong to the whites."[109]

Sui Sin Far's Chinatown fictions critiquing systems of prejudice and the era's racialized discourses of public health anticipate what is now known as the social model of disability. Literary historians Jennifer C. James and Cynthia Wu define disability, within such a framework, as a "discursively engineered social category" that "call[s] attention to how built and social environments" disadvantage and harm "those with physical, sensory, or cognitive impairments" and also "privilege those who are normatively constituted" along the lines of race, class, and gender.[110] Consequently, understanding how "categories of race/ethnicity and disability are used to constitute one another" requires an awareness of how systems of oppression intersect.[111] In her own day, Sui Sin Far demonstrates that it is not any individual person's disabled, disfigured, or diseased body that poses a "problem" that requires correction (or somehow signals deviancy or divine punishment); rather, it is a surrounding environment—an entire set of legal and political structures—that harms racialized individuals and disadvantages entire populations.

"The Chinese Lily" almost conforms to a normative chivalric romance—yet not quite. Even when Sui Sin Far is writing in the Chinese male persona of "Wing Sing," she recognizes Jewish American proximity to whiteness and implicitly acknowledges the partial access that Japanese can claim to honorary whiteness, all the while implying that whiteness itself is a condition that Chinese in North America can never claim. Whether she writes as an omniscient narrator or in the persona of a Chinese male narrator specifically, Sui Sin Far transforms "Yellow Peril" discourses to challenge her audience's preconceptions, and her interests in cross-ethnic solidarities engage in a productive dialogue with works by Wong Chin Foo. Wong resists white Christian scripts of conversion and assimilation while also rebuking manifestations of toxic chivalry. Both authors not only humanize their Chinese characters, but they also open up possibilities for expansive forms of empathy with Jews, disabled people, and "others" stigmatized by rhetorics of contagion.

---

106 Ibid.
107 Ibid.
108 Ibid., 99.
109 Ibid., 101.
110 James and Wu, "Race, Ethnicity, Disability, and Literature," 3.
111 Ibid., 4.

Engendering Community

Wong Chin Foo and Sui Sin Far—writing against the era's medievalizing discourses of white Christian supremacy—use their journalism and autoethnographic publications to address dehumanizing discourses of "Yellow Peril" and plague, and they confront longstanding practices of racialized "othering" in urban spaces. Each author repurposes a submerged history of medieval antisemitic discourses within a modern urban context of "heathen" identities, segregation, and assimilation. Mindful of the potentials for queer intimacy through medievalism (journalistic and literary), my close readings of these authors trace strategies of addressing historical processes of dehumanization. Each writer asks what forms of racial belonging are available to Chinese people in North America, creating potentials for cross-ethnic and interracial alignments. In the process, they demonstrate how intersecting forms of structural oppression can engender new kinds of solidarity and community.

Chapter Three

PLACE: INDEFINITE DETENTION AND FORMS OF RESISTANCE IN ANGEL ISLAND POETRY

THIS CHAPTER COMBINES medieval literary analysis and ecocriticism to consider the poetic corpus (hundreds of lyrics) that Chinese detainees carved into the wooden walls of detention barracks of the Angel Island Immigration Station, a site in San Francisco Bay currently registered by the United States as a National Historic Landmark due to its cultural significance. Located in waters a boat ride away from the city of San Francisco, CA, this so-called "Ellis Island of the West" was where many newcomers from Asia were processed as they sought entry into the US and it also operated as an immigration detention center from 1910–1940. The majority of the detainees were Chinese with some staying as long as months or years before being deported or "landed" (granted entry into the US). Thick with literary allusions and references to imprisonment and injustice in Chinese myths and literary classics, the mostly anonymous and untitled

Figure 6: Two-story wooden barracks at the former US Immigration Station at Angel Island in the San Francisco Bay. It operated as a detention center primarily for Chinese migrants from 1910–1940, and the restored site is now a National Historic Landmark. July 2019. Photo by the author.

poems that the detainees composed while on Angel Island adapted medieval lyric forms (conventionalized in the Tang Dynasty) for a new geopolitical environment.

Crafting new poetic terms not used in medieval lyrics themselves, the detainee-poets repeatedly invoked the modern "wooden house" (木屋) or "wooden building" (木樓) as a prison and an uncanny home. The barracks of Angel Island, situated within a garden landscape inaccessible to the detainees themselves, were a site of frustration, humiliation, longing, and anger. In this chapter, I explore how detainees drew upon a rich tradition of medieval Chinese lyrics to testify to their own lived experiences of incarceration, and I conclude by reflecting on the importance of this "wooden building" as a site of cultural memory and activism today.

Previous chapters in this book have examined how elite Chinese Americans (or Chinese immigrants seeking US citizenship) used medieval imagery or genres to address urgent issues of racism, discrimination, and cultural belonging. During the earlier part of the twentieth century, Chinese immigrants who were scholars or merchants were not subjected to restrictions as harsh as those for incoming laborers, and my discussion of Angel Island poetry focuses on experiences of incarcerated migrants who were often less privileged and hailed from humble village origins.

This chapter has three main strands. First, I provide historical context and sociopolitical background for the composition of Angel Island poetry itself. Second, I discuss major stylistic features of Tang-era regulated verse forms, as well as some of their original medieval literary and cultural contexts. Third, I consider how Angel Island poetry adapts and reshapes the meanings of the physical environment to enact sustained forms of resistance to racial injustice. Not only has the adaptation of Chinese medieval poetry at Angel Island enabled new kinds of community and cultural memory even generations after the immigration station closed, but the Angel Island barracks themselves have become an important archive attesting to collective experiences of racial discrimination and forced incarceration. Most importantly, the site has set key foundations for activist solidarities across ethnic groups that carry over into the present.

Sociopolitical Landscape of Angel Island

I begin with some social and environmental context for Angel Island itself. In contrast to Ellis Island on the East Coast (where immigrants seeking entry into the US primarily from Europe were processed within hours), the Angel Island Immigration Station "was built in 1910 to better enforce the Chinese Exclusion Act of 1882, which barred Chinese laborers from the country," and most of the arrivals at this location came from Asia with over 70 percent of the detainees at any given time being Chinese,[1] and the vast majority of these were young men between 14 and 18 years of age.[2] After the 1906 San Francisco earthquake destroyed public birth records, many incoming Chinese circumvented restrictive racist exclusion laws by purchasing paperwork presenting themselves as blood relatives of US citizens; such newcomers were "landed" only if immigration offi-

---

1 Yung, "Poetry and Politics."

2 Angel Island Immigration Station Foundation, "Chinese Poetry of the Detention Barracks."

cials were satisfied they proved their cases. Upon their arrival Chinese migrants were segregated by gender, separated from their children, endured painstakingly grueling interrogations and invasive medical exams, and were held in crowded wooden barracks.

Even white observers deplored the poor living conditions of the detainees in the barracks; this space was a dark, cramped fire hazard,[3] and medical authorities associated the detained Chinese themselves with stench and vermin.[4] As social historian Nayan Shah has observed: "From the turn of the century until 1940, the ordeal of immigration for Chinese and other Asian migrants to San Francisco began with medical inspection at Angel Island," and an invasive "military-style" protocol that "required submission to nude physical exams and the inspection of body parts" formed "part of an emerging worldwide network of quarantine and health inspection" serving as "the 'imperial defence' against the potential invasion of epidemic diseases into metropolitan ports in North America and Europe."[5] Although white employees and their families could experience Angel Island's landscape as a cultivated space of enjoyment and leisure (including a tree-lined garden walk known as the Tar Path or the Natural Way),[6] Chinese detainees primarily experienced the island as a shameful prison and a dehumanizing space of confinement.

Chinese poetry brushed upon and carved into the walls of the "wooden building" attests to the power of anonymity as a strategy to critique racial injustice when no other options are available. Immigration Commissioner Hart Hyatt North, who initially supervised the station, ordered the "graffiti" on walls to be filled with putty and painted over within months after the station opened—but the detainees continued to write upon and carve into the walls anyway, with the shrinking putty revealing layers of poetry as the paint cracked over time.[7] Much of this poetry was documented and brought to public attention decades after the immigration station was closed, and I will discuss later in this chapter the story of the "rediscovery" of the poetry and activist efforts to preserve Angel Island as a site of cultural memory. During the decades over which these poems were composed, the detainees looked to the distant past to express their current feelings, with their acts of writing and inscribing as collaborative forms of resistance.

In composing their lyric inscriptions, the detainee-poets drew primarily upon literary conventions that had been established in the Tang Dynasty (618–907 CE), which scholars of Chinese literary history such as Manling Luo identify as China's "late medi-

---

3 Lai, Lim, and Yung, *Island*; on "Yellow Peril" discourses, 5; on crowded conditions, 24.

4 Lee and Yung, *Immigrant Gateway*; on Angel Island being deemed "unfit for habitation by reason of vermin and stench," 60. M. W. Glover, Assistant Surgeon, stated: "The walls and ceilings are sheathed with soft wood, unpainted ... This covering absorbs and retains the odorous emanations of the aliens; it affords a safe hiding place for the vermin also common among Asiatics and it lends itself to drawings and writings. The character of the latter I know not, but the obscenity of the former is apparent" (November 21, 1910) ("Detention Barracks" informational signpost, US Immigration Station, Angel Island State Park, San Francisco, CA).

5 Shah, *Contagious Divides*, 179.

6 Davison and Meier, et al., *Cultural Landscape Report*, 46–47 and n111.

7 Lai, Lim, and Yung, *Island*, 37.

eval" period with the formative conventions of literati poetry and its storytelling contexts extending into the Song Dynasty (960–1279 CE), a timeframe coinciding with Europe's medieval past.[8] Tang-era poetry is most familiar to Chinese diaspora audiences for recounting the experiences of dispersed and homesick literati (scholar-officials) in exile, and as Xiaofei Tian has observed, the language such poets use is classified linguistically as Middle Chinese (an era in the history of the language from the sixth through the twelfth century CE) to mark a transition from ancient or "classical" Chinese to a form of verse relying upon "balancing the tones of Middle Chinese prosody" which were "honored and perfected by Tang dynasty poets" to become the basis of what is often called "regulated verse."[9] Tsung-Cheng Lin has shown how Tang literati poets dispatched far from home often cast themselves as weary "knights-errant" (遊俠) or heroic figures in transit,[10] and modern Chinese migrants incarcerated in the barracks had some basic familiarity with Tang-era forms and conventions from their hometown educations.[11] These Chinese detainee-poets repurposed literary conventions from what was originally a far-flung medieval Chinese network of literati poets to suit a newly shared physical and sociopolitical environment.

Queer theorist and medievalist Carolyn Dinshaw has richly explored her own racial positioning as an Asian American and the process of "making affective connections … across time," making "histories manifest by juxtaposition, [and] by making entities past and present touch."[12] The wooden building which once had decades of inscriptions covering almost every surface of its walls renders disparate voices of detainees (and later, prisoners of war) tangible in physical form. Expanding on Dinshaw's tactile metaphors of time and space, queer medievalist Wan-Chuan Kao reflects on his own relationship to medieval texts as a scholar of Chinese ancestry and considers how thinking beyond "modernity's linear temporality" can create a "more intimate and queer understanding of the interconnections among objects, persons, and events."[13] Medieval lyrics produced by bodies in close proximity in physical space and written upon surfaces of the surrounding walls convey the lived experiences of Chinese detainees: their emplacement, collective memory, and conditions of their social and political environment. Metaphors of touch, and attention to intimate connections among persons and objects, are appropriate for exploring both the architectural and environmental grounds of detention poetry.

---

8 Luo, *Literati Storytelling*, 4–5.

9 Tian, "Pentasyllabic *Shi* Poetry," 141.

10 Lin, "Knight-Errantry."

11 So crucial is the Tang Dynasty in diasporic Chinese culture that the term for "Chinatown" used in San Francisco and early Chinatowns elsewhere is 唐人街 ("Tang People Street").

12 Dinshaw, *Getting Medieval*, 12. See also Dinshaw, "Pale Faces," 20.

13 Kao, "#palefacesmatter?"

Fixed Forms and Ecopoetics

In terms of their poetic structure, the vast majority of the Angel Island inscriptions are composed in "regulated verse forms" with fixed patterns of character-based line length, tonal patterns, and rhyme schemes established in the Tang era, as Steven G. Yao and many others have noted.[14] Yunte Huang further characterizes such poetry in its material form as *tibishi* (題壁詩 or literally "poetry inscribed on the wall"), a subgenre of Chinese travel poetry written on walls as a public outlet for anonymous travelers.[15] My analysis of these lyrics inscribed in the wooden building of the men's barracks contextualizes these poems as imaginative reinventions of Tang-era representations of the Chinese knight errant or literati scholar in exile. Tsung-Cheng Lin extends an established analytical framework of "knight-errantry" within Chinese literary scholarship to contextualize Tang "frontier poems" and the pervasive themes of injustice and homesickness exemplified in the poetry of prominent male literati poets,[16] and Ao Wang has attended to the deep intimacies of homosocial "literati friendship" in Tang-era poetry expressed by dispersed civil servants, who often communicated with one another via inscriptions on the walls of post houses.[17] In a marked contrast to medieval European chivalric genres, Chinese medieval poetry about men traveling far from home tends not to emphasize valiant deeds, adventure, and conquest so much as the protagonists' feelings of war weariness, anger at injustice, and empathy with fellow sufferers. During their time incarcerated on Angel Island, Chinese detainees adapted longstanding gendered literary expressions of thwarted mobility and powerlessness to suit the shared space of the men's barracks.

One of the most iconic poems of displacement and homesickness in Chinese literary tradition is a work by famous Tang literati poet Li Bai (李白). Commonly known as "Quiet Night Thoughts" (靜夜思), Li Bai's poem is anthologized in the famous later anthology *The Three Hundred Tang Poems* (唐詩三百首) and it remains familiar today to schoolchildren across the Chinese diaspora. This well-known pentasyllabic regulated verse form uses a strict structure of rhyme and total patterning and the text of the poem remains very faintly inscribed on a wall of Room 105 of the former men's barracks on Angel Island:

床前明月光
疑是地上霜
舉頭望明月
低頭思故鄉

Before [my] bed [the] moonlight [is] bright
[I] misbelieve [it] is frost on ground
Raise [my] head [and] look [at the] bright moon
Lower [my] head [and] think [of] hometown

---

14 Yao, "Transplantation and Modernity," 311–14; Lee and Yung, *Immigrant Gateway*, 103–4; Lai, Lim, and Yung, *Island*, 37; Liu, "Analysis of Poems Inscribed"; Leong, *Wild Geese Sorrow*, xxi–xxiv and 164.

15 Huang, *Transpacific Imaginations*, 105.

16 Lin, "Knight-Errantry."

17 Wang, "Literati Friendship," 250–51.

Even though the poems carved into the walls of the Angel Island barracks are read in the traditional Chinese manner of columns of text reading from right to left, I present the Chinese poems in left-to-right horizontal lines in order to make the parallels to the English translations more evident. My unpoetic literal translation supplies first-person pronouns ("I" and "my") not used in traditional Chinese poetry but grammatically required when translating such poetry into English. Punctuation is not present in the original Chinese poems, but it is usually supplied by later textual editors. In this work, the poetic speaker is displaced or in exile; moonlight coming through a window is ambiguously mistaken for ground frost, troubling distinctions between a built interior space (a bed chamber) and an external environment (natural landscape). The speaker gazes at the moon—an implicit allusion to the annual Mid-Autumn Festival when family reunions occur—which reminds the poet of home.

One moving modern transformation of Li Bai's poem among the lyrics written at Angel Island is the rare occurrence of a poem bearing a title: "Mid-Autumn Festival" (中秋偶感). I quote the opening of this poem in Chinese with modernized punctuation, followed by an English translation by Chinese American poet Jeffrey Thomas Leong:

夜涼僵臥鐵床中，
窗前月姊透照儂。
悶來起立寒窗下 [...]

Cool nights lying on the steel bunk.
Through a window, the moon goddess shines down on me.
Bored, I rise and stand beneath cold glass. [...][18]

Marking the temporal and natural cycles of Li Bai's medieval poem with its new title, this modern anonymous poem transfers moonlight of Li Bai's dwelling into the space of a wooden barrack with a cold glass window and a steel bed (床 which Leong translates as "bunk"). Another anonymous modern poem begins with the two characters for "wooden house" (木屋) followed by a reference to an open window, the moon, and homesickness:

木屋閒來把窗開，
曉風明月共徘徊。
故鄉遠憶雲山斷，
小島微聞寒雁哀。
失路英雄空說劍，
窮途騷士且登台。
應知國弱人心死，
何事囚困此處來?

Bored in the wood house I held open a window,
Dawn breezes, the day-bright moon, linger together.
In distant memory, an old village, hills obscured by clouds,
On this small island, tiny cries of wild geese sorrow.

---

18 Leong, *Wild Geese Sorrow*, Poem 29, pp. 62–63.

The mighty hero who's lost his way speaks emptily of the sword,
A troubled scholar on a poor road writes only high poems.
You should know when a country is weak,
    the people's spirit dies.
How else have we come to be trapped here as prisoners?[19]

One line in this poem has a strong localizing effect: 小島微聞寒雁哀 ("On this small island, tiny cries of wild geese sorrow").[20] This image touchingly evokes the environment of Angel Island: the experience of looking out a window to see "migratory waterfowl" flying over San Francisco Bay.[21] In this poem, the image of freely moving migratory birds marks a contrast to the incarcerated detainees or "prisoners," who are either positioned as thwarted knights-errant whose lives are now deprived of meaning ("The mighty hero … speaks emptily of the sword"), or as literati or civil servants (the "troubled scholar on a poor road") who are dispatched to bleak environments far from community or opportunities for social advancement.

A modern poem entitled 深夜偶感 ("Deep Night") makes yet another nod to Li Bai through its title, and the anonymous poet who signs the work as 台山余題 ("Yee of Toishan") recreates Angel Island's soundscape and atmosphere even more vividly: through the sound of the wind, feeling of fog, and surrounding inhuman noise (crickets).[22]

夜靜微聞風嘯聲，
形影傷情見景詠。
雲霧濛濛也暗天，
蟲聲唧唧月微明。
悲苦相連天相道，
愁人獨坐倚窗邊。

In the still of night, small sounds are a howling wind.
Shadows, an ache of old wounds, so I recite verse:

Fog and mist drift, a gloomy sky,
Insects rub crick-crack beneath the moon's faint light.
My sad and bitter face matches these heavens.
A worried man sits alone, leans at the window's sill.[23]

The surrounding environment shapes this poem's composition, with "the natural landscape … represent[ing] inner terrain, with natural scenes both reflecting and expressing the poet's affective state."[24] I would emphasize in this context how both built structures and natural metaphors interact to produce the poet's affective states. A similar poem 感景拙詠 ("Perceiving the Landscape, I Compose This Worthless Verse") enmeshes the built environment with its beyond-human surroundings: 滄海圓孤峰，／ 崎嶇困牢籠。

---

19 Ibid., Poem 10, pp. 22–23.

20 Ibid.

21 Ibid., 160.

22 Ibid., "Deep Night," Poem 20, pp. 44–45; Lai, Lim, and Yung, *Island*, Poem 24, pp. 66–67.

23 Leong, *Wild Geese Sorrow*, Poem 20, pp. 44–45.

24 Bashford, et al., "Geographies of Commemoration," 20.

[...] 鴻使莫尋蹤 ("Blue-green ocean encircles a solitary peak, / Rugged hills edge this prison cage. [...] Wild geese make no trace").[25]

I have chosen to present these poems along with modern English translations by Jeffrey Thomas Leong, a Chinese American poet whose father was a "paper son" who entered the US via Angel Island. Leong preserves the line length and imagery of the Chinese poems and at times uses the term "detained/detainee" rather than a more poetic "prisoner" or "captive."[26] Leong aims for English equivalents that avoid being "wooden or bizarrely 19th century and incomprehensible."[27] A "wooden" metaphor is often used by translators to describe unpoetic, word-for-word renditions of texts, but I suggest that the materiality of the wood metaphor warrants careful attention in the context of the barracks as a "wooden building." Tang poetry proved useful for Chinese detainees to express affective longing and environmental displacement while also physically transforming their living space through acts of inscription. The fixed structures of "regulated verse" convey a strategy of working within constraints, demonstrating how detainees bore witness to, and resisted, their own restricted mobility. One poem even embeds a political statement through an acrostic, with the first character of each column of text reading in sequence as 埃崙待劂 or "Island awaits leveling" (i.e., raze or abolish Angel Island).[28]

A number of the poems evoke both the interior and environmental space of the barracks through allusions to medieval narratives. One untitled poem alludes to the *Ballad of Mulan* (木蘭辭), the famous oral legend, possibly composed as early as the sixth century CE,[29] about a woman who dons masculine armor and acquires weapons to fight on her father's behalf. Through its oblique references to the story of Mulan, this lyric subtly transforms the gendered dimensions of the medieval Chinese knight-errant motif.[30] The original text opens with the sounds of the female protagonist who sighs as she is weaving in front of the door,[31] but the modern Angel Island poem adapting this scene opens with the Chinese characters for "four walls" (四壁) and the sound of outdoor crickets (蟲唧唧 or "the insects chirp") and then constructs the barracks as a space crowded with many sighing inhabitants (居人多歎息 "The inmates often sigh").[32] In contrast to the exceptional woman warrior Mulan—who honorably fights in battles in far-off lands on her father's behalf, and who also returns home to reunite with family—these incarcerated men collectively languish and sigh in inglorious frustration.

---

25 Leong, *Wild Geese Sorrow*, Poem 62, pp. 134–35.

26 Ibid., Poem 23, pp. 50–51; Poem 68, pp. 148–49.

27 Ibid., xxi.

28 Ibid., 170, note 57, about Poem 57. A number of poems suggest anger and revenge; e.g., a poet abandons the brush (vocation as a scholar) and closes by evoking a warrior awaiting vengeance against "barbarians" (Lai, Lim, and Yung, *Island,* Poem 66, pp. 100–101).

29 Lai, Lim, and Yung, *Island,* Poem 26, pp. 68–69.

30 On the female warrior motif in medieval Chinese literati poetry, see Luo, "Woman Avenger."

31 Feng, "Ballad of Mulan." See also Chin, "Ye Asian American Writers," 4–6.

32 Lai, Lim, and Yung, *Island,* Poem 26, pp. 68–69.

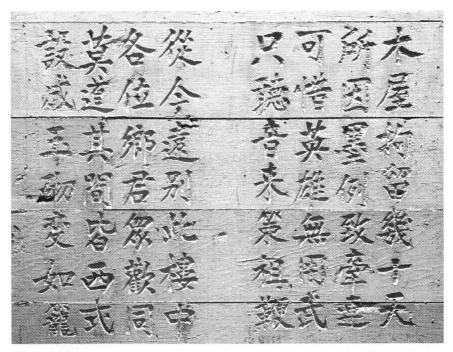

Figure 7: Chinese poetry based on Tang-era lyric forms, composed by an anonymous Mexican migrant, carved into a wooden wall of the former men's barracks of the US Immigration Station at Angel Island in the San Francisco Bay. The first two characters (reading top down from the rightmost column) are 木屋, "wooden house." July 2019. Photo by the author.

One Angel Island poem that transforms a medieval Chinese social environment by drawing attention to the physical conditions of incarceration derives from a lyric originally entitled 陋室銘 (often translated as "Inscription on a Crude Dwelling") by Tang literati poet Liu Yuxi (劉禹錫).[33] The modern anonymous Angel Island counterpart bears the title 木屋銘 or in Leong's rendition "Muhk Nguk Ming (Inscribed Upon the Wood House)," the first two characters "Muhk Nguk" (木屋) materializing the "Wood House," and the second stanza of the poem transforms the Tang poet's secluded abode with its green moss-covered steps into a bleak modern wooden building of four walls (四壁) that are painted green (油漆綠) on the inside, and enclosed by the green grass (草色青) of the island itself.[34] Transplanting poetic conventions into a new geospatial environ-

---

33 Leong, *Wild Geese Sorrow*, Poem 31, entitled here "Lou Shi Ming (Inscription About a Crude Dwelling)," 66–67.

34 Ibid., Poem 32, pp. 68–69; Lai, Lim, and Yung, *Island*, Poem 44, pp. 82–83. The spatial coordinates are disorienting given the location of this poem carved into the barracks building. The barracks run in an east-west direction, making the poet's reference to seeing a hospital by gazing south impossible (the hospital and other buildings could be seen from the north window, but not the south). Lai, Lim, and Yung, *Island*, 82n31.

ment, the detainee-poets turn medieval Chinese solitary dwellings into confining modern barracks.

One visually striking poem found on a lavatory room wall originally covered with dark green paint was composed by a Chinese refugee from Mexico who had fled due to the Mexican Expulsion Order of 1931, and it ends with the vivid image of a cage (籠) made of jade (玉):

> 木屋拘留幾十天，
> 所囚墨例致牽連。
> 可惜英雄無用武，
> 只聽音來策祖鞭。
>
> 從今遠別此樓中，
> 各位鄉君眾歡同。
> 莫道其間皆西式，
> 設成玉砌變如籠。

> Detained in the wood house several weeks,
> It's because of Mexico's exclusion law which implicates me.
> It's a pity heroes don't use weapons.
> I await word to snap Zu's whip.
>
> From here on, I'll travel far from this two-story building.
> Each and every villager will share a happiness.
> Don't idolize everything that's Western-style.
> Even if cut from jade, these walls are
>   nothing but a cage.[35]

This poem not only attests to Chinese immigration beyond transpacific trajectories (i.e., transit via Mexico);[36] it also marks a noteworthy survival of skilled calligraphy by a talented author or scribe. The lofty reference to Zu Di (祖逖), a Chinese hero from the Western Jin Dynasty (265–316 CE) and a fierce and ambitious warrior, sets up what Yao calls "the bitterness of having one's dreams snuffed out by the cold reality of a racist national immigration policy that sanction[s] imprisonment of a select group of people" on the basis of their country of origin.[37] In lieu of taking arms and seeking justice, the detainee-poet carves into the "jade" walls. Within the Angel Island barracks today, a full-scale reproduction of this poem, covered with dark-green paint recreating the original hue of the painted wall, allows a visitor to literally touch the past.

By exploring how detention poetry transforms the meanings of a physical environment, I seek to understand the symbiotic relationship of built environment and organic matter. The repeated use of phrases such as "wooden house" (木屋) or "wooden building" (木樓)—epithets collectively invented by the detainees inhabiting a shared space—

---

35 Leong, *Wild Geese Sorrow*, Poem 23, pp. 50–51. The Chinese in this quotation follows Lai, Lim, and Yung, *Island*, Poem 135, pp. 162–63.

36 For an Angel Island poem by a migrant en route to Cuba, see Lai, Lim, and Yung, *Island*, Poem 131, pp. 158–59.

37 Yao, "Transplantation and Modernity," 303.

make the wooden inscriptions a resilient human counter-history to bleak systems of border policing and incarceration. Carving into the bare California redwood walls alters the building's organic matter, monumentalizing Chinese labor in the space of the detention barracks. Inscription was a recursive act of resistance as the "graffiti" was repeatedly filled and painted over, with freshly made poems accruing additional meanings through emplacement. The painted green walls become poetically transmuted from the Tang scholar's dwelling or home into an uncanny jade cage, and the physicality of writing surfaces richly layer the cross-historical resonance of the inscriptions.

In a thickly nuanced formal analysis of what Leong numbers Poem 10, Sheng-mei Ma considers how the modern detainee adapts "the imageries" of a medieval Chinese "literati tradition" into an "elegant poetic form," including a pictographic "word game" or set of visual puns through the literary phrase 囚困, which literally translates as "prisoner incarcerated."[38] The first character depicts a person (人) in a box (囗), and the second uses the Chinese radical or component symbol for wood (木) in a box (囗), and the "graffitist accrues power" by playfully transforming "the detainee's physical condition" of being "trapped inside the square" of the wooden two-storied detention center now converted into a two-storied "wooden tower" (木樓).[39]

Medieval literary scholars such as Marisa Galvez have developed robust critical modes for assessing the "whole book" of European lyric anthologies including "multiauthor and anonymous" anthologies "contained in a manuscript codex or volume of parchment leaves bound together in book form."[40] The "multiauthor and anonymous" poetic anthology that Chinese detainees constructed at Angel Island becomes discernable not as a "whole book" nor "manuscript codex" but as a set of inscriptions in three-dimensional space, and as an architectural miscellany the entire wooden building forms a poetic ecosystem. The Angel Island barracks, in codicological terms, can be understood as a mostly anonymous and collaboratively authored architectural miscellany.

As Carissa M. Harris states in a different context, anthologies of medieval lyrics can create "a transhistorical affective space" that builds empathy between readers across time,[41] and just as lyrics "[share] textual space in a manuscript," so too can "bodies occupying physical space with one another" create an "affective space of identification between real and fictional subjects across time, crackling irresistibly between past and present like electricity."[42] It is both the close quarters of the barracks, as well as the crowded placement of poetry on its walls, that energize circuits of affect between the past and present.

The placement of poems on the walls, especially in the case of paired poems directly echoing or revising one another, suggest a collaborating community of poets while also attesting to the lived presence of bodies sharing a physical space. The acrostic "abolish

---

38 Ma, *Asia in Flight*, 80.

39 Ibid., 80–81.

40 Galvez, *Songbook*, 2.

41 Harris, *Obscene Pedagogies*, 191.

42 Ibid., 193.

Figure 8: Faint sketch of an ancestral shrine (with multiple family surnames) carved into a wall on the second floor of the former barracks of the US Immigration Station at Angel Island in the San Francisco Bay. July 2019. Photo by the author.

Angel Island" poem cited previously is accompanied by a poem that primarily uses identical Chinese characters as its end-rhymes. The response poem begins: 同病相憐如一身 [...] ("I sympathize, the same illness, as if we shared a body..."), and the use of shared rhymes across the two poems formally embodies somatic empathy.[43] A simple drawing of a shrine on the second floor of the barracks creates a "surrogate space" of community with family names sharing an ancestral connection, and elsewhere sketches of ships and houses evoke previous journeys and hometown villages. Crowded writing all over the barracks evokes the immediate context of interrogations as well. Crammed with tiny text, ephemeral "coaching books" helped paper sons and daughters prepare for interro-

---

43 Leong, *Wild Geese Sorrow*, Poem 58, pp. 126–27.

gations by providing a detailed alternate backstory or mental map of a village they most often did not inhabit prior to their departures (and oral histories suggest a process for converting dense "coaching books" into song for memory).[44] In this broader context, the "wooden building" not only brings bodies together into a shared living space; the barracks themselves become a layered palimpsest and a polyvocal florilegium, a linguistic ecology as well as a cultural repository.[45]

Solidarity, Oral Histories, and Literary Legacies

The poetry of Angel Island has become an important cultural archive attesting to lived experiences of incarceration and a reminder of the injustices of racial discrimination, and the site of Angel Island itself, now designated as a National Historic Landmark and functioning as a museum and site of reflection, continues to create new forms of solidarity and community. The history of how Angel Island poetry has survived to this day is a story of collective struggle. Tet Yee (aka Yee Tet Ming) and Smiley Jann copied hundreds of poems by hand into notebooks while they were detained at Angel Island in the 1930s, which is how many of the poems survive to this day. In one oral history, Yee states that "the injustices that I witnessed on Angel Island motivated me to later become a political activist and labor organizer,"[46] and his experience informed his decision to fight in World War II "because we had to defeat fascism."[47] Revisiting Angel Island many years later, he found the former "prison" had become "now like a paradise," and he composed a new poem to mark the occasion.[48]

It is fitting to note that it was an immigrant—and a former child refugee—who helped instigate efforts to preserve the Angel Island poetry that had long been dismissed as mere graffiti. Alexander Weiss, a Jewish American who was originally born in Austria and later naturalized as a US citizen, fled the Nazis at the age of four and he was employed as a park ranger at Angel Island in May 1970 when plans to demolish the building were underway. Weiss was surprised to come across "entire walls ... covered with calligraphy," and without even knowing Chinese he grasped the site's significance.[49] Weiss contacted George Araki (whose mother came into the US via Angel Island as a Japanese picture bride) and photographer Mak Takahaski to document the surviving poetry, and Asian American activists Christopher Chow, Paul Chow, Connie Young Yu, and Philip Choy among others lobbied to preserve the poetry and to establish the Angel

---

44 Ruth Chan Jang recalls her illiterate mother "had another woman read [the coaching paper] to her, and she would sing it to herself like she would Chinese opera" (Lai, Lim, and Yung, *Island*, 17). For images of coaching papers, see Lai, Lim, and Yung, *Island*, 18–19; Goldman, "Coaching Citizenship."

45 For a different sense of "language ecology," see Hsy, "Language Ecologies."

46 Lai, Lim, and Yung, *Island*, 289.

47 Ibid., 290.

48 Ibid.

49 Lee and Yung, *Immigrant Gateway*, 302.

Island Immigration Station as a National Historic Landmark and commemorative site.[50] During his lifetime, Weiss maintained that he "didn't discover the poems. They had been there for years and other people knew they were there."[51] His words published before his death in 2014 remain prescient today: "We don't have exclusion laws anymore, but we could have them in an instant tomorrow. It could happen to some other group of people. That's why we need memorials like concentration camps and Angel Island, so that we will learn from our past and not repeat the same mistakes."[52]

The quotations I have cited draw from interviews and oral histories, and a rich and robust orature (a communal body of oral literature and shared stories) lends the Angel Island poetry an elevated status in collective memory. In their authoritative edition of Angel Island poetry supplemented with "oral history interviews with former detainees and employees," Him Mark Lai, Genny Lim, and Judy Yung describe "a personal quest to reclaim our history as Chinese Americans."[53] These oral histories attest to unwritten poems preserved in memory;[54] lost poems commemorating acts of suicide in the building itself;[55] interviews soliciting oral histories of the poetic space eerily repurposing social scenes of interrogation;[56] and self-described "miracles" of surviving the humiliating Angel Island experience.[57]

Chinese detention poetry claims a literary legacy beyond the site of Angel Island itself. One Chinese poem found in a building of the Ellis Island Immigration Station ends with a laughing reference to the medieval Chinese travel narrative *Journey to the West* (西遊),[58] and a Chinese detention poem from the now-demolished Federal Immigration Detention Hospital in Victoria (British Columbia, Canada), suggests that both white and black government employees were sources of Chinese humiliation.[59] Ethnocentric Chinese terms for Western "barbarians" appear throughout such poetry composed across dispersed detention centers, but in the Angel Island context specifically a term such as 鬼佬 ("ghost person" or "foreign devil") subverts white anglophone perceptions of "Angel Island" as a pastoral island paradise.[60]

Postcolonial approaches have the potential to situate Angel Island within a broader comparative framework of incarceration systems beyond North America as well, reveal-

50 Ibid., 303 and 305.

51 Ibid., 303.

52 Ibid., 304.

53 Lai, Lim, and Yung, *Island*, ix.

54 Ibid., 290 (Tet Yee), 333 (Lee Puey You).

55 Ibid., 282 (Xie Chuang); see also Poem 111 and Poem 112 (pp. 140–41).

56 Ibid., 197–202, esp. 201–2.

57 Ibid., 251–53 (Soto Shee).

58 Ibid., Ellis Island, Poem 1, pp. 180–81.

59 Ibid., Victoria, BC, Poem 2, pp. 186–87, refers to "foreign slaves" (番奴) or white Westerners; Poem 3, pp. 186–87, refers to a "black ghost" (黑鬼) or African Canadian.

60 On the mythologizing of Angel Island along such lines in a prose novel, see Kingston, *China Men*, 53–60.

ing how island prisons or what Su Fang Ng calls "detention islands" operate in global mechanisms of social control.[61] Ato Quayson theorizes Robben Island off the coast of Cape Town, South Africa, as one such "repeating island" of displacement, settler colonialism, quarantine, imprisonment, and trauma.[62] Angel Island itself was converted after its closure (due to a fire in 1940) into a "prisoner of war processing center" as well as space for the forced internment of hundreds of immigrants of Japanese ancestry during World War II.[63]

Detention poetry such as the Angel Island lyric adapting the *Ballad of Mulan* for the space of the men's barracks, and a Chinese work dating from around 1911 entitled 妻囑情 or "My Wife's Admonishment" (recovered from a wall of a concrete cell in the immigration and detention center in Victoria, BC), can invite reassessments of the relationship between poetic anonymity and gendered authorship in both medieval Chinese and modern Chinese American contexts.[64] Grace S. Fong has examined the complexity of female-voiced medieval Chinese lyrics, interrogating the "non-gender-specific" or "universal" status ascribed to male Tang literati poets,[65] and she reveals how poetic anonymity forces readers to question their own assumptions about gendered authorship and the "manipulation of the female persona and its implications for role-playing, masking, and self-revelation" at play even in works attributed to male poets.[66] Contemporary poet Jennifer Chang interweaves locodescriptive and pastoral themes into her collections *The History of Anonymity* (2008) and *Some Say the Lark* (2017) while inscribing her own Chinese American name into modern English lyric forms.[67] Chinese American poet Brandon Som incorporates the story of his own grandfather's arrival as a paper son at Angel Island into *The Tribute Horse* (2014), a poetic anthology that features a series of English homophonic translations of Li Bai's "Quiet Night Thoughts" that perpetually reconfigures the relationship between lyric speaker and audience (the first lines of these iterations invoke grammatical subjects as varied as "me and you," "we," "a nun," or a "monk.").[68]

The poetry of incarceration as a sustained response to racist government policies in particular is a practice that extends beyond the particular experience of Chinese people in North America to additional communities of color. Toyo Suyemoto, a Japanese American whose family was forcibly relocated and interned during World War II along with thousands more in the US and Canada solely due to their Japanese ancestry, wrote lyric

61 Ng, "Detention Islands."

62 Quayson, *Aesthetic Nervousness*, 174–204.

63 Angel Island Immigration Station Foundation, "History of Angel Island." See also Lei, "Japanese Internment."

64 Lai, Lim, and Yung, *Island*, Poem 4, pp. 188–89.

65 Fong, "Engendering the Lyric," 114. On the rich life and works of prominent Tang women poets, see Samei, "Tang Women."

66 Ibid., 118.

67 Chang, *Lark*, "Dorothy Wordsworth," 54; Chang, *Anonymity*; see also Chang, "Asian American Lyric"; Chang, "Pastoral."

68 Som, *Tribute Horse*, 75–80 (at 75, 76, 77, and 79) and 95; see also 58–61 (in "Bows & Resonators").

poems in English during her years of incarceration in the pine plank barracks of the Topaz Relocation Center in Delta, UT, and she collected these poems about her experiences into her posthumous first-person memoir.[69] Suyemoto composed in poetic forms associated with European literary traditions (such as ballads and sonnets) as well as traditional Japanese forms (haiku and tanka), and Josephine Nock-Hee Park has observed that Suyemoto's "lyrics work through the experience of living in a space that cancels life," with poetry itself enduring as a "self-reflexive art whose powers of consolation and exposure resound within spaces of detention."[70] The medieval lyric forms reinvented and repurposed by Chinese detainees on Angel Island suggest just one localized collective strategy of resistance to racist exclusion and repeating systems of incarceration.

Archival Activism and Collective Action

Asian American literary and cultural studies is increasingly attentive (via oral history and archival recovery) to how Angel Island poems gain resonance through their physical locations of inscription around the "wooden building" and the divergent afterlives of medieval lyric forms today. A medieval literary, cultural, and ecocritical analysis opens up new geographies of commemoration and creates a broader appreciation for Angel Island as a thickly layered site of interethnic solidarity, resilience, and resistance to injustice.

Collective repurposing of medieval literature and orature at Angel Island not only testifies to the longstanding injustices of indefinite detention and racist exclusion. These enduring works also affirm the transformative powers of anonymity to speak to power, and they build a potent affective community across time and space that continues to motivate efforts to combat discrimination and create a more just society. As new coalitions of Asian Americans, including Chinese Americans and Japanese Americans, as well as Jewish Americans, act in solidarity with communities who are subjected to racist and xenophobic travel restrictions, forced incarceration, and indefinite detention today, there is hope that the lessons of Angel Island will be learned and not lost on future generations.[71]

---

69 Suyemoto, *Years of Internment*.

70 Park, "American Incarceration," 578–79.

71 Lee and Yung, *Immigrant Gateway*, "Epilogue," 315–25. See also Asian Americans Advancing Justice, "Testimony on Immigration Detention Centers"; Hayoun, "Japanese and Muslim Americans Join Forces"; Kandil, "Muslim-American Manzanar Pilgrimage"; Nodelman, "Jewish Activists on Front Lines Against ICE" [Immigration and Customs Enforcement].

Chapter Four

PASSING: CROSSING COLOR LINES IN THE SHORT FICTION OF ALICE DUNBAR-NELSON AND SUI SIN FAR

THIS CHAPTER CONSIDERS how two early multiracial authors in North America, Alice Dunbar-Nelson (1875–1935) and Sui Sin Far (1865–1914), transform the archetype (or stereotype) of the "tragic mulatta." First formulated in 1933 by African American poet and literary critic Sterling A. Brown,[1] the term "tragic mulatta" refers to a limiting set of representations for mixed-race characters that was pervasive throughout nineteenth-century American literature and sentimental romance, typically taking the form of a multiracial woman who lives as white (deliberately or ambiguously) and garners sympathy from the audience before her story comes to a tragic end. The issue of racial passing was a fraught and complex one in real life for multiracial individuals in the late nineteenth century through the turn of the twentieth, as Allyson Hobbs reveals in African American communities and Emma Jinhua Teng in a transnational "Eurasian" Asia-Pacific diaspora context,[2] and literary scholars have developed richly nuanced approaches for understanding stories of passing in sentimental romance traditions.[3]

In a contemporary Asian American literary context, Jennifer Ann Ho observes how "mixed race bodies ... create mobile subjectivities for their narrators" as a story passes "through genre, through identities, through countries—crossing multiple borders of form and content to create a passing story."[4] Ho's idea of the "theme of passing as a continually evolving strategy for dislocating one's racial and ethnic identity"[5] is evident in early passing stories as well. My discussion of "local color" sketches composed in the early careers of Dunbar-Nelson and Sui Sin Far traces how imagery of the Virgin Mary and Joan of Arc are associated with racial and gendered ambiguity and complex acts of passing and transformation. These feminine figures, deeply ingrained in the medievalism of the era, foreground nuanced traversals of language, race, gender, and sexuality.

1 Brown, "Negro Character by White Authors," 192–96.

2 Hobbs, *A Chosen Exile*; Teng, *Eurasian*.

3 Palumbo-DeSimone, "Race, Womanhood, and Tragic Mulatta"; Raimon, *"Tragic Mulatta" Revisited*.

4 Ho, *Racial Ambiguity*, 97. See also Skyhorse and Page, eds., *We Wear the Mask*.

5 Ibid.

Alice Dunbar-Nelson: Creolization and Francophone Medievalisms

Alice Dunbar-Nelson (1875–1935), author, journalist, and political activist, was the first woman of color to publish short stories, first in her collection of poems and short stories, *Violets and Other Tales* (1895), and then in *The Goodness of Saint Rocque, and Other Stories* (1899). Dunbar-Nelson's "local color" sketches (this term "local color" also devised by Sterling A. Brown)[6] explore nuances of life in and around New Orleans, and her narratives that ambiguously mark characters' racial identities and use careful representations of speech (including varieties of English and French) offer subtle indications of a person's class, race, and ethnicity. Understanding these "local color" sketches requires an appreciation for the complexities of black Creole identity in late nineteenth-century Louisiana, including local understandings of creolization and francophone Catholic traditions.

Louisiana, and New Orleans in particular, is often described as the northernmost point in the Caribbean, and it is in the context of French colonialism in the Caribbean that creolization and the local historical meanings of "Creole" and "people of color" are situated. In a much-cited food metaphor in her two-part essay "People of Color in Louisiana" (1916), Dunbar-Nelson states that a "person of color" in Louisiana would feel that "a Creole is a native of Louisiana," and the "mixed strains" of Creole identity include an "African strain slightly apparent" with the "true Creole" being much "like the famous gumbo of the state, a little bit of everything, making a whole, delightfully flavored, quite distinctive, and wholly unique."[7] Complicating and challenging a black/white racial binary predominant throughout the rest of the United States, free Creoles of color in Louisiana formed a vital third social grouping (in conjunction with black and white racial categories) with its own prestigious literary and cultural traditions and prominence in society.

The first poetic anthology of works by Americans of color was *Les Cenelles* [The Holly Berries] (1845), printed in New Orleans and composed in French by free black Creole men who dedicated the poems collectively "au beau sexe louisianais" (i.e., to the women of color of Louisiana).[8] Although these poems by men addressed to women might appear to be conventional love poems in form and style, there were unmistakably political dimensions to their use of discourses of love and devotion that were associated with French romanticism.[9] Most noticeably, Creoles of color in Louisiana aligned their sociopolitical interests with those of formerly enslaved black people in Haiti who had won the nation's independence from France in 1804, and Creoles of color in Louisiana proudly exhibited a mixed cultural and racial heritage. As Floyd D. Cheung has shown, the authors of *Les Cenelles* and Creoles of color aligned their values with Catholicism,[10] and Shirley Elizabeth Thompson observes that "the francophone black Atlantic" with its

---

6 Brown, "Negro Character by White Authors," 196–97.

7 Dunbar-Nelson, "People of Color in Louisiana: Part 1," 367.

8 Lanusse, *Les Cenelles*, reprinted by Coleman, ed., *Creole Voices*, xli.

9 Barnard, "Les Cenelles."

10 Cheung, "*Les Cenelles* and Quadroon Balls," 11.

"meeting of Catholicism and African religious practices" created an "elastic ritual space" of spiritual practices that could "incorporate political and social critique and vice versa."[11]

Attending to the francophone and Caribbean contexts for Catholic identity reveals how profoundly race, religion, and language intertwine. Throughout other parts of the United States, the anglophone category of WASP ("White Anglo-Saxon Protestant"), which Matthew X. Vernon observes "most insidiously" relies on a racialized understanding of the term "Anglo-Saxon" to mark "wealth, privilege, and whiteness,"[12] intertwines the social phenomena of language, religion, and race to construct a classed term strongly aligned with white supremacy and a Christian, i.e., Protestant, identity. Catholic identities and Catholic medievalisms throughout North America were not homogeneous. As discussed in this book's previous chapters, anti-Chinese violence incited by predominantly Irish American and Catholic brotherhoods mobilized medievalizing imagery and discourse to reinforce white supremacy and racism, including Denis Kearney's "The Chinese Must Go!" rhetoric in San Francisco and Catholic "rat libel" propaganda in New York's Chinatown.

Dunbar-Nelson's "local color" sketches reveal how place informs the lives of free people of color, and her early stories often rely on subtly encoded local cues to signal the sociocultural milieu of a setting. I concentrate on three prose narratives whose female protagonists are ambiguously racialized, usually by references to dark hair or eyes but also through vague references to color. As Thompson states, Dunbar-Nelson "only subtly hints at the African blood of her characters"[13] in her portrayals of "the hopes and dreams of the mixed-race Creole woman."[14] The indeterminacy of the term "Creole," which from the perspective of black Louisianans could include white Creoles as well as Creoles of color, allows Dunbar-Nelson's characters to be ambiguously "read" by an audience as white, black, or mixed. These stories, thick with Marian allusions and coded references to distant and unattainable whiteness, carry a particular significance once their central female characters are recognized as Creoles of color.

"Little Miss Sophie" tells a story drawing upon the "tragic mulatta" archetype, and Thompson has observed that "Creole of color women characters" of this kind serve to "delimit hard and fast racial and moral categories," becoming "tragic because they are trapped between them."[15] Sophie, "poor little Creole old maid,"[16] is a seamstress in Third District of New Orleans, and what seems to be a "slice of life" narrative changes course once Sophie overhears two men talking about the wealthy white man Neale who had abandoned his "little Creole love-affair" with a "dusky-eyed fiancée"[17] to marry a white woman. The text reveals that Neale had promised to marry Sophie (an arrange-

---

11 Thompson, *Exiles at Home*, 96.

12 Vernon, *Black Middle* Ages, 55.

13 Thompson, *Exiles at Home*, 177.

14 Ibid., 178.

15 Ibid., 173.

16 Dunbar-Nelson, *Goodness of St. Rocque*, 140.

17 Ibid., 145.

ment which would have been to her socioeconomic advantage), but he now needs back the ring he had previously given her in order to support his claim to a new inheritance. The subtext underlying Sophie's predicament is the local *plaçage* system, where a free woman of color could find romance and economic support with a wealthy white man (until he should choose to marry a white woman), and Cheung has explored the moral misgivings that Creoles of color expressed in response to this practice.[18] Throughout this story, Marian imagery not only associates the poor Sophie with tragic innocence and feminine beauty but also sets her against a vision of idealized whiteness; Sophie's worship of the Virgin introduces themes of suffering and sacrifice that set up a bittersweet irony when the story ends on Christmas day.

Medieval imagery pervades Sophie's story. When it opens, music is "dying away in distant echoes through the great arches of the silent church" as Sophie walks alone, "crouching in a little, forsaken black heap at the altar of the Virgin," and the "beneficent smile of the white-robed Madonna" elsewhere represented as a "calm white Virgin," initially "seemed to whisper comfort."[19] When Sophie enters a church and witnesses a wedding, the space is expressly described in medievalizing terms: "There it was, right in the busiest, most bustling part of the town, its fresco and bronze and iron quaintly suggestive of mediaeval times," and everything was "cool and dim and restful" inside "with the faintest whiff of lingering incense rising," with "the sweet, white-robed Virgin at the pretty flower-decked altar," as well as another statue of the Virgin "away up in the niche, far above the golden dome where the Host was."[20] This discourse of love and devotion to the Virgin shifts after the critical revelation of the story, when Sophie resolves to return the ring to her former fiancé:

> [O]nce you were his, and you shall be his again. You shall be on his finger, and perhaps touch his heart. Dear ring, ma chère petite de ma coeur, chérie de ma coeur. Je t'aime, je t'aime, oui, oui. You are his; you were mine once too. Tonight, just one night, I'll keep you—then—tomorrow, you shall go where you can save him.[21]

In this attentive display of code-switching (moving between English and French), the language of love addresses the ring as proxy for the former lover, and the language mixing reflects the other forms of cultural and racial mixing that shape Creole identities in Louisiana. This story ends with the ring described by the omniscient narrator in English as "clasped between her fingers on her bosom,—a bosom white and cold, under a cold happy face."[22] Throughout this story, the Virgin is repeatedly portrayed as distant, "white-robed," "white," and "calm"—and Sophie's pitiful death against the backdrop of Marian imagery implicates the church and legal institutions as "cold" and "silent," complicit in upholding idealizations of white supremacy and demanding sacrifices from

---

18 Cheung, "*Les Cenelles* and Quadroon Balls," 8.

19 Dunbar-Nelson, *Goodness of St. Rocque*, 137.

20 Ibid., 147.

21 Ibid., 150–51.

22 Ibid., 152.

women of color. Sophie in the story's conclusion is "white and cold," ironically becoming white only in the pallor of death.[23]

"Sister Josepha" is divergently rich in its medieval imagery and a nuanced play of linguistic registers through spoken dialogue. In this story, the woman known as Sister Josepha had started out an orphaned Creole infant named Camille, who has "big black eyes"[24] and "small brown hands."[25] After being taken into the convent she grows into a beautiful woman, but she flees the white man who would be her prospective adoptive father: "she could not divine the meaning of the pronounced leers and admiration of her physical charms which gleamed in the man's face," but "she knew it made her feel creepy" and she "refused to go" back to the household.[26] She takes refuge in the convent, but even Father Ray objectifies her, "linger[ing] longer in his blessing when his hands pressed her silky black hair."[27] With no family and "no nationality"[28] and no future prospects, she has no option but to shut herself into the convent.

The narrator uses Marian imagery to eroticize architectural and environmental space when she is in church. Although Sister Josepha looks at "her worn rosary" and "glanced no more at the worldly glitter of femininity," the "golden magnificence of the domed altar with its weighting mass of lilies and wide-eyed roses" infuses the space.[29] "Her heart beat quickly" and "rebellious thoughts ... surged in her small heavy gowned bosom"[30] when she exchanges glances in church with a boy with "waves of brown hair" and "pitying brown eyes" and she "briefly" falls in love.[31] Erotically-charged Marian imagery renders all the more vivid the tragedy of her foreclosed life path, and in a "flash" she experiences "the cruel self-torture of wonder at her own identity ... asking herself, 'Who am I? What am I?'"[32] The language of martyrdom and suffering or "cruel self-torture" forms the crux of her fraught identity.

The narrative ends with a return to prayer, rendered in three languages: "'Confiteor Deo omnipotenti,' [i.e., I confess to almighty God] murmured the priest" in Latin, and "tremblingly one little sister followed the words" in French saying: "Je confesse à Dieu, tout puissant—que j'ai beaucoup péché par pensées—c'est ma faute—c'est ma faute—c'est ma très grande faute" [I confess to God almighty that I have sinned greatly—it's

---

23 In an analysis of race and modern American visual culture, Ruby C. Tapia examines the "framing of whiteness as it is produced and reproduced in racialized images of the maternal," including in some cases Marian imagery, and she describes how maternal visual motifs that can be used in forms of "white self-making" that rely upon the "negation of the full humanity" of people of color and contribute to the production of their "social death." Tapia, *American Pietàs*, 21.

24 Dunbar-Nelson, *Goodness of St. Rocque*, 164.

25 Ibid., 156.

26 Ibid., 159.

27 Ibid., 160.

28 Ibid., 170.

29 Ibid., 165.

30 Ibid., 164.

31 Ibid., 167.

32 Ibid., 171.

Figure 9: Brown-eyed and brown-haired Joan of Arc in the Cathédrale Saint-Louis, Roi-de-France or St. Louis Cathedral (largely in its current form since 1850) in the French Quarter of New Orleans, Louisiana. Standing figure donated by the Sodalité de Sainte Jeanne d'Arc in 1920. October 2018. Photo by the author.

my fault, it's my fault, it's my most grievous fault].[33] The author's triglossia stratifies language within the space of the church: an omniscient English narration framing the action, a ritual utterance of the priest in Latin, and an internal expression of emotional "self-torture" or self-blame in French. This literary layering of three languages shows how social scripts and power structures constrain the life paths available to Josepha within a patriarchal and racially stratified society.

In these "tragic mulatta" stories, imagery associated with the Virgin Mary implicates institutionalized religion as a social and legal mechanism of control that is complicit in victimizing mixed-race women, but some of these texts invert Marian tropes by means of happy outcomes. "La Juanita" opens with the exotic beauty of a woman of mixed ancestry who revises the tragic archetype: "La Juanita, you must know, was the pride of Mandeville, the adored, the admired of all, with her petite, half-Spanish, half-French beauty" and "black curls."[34] The family patriarch Grandpère Colomés wants to preserve this family's mixed Creole identity and keep it "aloof" from white anglophone Americans, but Captain Mercer Grangeman, "this pale-eyed youth"[35] who is "big and blond and brawny,"[36] gains La Juanita's affections. Mercer names his boat "La Juanita," and during a boat race Grandpère Colomés "prayed a devout prayer to the Virgin that 'La Juanita' should be capsized."[37]

This prayer to the Virgin Mary goes unheeded, as Mercer proves himself valiant by braving the ensuing tempest on Lake Pontchartrain: "La Juanita was proud," and when her elders lead her "away in the storm, though her face was white, and the rose mouth pressed close," she stays silent "and her eyes were as bright as ever before."[38] Mercer lands safely "surrounded by a voluble, chattering, anxious throng that loaded him with questions in patois, in broken English, and in French" and Mercer was "no longer 'un Américain' now, he was a hero."[39] Grandpère Colomés admits "some time dose Americain can mos' be lak one Frenchman."[40] Fusing Marian imagery with Petrarchan conceits of love as a tempest, the family patriarch's "devout prayer to the Virgin" to *sink* a ship at sea (rather than a maiden's prayer to *save* a mariner from danger) inverts gendered conventions of medieval romance traditions, and forbidden love results in a happy mixed marriage.

Although Dunbar-Nelson uses medieval imagery as the atmospheric backdrop for tragic stories or objectified maidens, some of her medievalism recuperates the potential for an empowered womanhood through imagery associated with Joan of Arc. The young martyr-saint "Maid of Orleans" Jeanne d'Arc who adopted masculine arms and armor

---

33 Ibid.
34 Ibid., 197.
35 Ibid., 200.
36 Ibid., 198.
37 Ibid., 200.
38 Ibid., 205.
39 Ibid., 207.
40 Ibid., 208.

to lead French troops to victory against the English during the fifteenth century now enjoys prominence throughout Nouvelle-Orléans (New Orleans) in public sculpture and its divergently medievalizing church architecture,[41] and her role as a crusader fighting a just struggle was not lost on Creoles of color in the late nineteenth century. A poem by Creole of color poet Victor-Ernest Rillieux entitled "Amour et Dévouement" [Love and Devotion] is overtly politicized and dedicated to "Miss Ida B. Wells," African American anti-lynching crusader who is addressed as "vierge au teint brun, au pays du Sauvage" [brown-skinned virgin in the land of the savage][42] and compared to both "Judith et Jeanne d'Arc," i.e., the biblical Judith who beheaded a tyrant and sexual predator, and the medieval maiden and martyr Joan of Arc.[43] The phrase "pays du Sauvage" names the brutality of antiblack racism and white supremacy in the United States, redirecting the "savage" and "heathen" epithets to the white Americans who have used such derogatory terms to describe Africa or Asia, and the English phrase "le White Cap" (referring to the notorious white hoods of the Klu Klux Klan) disruptively code-switches from the French.[44]

One of the works in Dunbar-Nelson's *Violets* is "The Maiden's Dream," an enigmatic reverie on romance and desire, interspersed with verses, with medieval intertexts that thematize tragic love. "The maid had been reading love-poetry, where the world lay bathed in moon-light, fragrant with dew-wet roses and jasmine," with her thoughts "more caressing than the overshadowing wing of a mother-dove."[45] The text refers to Dante Alighieri, the "stern, dark, exiled Florentine poet, with that one silver ray in his clouded life—Beatrice,"[46] and an allusion to the doomed lovers Antony and Cleopatra locates heroism in an explicitly racialized African woman: "Egypt herself, her splendid barbaric beauty acting like an inspiration upon the craven followers, leads on, foremost in this fierce struggle" before "the tide turns" and they are defeated.[47] Marian devotion ("mother-dove") and erotic love coexist with religious iconography that casts an African woman as a figure of strength in a "fierce struggle," even if this imagery is not given a clearly politicized meaning.

Joan of Arc would become more significant to Dunbar-Nelson after World War I, when she adopts the figure in line with contemporaneous imagery of the "new woman" associated with modernity, and the queerness of Joan of Arc evident at the turn of the twentieth century (which I discuss elsewhere in this book) would become prominent in the author's later works. The erotic networks that would emerge among Dunbar-Nelson and contemporaneous African American women associated with the Harlem Renaissance are richly archived and documented in the research of Black feminist poet and

---

41 Vishnuvajjala and Barrington, "New Orleans's Medievalisms."

42 Coleman, ed., *Creole Voices*, 115–16.

43 Ibid., 117.

44 Ibid.

45 Dunbar-Nelson, *Violets*, 85.

46 Ibid., 90.

47 Ibid., 89.

literary historian Akasha Gloria Hull.[48] As far as francophone and activist contexts are concerned, Dunbar-Nelson writes a chapter "Negro Women in War Work" for a history on African Americans in the Great War, which elsewhere includes a story of Drum Major Sissle, a "man of color," movingly singing a song about Joan of Arc "in English and then in excellent French," honoring the "Maid of Orleans" who "liberate[d] the French at a time when their national existence hung in the balance."[49] In a reading journal on April 29, 1923, Dunbar-Nelson records reading a book about Joan of Arc "with text subservient to beautiful illustrations" by French artist Bernard Boutet de Monvel,[50] and her conclusion to an essay "The Negro Woman and the Ballot" on socioeconomic freedom of African American women in 1927 states: "Perhaps some Joan of Arc will lead the way."[51]

In Dunbar-Nelson's earliest "local color" works set in Louisiana, it is not yet Joan of Arc but the imagery of Marian devotion and more conventional models of maidenhood that invite her most focused attention, in conjunction with her subversions of the "tragic mulatta" trope. The author's early interests in linguistic creolization create vivid portrayals of local space and social environments, and the ambiguous racialization of characters in her "local color" sketches allows them to pass among perceived racial categories and enact subtly transformative deployments of medieval feminine imagery.

Yellow Medievalism: Sui Sin Far in Jamaica

Alice Dunbar-Nelson's "local color" sketches and "tragic mulatta" stories bear fruitful comparison with the works by a contemporaneous biracial woman author, journalist, and poet: Sui Sin Far (1865–1914). Sui Sin Far was the most commonly known pen name of Edith Maude Eaton, who was born in England to a white English father and a Chinese mother (who had been adopted by white English missionaries); the author spent her childhood in Montreal before her family relocated to Jamaica. In 1898 between the publication of Dunbar-Nelson's first two story collections, Sui Sin Far published a story "Away Down in Jamaica" featuring a tragic brown Clarissa on the Caribbean island. The white woman who frames the story is told the character's backstory: "Clarissa is a brown girl, Missus. She was adopted when a little child by some rich white people. They brought her up like a lady, but some years ago she ran away from them."[52] The interlocu-

---

48 Hull, *Color, Sex, and Poetry*; Hull, *Diary of Alice Dunbar-Nelson*. On medievalism and the Harlem Renaissance, see also Whitaker, "B(l)ack in the Middle Ages"; Whitaker, *Harlem Middle Ages*; Chang, "Pastoral."

49 Scott, *American Negro in World War*, 309; this text includes Dunbar-Nelson's Chapter XXVII, "Negro Women in War Work," 374–97.

50 Alice Dunbar-Nelson, Journal II, Record Book No. 3, MSS 113, University of Delaware Library, Newark, DE. Jesse Ryan Erickson, *Alice Dunbar-Nelson Reads*. https://sites.udel.edu/alicereads/journal-ii/1923-2/.

51 Dunbar-Nelson, "Negro Woman and the Ballot."

52 Sui Sin Far [Edith Eaton], "Away Down in Jamaica." Chapman, ed., *Becoming Sui Sin Far*, 171–180, at 174.

tor responds: "Indeed! Quite a romantic history!" and the story ends with a quotation of verses from Harriet Beecher Stowe's abolitionist novel *Uncle Tom's Cabin*.[53]

Sui Sin Far's sympathy for the "tragic mulatta" figure is most evident in a column published in Jamaica about the opening of a new theater in Kingston, and she remarks that the stage is "next to literature ... the most potent influence that is working in the modern world" and it "links us to the past" while it also "keeps us in close touch with all the great hopes, enthusiasms, and interests of the nineteenth century."[54] She is moved by a show about a "Vaudeville girl" that features a song about a mixed-race Caribbean woman, a "yellow girl [at] whom we decent people hurl / Anathemas, and jokes."[55] This song names the mixed-race woman as a spectacular figure targeted by both misogyny and racism, and the lyrics name the figure herself as a trope: "You are a poem, or a song— / A wicked one, they say— / A bit of colour thrown along / A drab old world and gray."[56] The term "yellow" in this context has its own ambiguity; it can refer to the pseudo-scientific racism of the day which uses "yellow" as a third term for mixed-race black people (Dunbar-Nelson herself uses "white and black and yellow" in a story about male racial passing that she published posthumously),[57] and Christine "Xine" Yao notes that "yellow" is simultaneously the "shade of Asian racialization triangulated between black and white."[58]

In a later essay entitled "Leaves of the Mental Portfolio of an Eurasian" (1909), Sui Sin Far would recount her refusal of the advances of a white English naval officer and her own act of identifying with the "brown people" of the world.[59] In her earlier account of a theatrical performance in Jamaica in 1897, Sui Sin Far's implicit sympathy for and identification with the "yellow girl" in the song signals the multivalent associations of "yellow" within a shared mixed-race diasporic Black and Asian context. The author's empathy for the "yellow" mixed-race woman enacts a form of what José Esteban Muñoz calls "disidentification," a politicized strategy by which queer people of color transform social perceptions of their own marginalized positionings through performances or cultural productions that are not typically "coded" as properly belonging to them.[60] In this earlier context in Jamaica, Sui Sin Far, a "yellow" biracial (white and Asian) author, finds a subtle way to signal disidentification with a "yellow" (or "brown," depending on context) mixed-race woman—even if such a woman does not precisely share her own racial or ethnic background. In this process, the author creates literary and theatrical space for new kinds of interracial "yellow" solidarity between women.

---

53 Ibid. See also 180.

54 Sui Sin Far [Fire Fly], "The Girl of the Period: The Theatre." Chapman, ed., *Becoming Sui Sin Far*, 119–21, at 119.

55 Ibid.

56 Ibid.

57 Dunbar-Nelson, "Stones of the Village," 5.

58 Yao, "Reading Sui Sin Far in Jamaica," 200.

59 Ibid., 199–200.

60 Muñoz, *Disidentifications*; also see this book's introduction.

By inviting audiences to consider the rich sociopolitical implications of the term "yellow," Sui Sin Far's medievalism (discussed in the previous chapter and below) could be considered a recuperative form of "yellow medievalism," a social corrective to the era's stigmatizing anti-Asian discourses of "Yellow Peril" and the sensationalist fearmongering "yellow journalism" associated with newspaper publisher William Randolph Hearst before and after the Spanish-American War of 1898.[61] The ambiguously racialized "yellow girl" in the Jamaican theater names and subtly reworks the "tragic mulatta" archetype, allowing for what Yao has called "counterintimacies" between Black and Asian women. Sui Sin Far's queer act of disidentification in the theater opens up a seemingly constraining trope of cultural representation.

Tricksters and Fictive Voicing

I end this chapter by addressing Sui Sin Far's own "local color" sketches, including her early narratives and essays, and I attend to the author's own flexible vernacularity and mobile acts of fictive voicing across genres (journalism, short fiction, and memoir). Sui Sin Far's earlier works have been described as having the hints of the "trickster" hero not only associated with later Asian American traditions but also with medieval European beast-fables and African folklore.[62] Sui Sin Far's "local color" sketches located in Montreal, Jamaica, and across the US construct varied acts of racial passing while in transit. She implicitly passes as a white Englishwoman in Canada writing as "E. E." (Edith Eaton) in order to speak against white anti-Chinese racism in "A Plea for the Chinaman" (1896),[63] but elsewhere she adopts a persona and literary voice of a Chinese man whose racial positioning shifts across North American locations and navigates varied spaces of solidarity among Jews, Japanese, and Chinese in New York's Chinatown (as discussed in the previous chapter). In addition to her "white" and "Chinese" racial personas, the author also writes *in propria persona* as an "Eurasian" hybridizing complex positionings.

Sui Sin Far's acts of racial and gender passing are most evident through her multiple pseudonyms. In some of her early pieces published as if they were journalistic travel sketches, she writes as a "Chinaman" named "Wing Sing" using a stylized and affected "accent" or pidgin English. In a description of travels from Los Angeles through Canada, "Wing Sing" includes an episode entitled "He Hears Habitant French" where the narrator reports hearing "very strange talk" in the railway car and the "Irishman he say 'That is the French talk. We have plenty French people in Canada.'"[64] Another "Wing Sing" report from Montreal during Chinese New Year opens: "Gung Hee Sun Neen, Happy New Year," and it describes a meeting with "Lee Chu, he Chinaman, but he all same Canadian man" who "wear fur coat and fur hat and he drink plenty beer" and is "interpreter in Montreal

61 On the long history of such "Yellow Peril" discourses, see Tchen and Yeats, *Yellow Peril!*

62 White-Parks, "Sui Sin Far as Trickster Authorship."

63 Sui Sin Far [E. E.], "Plea for the Chinaman."

64 Sui Sin Far [Wing Sing], "Wing Sing of Los Angeles on His Travels." Chapman, ed., *Becoming Sui Sin Far*, 209–11, at 211.

court."[65] Chu "[s]ometime he talk English, sometime he talk Chinese and sometime he talk the French talk," and "[w]hen I go to bid him good-bye, he say 'Au Revoir'" and he asks his cousin what that means and "my cousin he say, 'I think he mean to tell you he know something you not know.'"[66] This play on what the "native informant" does and does not know sets up a clear winking pun on the author's own pen name: "The Chinese lily, the Chinaman call the Sui Sin Far, it bloom in all the house of the Chinese at this time and its fragrance greet me like a friend."[67]

In her earlier work before the turn of the century published as "Fire Fly," Sui Sin Far seemingly adopts the social positioning of the white English colonizer. Fire Fly's "The Departure of the Royal Mail" (January 1897) describes "English voices mingled with the soft southern accents of the West Indians," reminding her that "Jamaica is English" and the piece ends with a quotation from William Watson's imperialist and colonial verse.[68] Fire Fly's "Alpha Cottage" sketch (February 1897) describing the Convent of Mercy finds the "sunny institution" an appealing shelter.[69] She notes that "they welcomed me most courteously and kindly,"[70] and the "ideal school, located healthily and beautifully supplied" and "taught by gentle, refined ladies," features paintings of former mothers and a "lady whose fresh youthful face beamed so happily upon me that for a moment I almost wished I myself were a member of her sisterhood."[71] The medieval atmosphere of the Convent of Mercy Chapel is so idyllic and charming that the narrator "almost" wishes herself "a member of [the] sisterhood," and Sui Sin Far signals her fascination with, yet marked distance from, this community whose grounds she visits.

The notion of the Convent of Mercy as an "institution" providing safety for marginalized women invites fruitful comparisons with Dunbar-Nelson's contemporaneous stories. According to the community's own lore, the Convent of Mercy was first founded as Alpha Cottage School by Justina "Jesse" Ripoll, a Jamaican-born Creole of "mixed" black, Portuguese, and French ancestry, and one account of the Convent's origins in May 1880 begins with her "holding the hand of a little orphan girl, walk[ing] up the path" to Alpha Cottage.[72] As much as "Fire Fly" aligns herself with the white English colonizer class in Jamaica, she nonetheless comes close to identifying with the perspectival protagonists of Dunbar-Nelson's contemporaneous fiction.

Sui Sin Far's first and only collection of short stories, *Mrs. Spring Fragrance* (1912), engages both with medievalizing romance traditions as well as new configurations of

65 Sui Sin Far [Wing Sing], "Wing Sing of Los Angeles on His Travels," Chapman, ed., *Becoming Sui Sin Far*, 211–13, at 211–12.

66 Ibid., 212.

67 Ibid., 213.

68 Sui Sin Far [Fire Fly], "Departure of Royal Mail." Chapman, ed., *Becoming Sui Sin Far*, 116–18, at 118.

69 Sui Sin Far [Fire Fly], "Girl of the Period." Chapman, ed., *Becoming Sui Sin Far*, 121–25, at 122.

70 Ibid., 123.

71 Ibid.

72 Little, *You Did It Unto Me*, 2–3.

the "tragic mulatta" figure within a new set of "yellow" biracial (white and Chinese) contexts. The short story "Sweet Sin," written in Montreal and published in 1898, is the author's first narrative featuring a "Eurasian" (Chinese and white American) protagonist, and the narrative describes a woman similar to Dunbar-Nelson's Sister Josepha whose identity crisis is a form of "self-torture."[73] In Sui Sin Far's story, the biracial protagonist named Sweet Sin kills herself because she cannot marry the Chinese man whom her father favors due to her love for a white American, but she cannot marry the white American either—and in Arthurian fashion her story ends with the image of her enclosed remains floating on the water while a posthumous letter reveals the tragic circumstances of her death.[74]

The biracial woman's identity conflict is expressed in terms of dueling selves: "My Chinese half is good and patient, like all the Chinese people we know," but "my American half ... feels insulted for the Chinese half and wants to fight," and "you don't know what it is to be half one thing and half another," and "I feel all torn to pieces," and "I don't know what I am, and I don't seem to have any place in the world."[75] What Dunbar-Nelson calls "the cruel self-torture of wonder at her own identity" in Sister Josepha, and here expressed by Sui Sin Far through Sweet Sin, is a medievalized form of the internal suffering and "double-consciousness" famously formulated in 1903 by African American sociologist and historian W. E. B. Du Bois: the "peculiar sensation ... of always looking at one's self through the eyes of others," a "two-ness" of "two souls, two thoughts ... two warring ideals in one dark body, whose dogged strength alone keeps it from being torn asunder."[76] It is a theme that Sui Sin Far develops at length in her essay "Leaves of the Mental Portfolio of an Eurasian" (1909) relating episodes in her life spanning childhood and young adulthood across England, Montreal, New York, and San Francisco's Chinatown.[77]

Although Sui Sin Far often aligned herself explicitly with her Chinese background (in her texts and in real life), her first-person "Eurasian" narrative—related in a perpetual present tense—reveals the shifting ways she was perceived across time and space, and her autoethnographic turn conjoins white heroism and Chinese victimhood in one body. The first encounter with racist violence transpires after the family enters the US. In New York, white children on the street find out she and her brother are Chinese and hurl insults: "Chinky, Chinky, Chinaman, yellow-face, pig-tail, rat-eater."[78] The narrator proclaims that she (and by extension her brother) "would rather be Chinese than anything in the world," and in an ensuing skirmish "the white blood in our veins fights valiantly

73 Sui Sin Far [Sui Seen Far], "Sweet Sin." Chapman, ed., *Becoming Sui Sin Far*, 166–71.

74 On the medieval trope of the deathbed letter, see the story of "the lily maid" Elaine of Astolat (or Ascolat) in Malory, *Le Morte Darthur*, bk. 18, chap. 20, 435; Tennyson, *Idylls of the King*, "Elaine," 147–22, esp. 212–17.

75 Sui Sin Far [Sui Seen Far], "Sweet Sin." Chapman, ed., *Becoming Sui Sin Far*, 168.

76 Du Bois, *Souls of Black Folk*, 3. On Du Bois and the Middle Ages, see Achi and Chaganti, "Medieval African Art"; Vernon, *Black Middle Ages*, 19–22 and 108–11; Whitaker, *Black Metaphors*, 125–29 and 144–52.

77 Sui Sin Far, "Mental Portfolio of an Eurasian," in *Mrs. Spring Fragrance*, ed. Hsu, 221–33.

78 Ibid., 222.

Figure 10: Sculpture of Joan of Arc standing next to the altar at the Basilique Notre-Dame de Montréal in Old Montréal, Québec, a masterpiece of Gothic Revival architecture. May 2018. Photo by the author.

for the Chinese half of us."[79] Informing her proud mother afterwards that the siblings "won the battle," the narrator awakes in the morning shouting lyrics to "Sound the battle cry" —a hymn laden with chivalric imagery.[80] Alluding to anti-Chinese violence through this tale of childhood harassment, Sui Sin Far uses medieval imagery to express a racialized dual identity. Internalizing "white savior" tropes of progressive missionary uplift, she imagines a chivalric white self who fights on behalf of another self that is vulnerable and Chinese.

---

79 Ibid.

80 Ibid., 222–23. Sui Sin Far records the opening two lines of the hymn by William Sherman, "Sound the Battle Cry" (1869).

This episode with its imagery of Christ-like martyrdom and the cross evokes the "crossings" and burdens of mixed-race identity. Hsuan L. Hsu has argued that the "cross of the Eurasian" invokes both the "crucifix and the biological crossing of blood that marginalizes the author from both Chinese and white communities"[81] in line with the themes of martyrdom that Min Hyoung Song finds pervading Sui Sin Far's sentimental romances.[82] Expanding the Du Bois style "conflict" in "Sweet Sin" from a decade earlier, the author claims and reframes the "tragic mulatta" or "yellow girl" motif in her own voice. Sui Sin Far's biracial positioning allows her to mobilize the "tragic mulatta" motif and also embody a "white savior" archetype. In the form of a prophetic dream, the narrative reaches a hagiographical apotheosis in third-person voice. The author reads an article from a Chinese writer in New York stating: "The Chinese in America owe an everlasting debt of gratitude to Sui Sin Far for the bold stand she has taken in their defense."[83] In her later work as a journalist and advocate, she would write movingly on behalf of immigrants in Chinatowns (Los Angeles, San Francisco, Seattle, Montreal).[84] Sui Sin Far would reroute what might otherwise become tropes of toxic chivalry, expressing through medieval intertexts a commitment to racial justice.

One of the most revealing medieval motifs in the "Eurasian" essay is Sui Sin Far's invocation—and transformation—of Joan of Arc. The author declares that she loves "poetry, particularly heroic pieces [and] fairy tales" and "dream[s] of being great and noble."[85] She takes "glory in the idea of dying at the stake and a great genie arising from the flames and declaring to those who have scorned us: 'Behold, how great and glorious and noble are Chinese people!'"[86] By invoking progressive prophesy and potent martyrdom imagery associated with Joan of Arc, Sui Sin Far anticipates the more famous women warriors that would emerge throughout later Chinese American writing.[87] Within its own time, the Joan of Arc imagery is complexly racialized. Sui Sin Far's hagiographic prophesy as a Chinese Joan of Arc revises the "tragic mulatta" tropes by envisioning progressive potentials. This prophetic moment anticipates one of Sui Sin Far's fictional narratives of a white woman who witnesses a prophesy about her "half-breed" child "of Chinese blood," proclaimed by "the old mulatto Jewess who nursed me."[88]

---

81 Hsu, ed., *Mrs. Spring Fragrance*, "Introduction," 19.

82 Song, "Sentimentalism and Sui Sin Far."

83 Sui Sin Far, "Mental Portfolio of an Eurasian," in *Mrs. Spring Fragrance*, ed. Hsu, 226.

84 Sui Sin Far [E. E.], "Plea for the Chinaman."

85 Sui Sin Far, "Mental Portfolio of an Eurasian," in *Mrs. Spring Fragrance*, ed. Hsu, 225. See also "In Fairyland," *Dominion Illustrated* 5, no. 120 (October 18, 1890): 270; Chapman, ed., *Becoming Sui Sin Far*, xxxii–xxxiii and 33–39.

86 Ibid.

87 Born in 1905 in Los Angeles, Louise Leung Larson was given the name "Lau Lan, after the most famous woman in France, Joan of Arc" (*Sweet Bamboo: A Memoir of a Chinese American Family* (Berkeley: University of California Press, 2001), 225); see also Kingston, *Woman Warrior*; Hwang, *FOB*; and Yang, *Boxers & Saints* (listed in the "Creative Works by People of Color" bibliography at the end of this book). Note also Chin, "Ye Asian American Writers," 2–7.

88 Sui Sin Far, "My Chinese Husband," in *Mrs. Spring Fragrance*, ed. Hsu, 104–10, at 109. The child

Through such ambiguously racialized figures, Sui Sin Far offers possibilities for a revised heroic or transformative "mulatto" identity, and her vision of European Christian martyrdom or "glory in ... dying at the stake" uses a distinctly orientalist discourse: "a great genie arising from the flames." In a contemporaneous white-authored Chinatown narrative, Willa Cather's omniscient narrator adopts a white missionary gaze through a character visiting a Chinatown shop run by a "Chinaman, so smooth and calm and yellow," and he finds the store full of "glowing primitive colors" and infused with "odors [that] flashed before his eyes whole Orient landscapes, as though the ghosts of the Old World cities had been sealed up in boxes, like the djinn in the Arabian bottle."[89] Sui Sin Far's own orientalizing transformation of Joan of Arc into a "great genie rising from the flames" crafts a conspicuous hybridity conjoining old and new worlds.

Sui Sin Far's short stories, contemporaneous with Dunbar-Nelson's "local color" narratives laden with intense Marian imagery, deploy the figure of the Virgin not only for emotional impact but also for ethnographic ends. Dunbar-Nelson associates Mary with patriarchal and institutional forms of complicity in white supremacy and the devaluation of women of color in Caribbean cultural frameworks, but Sui Sin Far uses her journalistic and fictional "local color" sketches to make the Virgin Mary represent the cultural syncretism evident throughout Chinese diaspora contexts, and the author subtly subverts normative scripts of the racialized maiden as a tragic love object.

In her story "The Chinese Lily" (1908), originally published within a year of her "Eurasian" essay, Sui Sin Far features a beautiful Chinese maiden who shares the author's pen name (as discussed in the previous chapter). In the 1912 reprinting of the story, the character's name diverges from the author's full moniker of "Sui Sin Far,"[90] or the English transcription of the Cantonese 水仙花 (literally "water fairy/immortal flower"), which is often translated as "water lily" in reference to the fragrant white narcissus which can grow in water alone and is associated with Chinese Lunar New Year traditions.[91] The name of the maiden as specified in *Mrs. Spring Fragrance* (1912) is instead "Sin Far" and the name's English meaning is glossed within this version of the text as "Pure Flower, or Chinese Lily."[92] The author's naming of the flower through two possible designations multiplies the range of interpretations that readers can bring to the blossom in question, as the phrase "pure flower" could potentially evoke the idea of the sacred lotus— an entirely different plant which also emerges from water and which carries deep religious significance in Chinese Buddhist and Daoist iconography.[93]

The range of meanings that the author attributes to the name "Chinese lily" increases the symbolic resonance of flowers and their myriad religious associations. The imagery

is born with a "veil over his face," which Hsu suggests evokes W. E. B. Du Bois's observation that "the Negro is ... born with a veil, and a gifted second-sight in this American world." Hsu, Ibid.

89 Cather, "Conversion of Sum Loo," 263.

90 Sui Sin Far (Edith Eaton), "The Chinese Lily," *Out West:* 508–10. In the first iteration of the text, the protagonist's name is "Tin-a" and the other woman is named "Sui Sin Far."

91 Li, "Chinese Flower Arrangement," 35 and 49; Yin, *Chinese American Literature,* 54 and 112.

92 Sui Sin Far, "The Chinese Lily" (1912), in *Mrs. Spring Fragrance,* ed. Hsu, 129–32, at 130.

93 Li, "Chinese Flower Arrangement," 32.

Figure 11: White-robed statue of Guanyin and other female deities in Honolulu's Chinatown. Honolulu, Hawai'i, November 2017. Photo by the author.

of a "little bird with a white breast" outside the window with Sin Far "extending ... a blossom from a ... lily plant" at the threshold of a feminized domestic space might suggest to Christian readers the white lily flower so often associated with the Virgin Mary in European literary and artistic traditions, especially representations of the Archangel Gabriel's appearance to Mary in the Annunciation.[94] Foregrounding fully humanized Chinese characters, this story offers a syncretic and ambiguously racialized annunciation scene. Mermei sits indoors while Sin Far arrives with a "lily" betokening good news. The queer intimacy of this moment also tweaks heteronormative scripts of erotic love, casting Sin Far as the Archangel Gabriel and Mermei as a disabled and deformed Chinese

---

94 Sui Sin Far, "The Chinese Lily" (1912), in *Mrs. Spring Fragrance*, ed. Hsu, 129–32, at 130.

reincarnation of the Virgin Mary.[95] It's unclear from the text what the Chinese meaning of "Mermei" might be, but the character "mei" (美), often used in Chinese female names, means "beautiful" or can refer to America ("Mei Guo" or 美國, the "Beautiful Country").

Elsewhere in Sui Sin Far's "local color" sketches, the author signals an awareness of the syncretic practice and belief systems of Chinese diaspora communities, where traditional Daoist and Buddhist forms of worship meld with Christian iconography. In Chinese Catholic contexts across Taiwan, Fujian, and the Philippines, Guanyin (觀音, dubbed the "Goddess of Mercy" by Jesuit missionaries in China) or the Daoist or Buddhist figure of Mazu (媽祖), the "Queen of Heaven" (天后) or "Empress of the Sea" who saves mariners and fishermen in danger, is often aligned with the *Stella Maris* (Star of the Sea) or Virgin Mary.[96] A beautiful compassionate white-robed woman bearing a "Chinese lily" or some other kind of blossom associated with deep religious meaning could be read as Mazu, Guanyin, or Mary, depending on the reader's particular cultural orientation.[97]

In an unsigned piece by Sui Sin Far in the *Montreal Star* (September 1895), an unnamed "Lady" interviewing "Montreal Chinamen" reports that her informant "Mr. Cheeping declared emphatically that the Chinese worship spirits, not images," and he states: "We worship … in the same way that I have seen people worship in Notre Dame Church here," concluding: "We kneel before 'Mother' (Ahmah) (a Chinese goddess) as the Catholics kneel to the Virgin Mary."[98] This term of familiarity "Ahmah" is consistent with Chinese practices of affectionately referring to Mazu by names along the lines of "Granny Mazu" (媽祖婆). The analogy between "Ahmah" and the Virgin Mary "in Notre Dame Church here" refutes accusations that the Chinese engage in heathen "idolatry" by worshiping mere objects and not the spiritual entities they represent, and this particular argument is appropriately contextualized for a predominantly francophone Catholic setting.

Sui Sin Far's autoethnographic tropes of conjuring an "other" in order to clarify that non-Christian practices of worship are not mere "idolatry" reforms a discursive strategy as old as the medieval *Travels of Sir John Mandeville*, whose French-speaking English knight makes an analogy between simulacra used in Asia and icons of the Virgin Mary in Western Europe. Near the conclusion of the text the knight discusses "simulacra and idols," observing that people with "diverse laws" and "diverse beliefs" might claim that "there is no people who do not have simulacra," but "they say this because we Christians have images of Our Lady and other saints that we worship" and fail to understand that the powers reside not in "the images of wood or stone" themselves "but the saints in whose name they are made."[99] As Shirin A. Khanmohamadi has argued, the medieval

95 On the queerness of Sui Sin Far's "The Chinese Lily" and the author's sexuality in general, see Song, "The Unknowable and Sui Sin Far."

96 Dy, "Virgin Mary or Guanyin"; Andaya, "Water Cosmologies in Southeast Asia." On French Jesuits in China and links to the Notre Dame basilica in Montreal, see Madsen and Fan, "Catholic Pilgrimage to Sheshan," 81–82.

97 Song, "Many Faces of Our Lady."

98 Sui Sin Far [Unsigned], "Chinese Religion," in *Becoming Sui Sin Far*, ed. Chapman, 67–69, at 67.

99 Higgins, ed. and trans., *Book of John Mandeville*, 183–84.

traveler Mandeville at times "shows an openness to alternative perspectives and voices" and "highlights the limits of a single-point Latin Christian perspective on a diverse world,"[100] and the narrative's unfolding reveals how "the traveler is sufficiently othered, 'worlded' [by] travels around the globe."[101] Sui Sin Far's medieval iconography and adaptations of longstanding ethnographic discourses of travel attend to a complex texture of syncretic practices, fuse hagiographical narratives and devotional traditions, and create intricate patterns of linguistic code-switching and cross-cultural resonance. Sui Sin Far's "local color" sketches skillfully adapt medievalizing rhetoric to the multicultural milieux of her anglophone and francophone environments throughout the Caribbean and North America.

Local Colors Revisited

A comparative reading of Dunbar-Nelson and Sui Sin Far attends to ambiguously racialized characters within multiracial environments (Louisiana, Jamaica, and Montreal). These authors' shared Caribbean contexts bridge "yellow" racial formations (in Asian and multiracial Black contexts) and offer a complex reworking of Marian imagery from two francophone Catholic regions of North America. In their "local color" sketches, both writers grapple with a multifaceted deployment of Joan of Arc in conjunction with political movements at the turn of the century. The narrators' strategic passing through medieval genres, imagery, and conventions allow each writer to reinvent the figure of the tragic mixed-race woman and to generate new resistant and complex hybrid possibilities. It is this intricate play of racial positioning and literary voicing that I will examine in the next chapter on contemporary poets of color adapting Old English and Middle English traditions.

---

100 Khanmohamadi, *Light of Another's Word*, 114.
101 Ibid., 140.

Chapter Five

PLAY: RACIAL RECOGNITION, UNSETTLING POETICS, AND THE REINVENTION OF OLD ENGLISH AND MIDDLE ENGLISH FORMS

THERE'S A COMMON EXPRESSION in literary studies that "poetry is what gets lost in translation." Indeed, translating poetry is one of the most difficult things a writer can do. Can you capture the nuances of a text's language—including wordplay, irony, humor, or cultural references—for a new audience? How can a translator respect a poem's artistic form and its original social context while also creating a work that is meaningful to a new audience?

One persistent idea underlying the academic field of Western translation studies is the so-called "invisibility" of the translator.[1] When translators do their job properly, so the thinking goes, the audience isn't even aware that a translator exists—it's only when a text exhibits an awkward or stilted "translationese" or introduces confusing or unfamiliar words that an audience knows something has gone awry. Philosopher and cultural theorist Kwame Anthony Appiah argues for the value of "thick translation" and making acts of translation recognizable to the audience through annotations, glosses, and commentary; since translations can never enact word for word correspondences, a thick translation "seeks with its annotations and its accompanying glosses to locate the text in a rich cultural and linguistic context."[2] Translator, author, and cultural theorist Tejaswini Niranjana has argued that "translators can intervene to inscribe heterogeneity, to warn against myths of purity" and to offer "a more densely textured understanding of who 'we' are."[3] Poets of color often find themselves writing against Eurocentric traditions that assume the white (male) subject as the "default" (or universal "we"), and when poets of color translate or adapt European texts, they confront the choice of whether to make their racial positionings and sociopolitical stances explicit—or to conform to dutiful white norms of self-effacement. The "double bind" that translators and poets of color face is not only the obligation to convey the "rich cultural and linguistic context" of a work to a new audience, but also the question of when, or how, to make their (our) racial identities "visible," or recognizable, to a reading audience.

This chapter considers how poets of color adapt (or adopt) themes and structures of Old English and Middle English literature to address the illusory dimensions of translation and race, when the labor—and racial identity—of a poetic translator flickers in and out of view (to use an optical metaphor). Enacting my own "thick translations" of each

1 Kiaer, Guest, and Li, *Between Visibility and Invisibility*, "Introduction," 1–2.

2 Appiah, "Thick Translation," 427.

3 Niranjana, *Siting Translation*, 186.

work, I put each poet of color in dialogue with relevant European medieval works and literary traditions, while also providing a fuller context for each poet's cultural and racial positioning and sociopolitical objectives. Along the lines of Appiah and Niranjana, I cultivate a thick and textured understanding of each poet's work. Rather than sustaining the fiction of the white "universal" subject valuing self-effacement in translation, poets of color challenge readers to rethink whiteness as the "invisible" default or unmarked category of difference.

As poetry scholar Jahan Ramazani has observed, "race not only exists" as a "cultural category that constructs social difference," but also as "one of the most significant aspects of our lived experience," and as such race "shapes, styles, even gives rise to various forms of aesthetic enunciation, including poetry."[4] This chapter explores some of the advantages of making one's distinct cultural and racial positioning recognizable in a poetic translation, as well as the complex interpretive consequences of constructing a poetic speaker that disrupts or evades clear forms of racial categorization.

The first section of this chapter examines how contemporary poets of color reinvent Old English poetry. The second and third sections examine works by contemporary Native and multiracial poets, addressing adaptations of the abecedarian (alphabetic poem) and reinventions of medieval European vernacular lyric traditions. As suggested in the introduction to this book, I approach artistic works by poets of color as performing what José Esteban Muñoz calls strategic acts of "disidentification" with a longstanding cultural tradition that is coded as white and European.[5] Each poet offers a thickly contextualized reworking of medieval literary traditions and challenges the audience's preconceptions of what "counts" as a proper translation or adaptation of a medieval text, as well as questioning who traditionally claims the authority or expertise to craft such interpretations. Just as importantly, my focus on reinventions of foundational anglophone literary traditions (including works originally composed in Old English and Middle English) foregrounds the racial, cultural, and geographical heterogeneity of global anglophone communities today.

Riddles of Identity: Old English Poetry Reinvented

I begin, fittingly enough, with Old English poetry. Alliterative verse composed in Old English (the earliest historical form of the West Germanic language we now call English) is the earliest form of English literature. The phrase "Anglo-Saxon," problematically used inside and outside academia interchangeably with the term Old English, has deep historical associations with idealized notions of racial purity and discourses of white superiority throughout global anglophone contexts. As Mary Rambaran-Olm, Adam Miyashiro, and Matthew X. Vernon have demonstrated, the term "Anglo-Saxon" is profoundly aligned with white supremacy in anglophone societies, from Thomas Jefferson's valorization of a so-called "Anglo-Saxon" (i.e., white anglophone American) identity and his role in displacing Native people in favor of those of "Anglo-Saxon descent," to

---

4 Ramazani, "Poetry and Race," vii.

5 Muñoz, *Disidentifications*; see also this book's introduction.

ongoing systems of white anglophone colonization and imperial expansion around the globe.[6] Rambaran-Olm names a longstanding erasure of Black scholars in Old English literary studies,[7] and Dorothy Kim observes that J. R. R. Tolkien's foundational scholarship on the anonymous Old English poem *Beowulf* "solidif[ies] white Englishness and English identity," establishing Old English or "Anglo-Saxon" literature as white property for generations of scholars—to the exclusion of Black intellectuals and writers.[8] In this section of the chapter, I consider how three poets of color (of Native, Black, and Asian ancestry respectively) question the longstanding alignment between Old English poetic traditions and racialized "Anglo-Saxon" identity. I trace how each poet uses Old English poetic traditions to challenge hegemonic whiteness and to dismantle ideologies of racial purity.[9]

The first poet-translator I discuss is Carter Revard, a renowned Native American author and storyteller as well as an accomplished scholar of medieval literature. Revard, who is of Osage and European American descent, was born on the Osage Indian Reservation in Pawhuska, OK, and his many literary and scholarly awards include the Lifetime Achievement Award from the Native Writers' Circle of the Americas as well as a Rhodes Scholarship to pursue graduate work at Oxford University. Revard's "double life" as both a Native author and as a scholar of medieval European literature finds vivid expression through his creative reinventions of Old English riddle poems.[10]

The most famous Old English riddle poems survive in the tenth-century manuscript known as the Exeter Book (also known as the *Codex Exoniensis* or Exeter Cathedral Library MS 3501). Composed anonymously in alliterative verse, these texts usually feature a first-person poetic speaker who describes the physical world or familiar everyday objects in oblique terms and concludes with a call to "say what I am called," inviting the audience to guess the "answer" to the riddle (there isn't always one clear or correct answer). In an essay entitled "Some Riddles in Old English Alliterative Verse" (2001), Revard compares "the Old English Riddles" to "glass-bottomed boats that let us see ... below us [into] the depths of everyday things and common beings," and the poet-translator seeks to "revive the riddle-form by looking at the mysterious inwardness of ordinary things here and now," in "our own world" of "North America in the twentieth and twenty-first centuries" and what is, for him and his audience, a shared "present time" and place.[11]

---

6 Rambaran-Olm, "Misnaming the Medieval"; Adam Miyashiro, "Decolonizing Anglo-Saxon Studies"; Miyashiro, "Our Deeper Past," 5–6; Vernon, *Black Middle Ages*, 3–5.

7 Rambaran-Olm, "Erasing Black Scholars."

8 Kim, "Question of Race in Beowulf." On white property, see this book's introduction.

9 On "new" Old English poetry, see Chris Jones, *Strange Likeness: The Use of Old English in Twentieth-Century Poetry* (Oxford: Oxford University Press, 2006) and *Anglo-Saxon and Linguistic Nativism in Nineteenth-Century Poetry* (Oxford: Oxford University Press, 2018). All of the poets discussed are white.

10 On the Exeter Riddles as enigmatic "life writing" and the "third space" of Revard's literary positionings, see Lundquist, "Revard as Autoethnographer," 45–57.

11 Revard, "Riddles in Old English Verse," 1.

Revard translates one Old English poem (which does not have any title in the Exeter Book) as "The Swan's Song," and the poet-translator maintains the alliterative verse form:

> Garbed in silence   I go on earth,
> Dwell among men   or move on the waters,
> Yet far over halls   of heroes in time
> My robes and the high   air may raise
> And bear me up   in heaven's power
> Over all nations.   My ornaments then
> Are singing glories   and I go in song
> Bright as a star   unstaying above
> The world's wide waters,   a wayfaring soul.[12]

In his rendition of this poem, Revard marks the pause in each line (called a caesura, indicated by a blank space in each line of verse) and each line has a pair of words that alliterate (repeat a shared stressed consonant sound): Garbed/go, among/move, halls/heroes, robes/raise, etc. Revard observes that "this creature" (the swan) "telling its life-story lives in silence among human beings or on the water," then "takes to the air" and "rises far above human habitations," with the closing lines of the poem symbolically transforming the swan into an "emblem of the immortal soul"—or a figure in flight as "a pilgrim soul."[13] Revard carefully guides the reader through his translations of Old English poetry, offering a "thick translation" through his text-and-gloss commentary. He not only discloses to the reader his own strategies of literary translation but he also pro-vides a rich interpretive context for the work (its original Old English cultural context, as well as its meanings for us today).

Revard's thick translations are especially fruitful when he demonstrates how Old English alliterative verse can be adapted to address cultural and spiritual practices of living Native communities. One of Revard's "new" Old English poems (not based on any existing poem in any medieval manuscript) is entitled "What the Eagle Fan Says," and its first-person speaker is an eagle-feather fan that plays a key role in a ceremonial dance:

> I strung dazzling thrones   of thunder beings
> On a spiraling thread   of spinning flight
> [...]
> lightly I move now   in a man's left hand,
> above dancing feet   follow the sun
> around old songs   soaring toward heaven
> on human breath,   and I help them rise.[14]

Revard's new "eagle fan" poem adapts to Native practices and expresses the importance of dance as a living spiritual practice. In this poem, the first-person poetic speaker is not the human dancer but the eagle itself (whose feathers create the fan). "Here, the eagle describes how it circles heaven" in the same way as "the beads are sewn around and

---

12 Ibid., 4.

13 Ibid.

14 Ibid., 5.

around the handle of an eagle-feather fan," in addition to how "dancers, carrying such fans, circle around the drum."[15] In the closing lines, the "feathers remain alive in the fans, whose motion sends up the dancers' and singers' prayers."[16] The reinvented Old English riddle form now expresses the inextricable ties between human and nonhuman life—with the eagle, feathers, drum, and human dancers each playing a role in a living song and dance tradition.

Revard's clearest use of the alliterative riddle-form to inhabit Native worldviews and confront ideologies of racial purity is his "new" Old English poem entitled "Birch Canoe." When he introduces readers to this poem, Revard lets "a Birch Canoe [tell] its story" but it is also "my story," a "bringing into being of a mixed self, afloat between cultures" that reflects his dual European American and Osage ancestry.[17]

> Red men embraced   my body's whiteness
> Cutting into me   carved it free,
> Sewed it tight   with sinews taken
> From lightfoot deer   who leaped this stream—
> Now in my ghost-skin   they glide over clouds
> At home in the fish's   fallen heaven.[18]

The opening lines acknowledge a coexistence of Native (red) and European (white) identities in one body and prepare the reader to consider histories of race and environmental violence. The poem names the violence enacted upon a birch tree and the deer who gave their lives to create the "body" and "ghost-skin" of this canoe. The closing phrase "fallen heaven" evokes the image of clouds in the sky reflected on the surface of the water (where fish find their home), but the phrase also obliquely suggests the displacement of Native peoples from their homelands. Revard's poem simultaneously acknowledges "my body's whiteness" and his Native identity, and the fact of his own body's whiteness does not make him any less authentically Native. This canoe, or this "American Indian 'space ship,'"[19] moves between "red" and "white" identities and disassociates the Old English riddle-form from monolithic notions of racial belonging.

Another modern poet of color who uses his writing to address race and violence is the Pulitzer Prize winning Yusef Komunyakaa, most widely known for his autobiographical work in witness to African American soldiers fighting in the Vietnam War as well as works that address Black resistance to white supremacy in the American South. One of his most intriguing poems describing a landscape and environmental destruction is his translation of an Old English poem known as "The Ruin" (which survives, incompletely, in the Exeter Book); this poem depicts a landscape of broken and decayed buildings, perhaps the faded glory of some ruined Roman city whose mere traces survive in early medieval Britain. Komunyakaa's "The Ruin" appears in a cluster of "Poems About Dying"

---

15 Ibid.
16 Ibid.
17 Ibid., 6.
18 Ibid.
19 Ibid.

in an anthology of works by contemporary poets entitled *The Word Exchange: Anglo-Saxon Poems in Translation* (2011), and Komunyakaa has the conspicuous position of being a Black poet in what is otherwise an overwhelmingly white "Anglo-Saxon" (Old English) poetry collection.

Komunyakaa's "The Ruin" presents clear stylistic contrasts with Revard's practices of Old English literary translation. Rather than seeking to preserve the Old English form of the original (e.g., alliteration and caesura in each line), Komunyakaa composes in free verse:

> Look at the elaborate crests chiseled into this stone wall
> shattered by fate, the crumbled city squares,
> and the hue and cry of giants rotted away.[20]

The opening lines of the original Old English poem are printed in *The Word Exchange* as "Wrætlic is þes wealstan, wyrde gebræcon; / burgstede burston, brosnað enta geweorc,"[21] which means "Wondrous is this wall-stone; the fates have broken it and shattered the city; the work of giants is crumbling" [awkward translation my own]. Komunyakaa makes crucial changes to the Old English poem's narrative voice, crafting a vivid sense of the poem's implied environment. His opening phrase "Look at..." (not in the original Old English) transforms the entire poem into a direct address to an audience who is physically present at the location along with the speaker, an impression reinforced by the phrase "this stone wall" (recalling the opening phrase of the original). Komunyakaa invites the audience to inhabit the environmental space of this poem, forging a relationship between the audience and poetic speaker.

Komunyakaa's rewritten "Ruin" poem subtly shifts the cultural context for the work, obscuring its origins as an early meditation on remnants of a Roman presence in Britain and making the poem accessible and meaningful to present-day audiences who may or may not be aware of the Old English poem itself. His rendition of the text evokes strikingly modern imagery of environmental destruction and urban violence: "This wall, mapped and veined by lichen, / stained with red [...] lofty and broad, it has fallen."[22] Black poet Toi Derricotte discerns a vivid assertion of humanity for a wide range of people throughout Komunyakaa's poetry: "whether it embodies the specific experiences of a black man, a soldier in Vietnam, or a child in Bogalusa, Louisiana," his poetic voice "shows us in ever deeper ways what it is to be human."[23] Indeed, Komunyakaa's rendition of "The Ruin" emphasizes "deeper" lived human experience of a space as much as the physical place itself, animating the city with motifs of blood and life ("veined by lichen" and "stained with red" refer to the inanimate stone wall surfaces but also evoke a living body). The poem centers the experiences of the city's inhabitants, and after the location becomes a "tomb" for soldiers, the "city rotted away,"[24] as if by an organic process or by neglect.

---

20 Komunyakaa, "The Ruin," in *Word Exchange*, ed. Delaney and Matto, 298–302, at 299.
21 Ibid., 298.
22 Ibid., 299.
23 Komunyakaa, *Neon Vernacular*, back cover.
24 Komunyakaa, "The Ruin," in *Word Exchange*, ed. Delaney and Matto, 301.

Although there is a universalizing aspect to Komunyakaa's "The Ruin" (which would make it accessible to "everyone"), a fuller appreciation for the poet's broader *oeuvre* brings this translation of an Old English text in line with Komunyakaa's abiding interests in race, place, and memories of violence. Komunyakaa's most famous and much-anthologized poem, "Facing It," takes place at the Vietnam Veterans Memorial in Washington, DC, and this work offers a deep meditation on race, violence, and memory. It begins:

> My black face fades,
> hiding inside the black granite.
> I said I wouldn't,
> dammit: No tears.
> I'm stone. I'm flesh.[25]

The Vietnam Veterans Memorial is a politically resonant site of memory in a public park, designed by an Asian American architect (Maya Lin) and commemorating a war in which Black Americans were disproportionately drafted with a rate of combat death higher than their white peers.[26] The poem's opening two lines announce the poetic speaker's own blackness as well as his deeply personal emotional experience at this site of reflection. The physical site is a wall of "black granite" upon which the names of dead and missing veterans are inscribed, and the audience is put in the perspective of the first-person "I" whose "black face" is reflected—and obscured—by the names inscribed on the stone wall. The poet-speaker tries not to weep, becoming "stone" in the process.[27] The speaker "touch[es] the name Andrew Johnson" (who could possibly be Black, like the speaker himself) and he relives the trauma of witnessing Johnson's death ("I see the booby trap's white flash").[28] The poet's reflections at this site of memory are highly individualized, yet the poem also "stands in" for the experiences of innumerable war veterans, survivors, and witnesses.

In this broader context of the poet's deep meditations on place, race, and war—which so often foreground the experiences of Black soldiers and Black resistance to violence—the vivid locodescriptive dimensions of Komunyakaa's rendition of "The Ruin" take on a new sociopolitical resonance. Readers of this anthology of translated "Anglo-Saxon" poetry in which "The Ruin" appears might consider how the poet's own blackness informs a translation of an Old English poem that might not, on the surface, appear to be "about" race at all.

This discussion of Old English poetic translations ends on a lighter note, addressing how one poet of color uses humor to dismantle preconceived notions of white "Anglo-Saxon" identity. In the poetry collection *100 Chinese Silences* (2016), Asian American literature professor and poet Timothy Yu composes a series of satirical poems that mock Western stereotypes about Asians and people of Asian ancestry. Many of these poems take the form of homophonic translations, or renditions of a text that adhere to

---

25 Komunyakaa, "Facing It," *Neon Vernacular*, 159.

26 Rothman, "Vietnam and the Black Soldier."

27 Komunyakaa, "Facing It," *Neon Vernacular*, 159.

28 Ibid.

the sounds of a previous work but with no desire to maintain the literal meaning of the original text. Homophonic translations can result in humorous nonsense or ironic juxtapositions of meanings that are clear only to people who understand the language of both the source text and its adaptation.

Yu's "Chinese Silence No. 85" grapples directly with questions of race, inclusion, and the genre of the multiauthored poetic anthology.[29] The poem is preceded by a quotation from a published review by a (white) academic of an anthology of poetry by Asian Australians; the reviewer deems it "puzzling" that the collection includes some "male poets with Anglo-Saxon names" who do not specify that they "actually have Asian ancestry" in their "biographical notes," and the "discomforting question" that arises in the mind of the reviewer is whether "mateship" is what "garner[s] a place in [the] collection."[30] The opening of Yu's poem mocks the sentiments of the reviewer, and its verse takes the form of a homophonic translation of the opening lines of the anonymous "Anglo-Saxon" (Old English) poem *Beowulf*.

> Hwaet! Of Asians   living among us
> we have heard   hushed stories   and breathless buzz
> of anthologies   they have assembled.[31]

The opening lines preserve the alliterative form of Old English verse, including the caesura and alliterative patterns: Asian/among, heard/hushed, breathless/buzz, anthologies/assembled. If you happen to know the opening lines of *Beowulf*, you will recognize how closely the sound patterns of this modern English poem evoke the Old English, and the opening word "Hwaet!" remains untranslated. By invoking "Asians ... among us," Yu mocks perceptions that people of Asian ancestry living in predominantly white anglophone societies are secretive perpetual "aliens," and the next few lines address stereotypical representations of Asian immigrant labor:

> Oft some silence   signaled their prowess
> at making machines   or mending dresses,
> awaiting our word.[32]

By conjoining the literary context of the academic book review (of an Asian Australian poetic anthology) and a broader history of Asian stereotyping, Yu exposes the folly of equating "Anglo-Saxon names" with a presumed white identity: "But since they have snuck / under our noses with Anglo-Saxon names / we are taken by terror [by] these 'discomforting' questions [...] of who is Asian [...] That was a bad thing!"[33] Yu's playful verse is "faithful" to the sound and form of Old English verse while radically transforming its meaning. Through this parody of "Anglo-Saxon" poetry, Yu makes the point

---

29 Yu, *100 Chinese Silences*, 116.

30 Ibid. See also Lesley Synge, "Book Review: *Contemporary Asian Australian Poets* edited by Adam Aitken, Kim Cheng Boey and Michelle Cahill," *Transnational Literature* 6, no. 1 (November 2013): 1–4.

31 Ibid.

32 Ibid.

33 Ibid.

that a person of Asian ancestry who has an "Anglo-Saxon" name is no less authentically Asian than someone with an identifiably non-anglophone name. Self-identified Asian poets—regardless of how their names might "signify"—should not have to prove to any reviewers that they are somehow "Asian enough" to belong within an Asian anthology. The title of Yu's poetry collection and the content of his poems make clear his own Asian American (and specifically Chinese American) racial positioning, and acknowledging the sociopolitical and academic context for this poem is crucial. Each of the poet-translators I have discussed, in their own way, use Old English forms to bring visibility to their racialized positions rather than effacing them. These "new" Old English poets of color collectively urge their audiences to face a long history of aligning "Anglo-Saxon" language and literature with white supremacy and false ideologies of racial purity.

Alphabetic Forms and Systemic Violence

In this section, I consider how poets of color repurpose the abecedarian form—a poetic structure whereby the first letter of each line or stanza follows sequentially through the alphabet. In particular, I trace how each poet uses the literary form itself to address long histories of racial violence. The oldest examples of abecedarian works in English include an Old English rune poem which does not employ Roman letters but rather the letters of the runic alphabet (the name of each runic letter describing its shape); in this poem, each runic letter has its own poetic stanza.[34] Throughout the later Middle Ages, the abecedarian poem adopted a form based on the Roman alphabet and the genre came to be associated with childlike innocence and devotion. Geoffrey Chaucer's Middle English alphabetic poem commonly known as An ABC (translated from a French source) offers a prayer to the Virgin Mary with each stanza beginning with a letter of the alphabet in sequential order, and there is a long historical tradition of associating alphabetic poems with children and learning.[35] Medieval scenes of childhood education and prayerful devotion have a sinister legacy, however; Marian miracle tales and antisemitic violence were often intertwined in medieval English texts.[36] Geoffrey Chaucer's "Prioress's Tale," for instance, features a "litel clergeon" (schoolboy) who performs an intense devotion to the Virgin Mary while he is learning to read in school, and he is murdered by villainized Jews (who in turn suffer gruesome executions en masse at the end of the story).[37] In this discussion, I consider how Native poets grapple with the sinister history of the abecedarian, connecting this seemingly childlike and "innocent" poetic form with systemic racial violence past and present.

Natalie Diaz, a queer poet who is Latina and Mojave and was born and raised in the Fort Mojave Indian Village (Needles, CA), uses the alphabetic poem structure to make a scathing critique of white settler colonialism and missionary intrusions into Native envi-

---

34 Delaney and Matto, eds., *Word Exchange*, "The Rune Poem" (trans. James Harpur), 207–15.

35 Brogan and Colón, "Abecedarius" (abecedarian)," 1.

36 Heng, *England and Jews*, 80–84; Rubin, *Gentile Tales*, 7.

37 Chaucer, *Canterbury Tales*, "Prioress's Tale," lines 489–508.

ronments. Entitled "Abecedarian Requiring Further Examination of Anglikan Seraphym Subjugation of a Wild Indian Rezervation" with key words deliberately "misspelled," its opening lines evoke the social environment of the reservation and the external threats that its inhabitants face. "Angels" (as the poem reveals) are associated with white missionaries (i.e., the "Anglikan Seraphym"), and nonhuman creatures such as bats, coyotes, and owls first appear in the poem as omens of death:

> Angels don't come to the reservation.
> Bats, maybe, or owls, boxy mottled things.
> Coyotes, too. They all mean the same thing—
> death.[38]

The critique of "angels" (white missionaries) becomes clear by the midpoint of the poem, which illustrates ongoing efforts to erase and replace Native cultures:

> Like I said, no Indian I've ever heard of has ever been or seen an angel.
> Maybe in a Christmas pageant or something—
> Nazarene church holds one every December,
> organized by Pastor John's wife. It's no wonder
> Pastor John's son is the angel—everyone knows angels are white.[39]

This poem's reference to "a Christmas pageant" and the pastor's child playing an angel may generate fond and nostalgic memories for white Christians, but Diaz frames this entire performance long associated with medieval Nativity plays as a recurring demonstration of white supremacy—an annual tradition that ideologically aligns whiteness itself with virtue. Diaz's sinisterly disenchanted representation of a Christmas pageant reveals how, in the words of Maria Sachiko Cecire, "[m]edievalist fantasy and mainstream representations of Christmas magic" enact an "obsession with a form of innocence" that idealizes whiteness and effaces "the political and cultural conditions from which [cultural] norms arise, and the groups of people that their spaces of wonder tend to exclude."[40] In the context of Native exclusion from Christmastime "spaces of wonder," it is "no wonder" that the pastor's wife casts her own son as an angel.

The closing lines of Diaz's poem most clearly announce the role that white missionaries play in the displacement of Native peoples and ongoing processes of settler colonialism:

> You better hope you never see angels on the rez. If you do, they'll be marching you off to
> Zion or Oklahoma, or some other hell they've mapped out for us.[41]

These final lines reveal how white missionaries may present themselves as "angels" or "saviors" but their ideas and actions are ultimately anything but innocent. Even the child portraying an angel at the Christmas pageant is part of a social system and a power structure that seeks to eradicate Native cultures and relocate Native communities from

---

38 Diaz, "Abecedarian."

39 Ibid.

40 Cecire, *Re-Enchanted*, 132.

41 Diaz, "Abecedarian."

ancestral homelands to a "hell they've mapped out for us." The poet's reference to "Oklahoma" alludes to the notorious Trail of Tears, the forced relocation of Native communities from the southeastern United States in the mid-nineteenth century to what the federal government had designated as "Indian Territory." For Diaz, the abecedarian—a poetic form long associated with childlike innocence—becomes a mechanism to expose systemic violence and to name the destructive forces of white supremacy and settler colonialism.

Writing from a different region of the North American continent, Karenne Wood (member of the Monacan Indian Nation in Virginia) writes a poem "Abracadabra, an Abecedarian" which makes invisibility its key theme. "Abacadabra"—the nonsense word that magicians utter before making things disappear—is a fitting title for Wood's urgent commentary on the lack of visibility and justice for missing and murdered (i.e., "disappeared") Native women throughout North America. The poem opens by describing (white) feminist efforts to advocate for (all) women: "All this time I've been looking for words for certain difficult women / because they aren't able to speak for themselves," but recently the "Clinton Foundation has come up with a brilliant campaign—they / decided, for International Women's Day" to use "digital magic to / erase women on the cover of *Condé Nast*" glamor and fashion magazines.[42] Using "digital magic" (photoshop or other manipulation) to remove women from a photograph creates an "empty space" that metaphorically shows how "women have not yet achieved / gender equity."[43]

Although the first-person speaker agrees that gender equity has not yet been achieved, the poem shifts from a symbolic visual erasure of women on a magazine cover to the real-life disappearance of Native women every day:

> I wasn't thinking about how women are not-there-yet, metaphorically, I
> just thought about women who are really not there, women and girls who
> keep disappearing (not from magazines, who don't make news in Manhattan)
> like they've evaporated, like illusions, hundreds in Juárez, twelve hundred
> missing and murdered Native women across Canada. The hands of men.[44]

This poem's abrupt turn enacts a "magic trick" of its own, suddenly deflecting the reader's attention from white feminist publications for an affluent readership to the blunt realities of murdered or missing Native women. Due to the poem's lengthy lines, its frequent use of enjambment, and its infrequent use of capital letters at the start of the lines, the alphabetic structure of this abecedarian might not be immediately apparent to all readers. Diaz forces the audience to confront the systemic silence and inaction that accompanies the disappearance of Native women throughout the continent (i.e., United States, Mexico, and Canada)—and all the while the alphabetic form of the poem itself threatens to vanish.[45]

---

42 Wood, "Abracadabra."

43 Ibid.

44 Ibid.

45 My quotations replicate the layout in Wood's book. In other iterations of the poem, the alphabetic structure is not clearly legible; compare Erdrich, ed., *New Poets of Native Nations*, 234.

Crafting Communities Through Medieval Lyric

The final section of this chapter explores how medieval lyric poetry can create new forms of cross-racial solidarity and community. Cedar Sigo, a queer Native poet raised on the Suquamish Reservation near Seattle, WA, crafts an enigmatic poem that evokes living Native ceremonial practices and indirect references to European medieval history. Entitled "Thrones," Sigo's poem addresses a range of literary figures beginning with two African American women writers:

> *For Phillis Wheatley:* A book of verse uncovered in cornerstones of a Moorish castle, purple and gold depicting souls in various stages of release, the pitch, anger and arc of the poems an unrhymed mirror to the long Atlantic.

> *For Jayne Cortez:* An intertribal grand entry of poets in cedar bark jackets split skirts and whalebones pinning them closed, a voice in praise and suspension of the drum.[46]

The quality of oral performance structuring "Thrones" recalls the social setting of the potlatch, which Native writer and activist Julian Brave NoiseCat (member of the Canim Lake Band Tsq'escen and descendant of the Lil'Wat Nation of Mount Currie) describes as a "traditional Indigenous ceremony here in the Pacific Northwest" that is "rooted in massive giveaways of art, goods and foodstuffs" and a generous reception of guests by the host community.[47] The first two addressees in Sigo's "Thrones" are Black women writers, and Sigo incorporates European medieval imagery into each ceremonial gift that the poetic speaker offers. The "book of verse" bound in "purple and gold" rediscovered on the site of a "Moorish castle" imaginatively recalls medieval Iberia. A procession of poets arrayed in "cedar bark jackets" with "whalebones pinning them closed" obliquely suggests an object such as the Franks Casket, a famous early medieval whalebone chest that could have been intended to enclose a psalter—such a holy book being a precious object that one of the riddles in the Exeter Book vividly attests would have been bound, or clothed, by wooden boards.[48] "Thrones" offers allusions to gift-giving as a vital ceremonial practice across medieval European cultures and also in living Native communities.

In addressing Black women writers and artists, Sigo affirms their visibility and importance in a capacious multiracial anglophone literary tradition. Wheatley is the first African American woman to publish a book of poetry in English, and Cortez is a performance artist and activist foundational in the Black Arts Movement. Sigo has observed that "Thrones" adopts a "form [that] has you presenting gifts on bended knee in a way and it forms this sort of totem, a twitching altar with an almost invisible frame."[49] Sigo is

---

46 Erdrich, ed., *New Poets of Native Nations*, 216.

47 NoiseCat, "Water Resources." See also U'mista Cultural Society, "Potlatch."

48 Delaney and Matto, eds., *Word Exchange*, "Some Enemy Took My Life" (trans. Jane Hirshfield), 164–67.

49 Mishler, "Cedar Sigo on Playfulness and Poetry." Sigo observes that "Thrones" was inspired by a recording of Philip Lamantia reading his poem *The Time Traveler's Potlatch*. Lamantia spent much of his life with Native communities but was not Native himself.

"interested in honoring (communicating with) certain essential African American artists through a (still living) coast Salish ceremony," but rather than "a flowing list of decadent gifts," the "form itself can also be seen as a gift to all poets."[50] "Thrones" enacts solidarity between the Native poet and Black artists, creating a sense of cross-racial artistic community through an ethos of gift-giving and celebration—and Sigo presents the poem itself as a gift through its very form.

Julian Talamantez Brolaski, who identifies as a "two-spirit and transgender poet and musician of mixed Mescalero and Lipan Apache, Latin@, and European heritages," offers a divergent model for how a poet of Native ancestry can create cross-racial affinities.[51] The title of Brolaski's poetry collection *Of Mongrelitude* (2017) makes a playful reference to the *Négritude* movement associated with intellectuals such as Aimé Césaire and other postcolonial francophone African diaspora thinkers who cultivated Black pride and resistance to assimilation into white Western cultural systems.[52] Brolaski's *Of Mongrelitude* (with its cover title typeset in a font resembling blackletter Gothic script) uses pervasive Middle English neologisms and vocabulary drawn from Indigenous and European languages to explore queer and racially hybrid identities.[53]

Brolaski describes the book as "a colloquy on the mongrel body, textual and actual, sexual, special, and racial"—the term "special" in this instance refers to species difference—and its "hybrid style ... makes the argument that everything can and does come into 'englyssh,' including neologisms, archaisms, vocables, Apache, Spanish, French, other romance and germanic tongues, tongues not yet named."[54] Finalist for the 2018 Lambda Literary Award for Transgender Poetry, Brolaski has characterized *Of Mongrelitude* as a "trans-literal, transmogrified body, the body of the poems figured as the body of the poet," an "ambiguous body" that is "cowboy and indian, male and female and a third and fourth thing."[55] The poet's discourse of a "trans-literal, transmogrified body" is intricately tied to what I elsewhere call a medieval "translingual" poetic practice—a capacity to "think and write across more than one language concurrently."[56] Brolaski's translingual poetics, drawing upon medieval forms of expression, creates a vivid idiom for a transgender and two-spirit voice.

The influence of medieval poetics throughout *Of Mongrelitude* is pervasive. Brolaski creates Middle English neologisms such as "gringitude,"[57] a word that conjoins "attitude" (English), *négritude* (French), and *gringo* (a term used by Spanish- and Portuguese-speaking Latin Americans to refer to foreigners, especially white anglophone Americans and Europeans). Elsewhere, Brolaski claims a style of "englyssh [...] so filled [with]

50 Ibid.

51 "Brolaski: 2019 Fellow-In-Residence." *The Pew Center for Arts & Heritage.*

52 Diagne, "Négritude."

53 Brolaski, *Of Mongrelitude*. Note also Poetry Center Digital Archive, "Caples and Brolaski."

54 "Author Notes: Julian Talamantez Brolaski," in *New Poets of Native Nations*, ed. Erdrich, 273.

55 Ibid.

56 Hsy, *Trading Tongues*, 6; see also Hsy, "Linguistic Entrapment."

57 Brolaski, *Of Mongrelitude*, 35.

periphrasis"[58] that cites lines from the Middle English poem "The Land of Cokaygne,"[59] and the poet crafts a work entitled "fowles in tha frith" after the opening words of the Middle English lyric that forms its template.[60] The book's titular poem "of mongrelitude" foregrounds a two-spirit and transgender identity, with Brolaski conveying the experience of living "across" gender binaries through puns on the meanings of the Middle English word "privy" (meaning toilet): "I am privy to these contradictory situations where I am told first the one and then the other bathroom is the wrong one."[61] Middle English neologisms and translingual literary strategies allow Brolaski to express a racialized and gendered position that evades monolithic or binary categories.

Brolaski's poetry also addresses how racism and misogyny inform medieval literary studies itself (including the translation, interpretation, and editing of medieval texts). In the final poem in *Of Mongrelitude*, the poet incorporates allusions to a *pastourelle* by the twelfth-century troubadour Marcabru who wrote in the Occitan vernacular. In the *pastourelle* genre, the poet-narrator, usually a knight, attempts to seduce (or prey upon) a vulnerable shepherdess who resists his advances. As Brolaski states: "marcabru uses the word 'mestissa' to describe the shepherdess his dickish narrator is poorly courting."[62] Building upon intersectional Black feminist approaches to cultural analysis, literary historian Carissa M. Harris has shown how the medieval European genre of the *pastourelle* exposes complex dynamics of social class and gendered power by depicting "well-off men targeting women who are young, poor, single, and alone" and "leveraging the women's multiple disadvantages to coerce them," but such poems can in certain instances model clear strategies of female resistance to sexual violence.[63]

Brolaski foregrounds the racial and gendered dimensions of the words that white male translators and editors have used in reference to the woman in Marcabru's poem. The Occitan term "mestissa" (which in its own day could signal Jewish ancestry) is translated by derogatory and racialized terms by William D. Paden, Ezra Pound, and W. D. Snodgrass respectively: "paden translates 'half-breed' and pound 'low-born' and snodgrass 'lassie.'"[64] Brolaski's narrator does not identify with the knight as the protagonist and poetic speaker of this *pastourelle*; instead, the modern poet discerns a resistant role for the shepherdess as a "mongrel, mestiza, mixedbreed."[65] Critiquing both the racism and misogyny evident in medievalist acts of linguistic translation and textual editing, Brolaski forges a seemingly unlikely cross-temporal identification with the medieval "mongrel" woman along the lines of Latinx ("mestiza") and Native ("mixedbreed") cultural frameworks. The poet rejects the collective mindset of modern white male inter-

---

58 Ibid., 16.

59 Ibid, 8–9.

60 Ibid, 78–79.

61 Ibid., 25.

62 Ibid., 91.

63 Harris, *Obscene Pedagogies*, 103–49, at 108; see also Harris, "Pastourelle Fictionalities," 248.

64 Brolaski, *Of Mongrelitude*, 91.

65 Ibid.

preters of the medieval poem and enacts what Muñoz might call a queer disidentification with the medieval "mestissa" across time, gender, culture, race, and place.[66]

The book's closing poem "as the owl augurs" announces solidarity with vulnerable communities of color in the wake of homophobic and racist violence: "I want namore of it [...] the killings of our familyes queer and black and brown and ndn / slaughter at orlando symbol of our hermitude."[67] The term "ndn" (or NDN = "Indian") is a colloquialism that Native people can use to refer to themselves. Presenting yet another play on the neologism "mongrelitude," Brolaski's "hermitude" suggests how vulnerable queer, Black, brown, and Indigenous communities set themselves apart from mainstream society (as if they are hermits) in order to create alternate "familyes" or safe spaces of gathering and mutual support.

The "slaughter at orlando" alludes to the violation of the safe space of Pulse, a gay nightclub in Orlando, FL, where fifty predominantly queer Latinx people and their allies were murdered by a gunman on June 12, 2016. A mournful litany of place names follows: "bear river   sand creek   tulsa   rosewood" [spacing as in the original].[68] These locations are all sites of massacres of Native and Black communities deeply harmed by longstanding histories of violent settler colonialism, as Dakota/Lakota writer Ruth Hopkins has noted.[69] Of Mongrelitude uses Middle English and translingual poetics to craft a new idiom for a racially hybrid voice evading binary notions of gender difference, while also addressing the harms of racism, misogyny, and violence against queer and transgender communities. The poet expresses solidarity for vulnerable groups (across differences in race, gender, and language), creating visibility for the resistant "mongrel" body.[70]

Poetics of Racial Recognition

In my exploration of heterogeneous writings by contemporary anglophone poets of color, I have suggested some of the multifaceted directions that medievalism can take. These poets all repurpose medieval European languages, cultural practices, and literary forms to toy with audience expectations regarding the legibility of race and identity and they create new configurations of cross-racial solidarity and community in the process. Revard, Komunyakaa, and Yu challenge readers to discern a racialized minority subject and voice even (or especially) in poetry derived from Old English literary forms that might in other circumstances be implicitly coded as white. Diaz and Wood repurpose the European form of the abecedarian to attest to histories of colonialism and violence against—and erasure of—Native peoples, and Native women specifically. Sigo and Brolaski evoke medieval European lyric conventions to suggest new forms of solidarity among Native communities and across vulnerable marginalized communities. Playfully

---

66 Muñoz, *Disidentifications*; see also this book's introduction.

67 Brolaski, *Of Mongrelitude*, 90.

68 Ibid.

69 Hopkins, "America's Legacy of Anti-Indigenous Violence."

70 On activist Latinx poetry see also Noel, "Queer Migrant Poemics of #Latinx Instagram."

subverting literary traditions and reshaping what Old English and Middle English poetics mean for anglophone readers in the present, poets of color bring vital forms of racial recognition to the combined forces of artistic craft, intellectual labor, and sociopolitical critique.

Chapter Six

PILGRIMAGE:
CHAUCERIAN POETS OF COLOR IN MOTION

GEOFFREY CHAUCER'S *THE CANTERBURY TALES* begins with "sondry folk, by aventure yfalle" [various people fallen together by chance] gathering in Southwark across the river from the City of London.[1] A mixed assemblage of people of different genders, ages, professions, and regional backgrounds, they form a temporary and at times fragile community (a "felaweshipe" or "compaignye") traveling to the shrine of Thomas Becket in Canterbury,[2] and along the route they tell stories on topics as varied as romantic love, violence, class conflict, religious devotion and conversion, geopolitics, philosophical matters, and sex. This chapter considers how modern-day poets of color use Chaucerian materials not only for the purposes of humor and light-hearted social satire (as they might be expected to do). They also—on a much more serious note—subvert longstanding Eurocentric cultural and linguistic norms, and they intertwine themes of race and migration to give testimony to long histories of violence and ongoing systems of oppression around the globe.

In modern-day Chaucerian adaptations by people of color, mobility—in both its physical and sociopolitical dimensions—drives the storytelling enterprise. In Chaucerian adaptations that transport the Canterbury pilgrimage into the present day while also relocating the pilgrimage to disparate locations worldwide, the storytelling narrators are always in motion, and it is impossible to disassociate the fictive speakers from their surrounding sociopolitical environments.[3] Writing from a Caribbean perspective, Barbara Lalla observes that "Chaucer's *The Canterbury Tales* assembles and confronts identities continuously on the move, displaced from their 'proper' categories, travelling light in the characteristically en route condition of the pilgrim,"[4] and "[p]ostcolonial writing in the Caribbean and elsewhere" is similarly "peopled by travellers. Travel facilitates shifting positions from which to view what is given out as reality … Implicated in travel is the denial of fixity."[5] Contemporary adaptations of Chaucer often use pilgrimage and its mixed storytelling potentials to explore present-day interplays of local and global phenomena and the "denial of fixity" that pervades transit, dislocation, and uprootedness, as well as ever-shifting ideas of home and (un)belonging. Although some modern Chaucerian poets focus on one city or neighborhood—or even a particular street—some explore a dispersal of voices and bodies across global trajectories.

---

1 Chaucer, *Canterbury Tales*, "General Prologue," line 25.

2 Ibid., lines 26 and 24.

3 Barrington and Hsy, "Afterlives"; Barrington and Hsy; "Chaucer's Global Orbits."

4 Lalla, *Postcolonialisms*, 44.

5 Ibid., 253.

Chaucerian poets of color, in other words, center racialized subjectivities in transit. Marking departures from the white "universal" subject or "global" citizen of the world who is free to move as he (usually he) desires, poetry by people of color inhabits the unequal conditions of mobility across national borders and geographies, as well as the culturally fraught meanings of "return" when a destination or desired place of return is inaccessible.[6] Attesting to historical forces of dispossession, displacement, and restricted mobility, poets of color demonstrate the "unfixed modernity" of an interconnected globe and reveal what Eleanor Ty calls the "fluidity of contemporary transcultural identities and the layering subject positions" of people in transit.[7]

In these sections to follow, I examine the relationship between race and transit in works by Chaucerian poets of color. When modern Chaucerian authors of color mark or disclose any particular racial identity, they challenge readers to ask if an unmarked narrator *necessarily* reads as white. Cord J. Whitaker has shown how metaphors of whiteness and blackness from the Middle Ages to the present create the rhetorical "shimmer" of blackness and "its simultaneous presence and nonpresence" in Western literary discourses of race,[8] and poets of color navigate the shimmering dimensions of racial disclosure beyond seemingly rigid black/white binaries that pervade racial thinking throughout predominantly white anglophone societies. Urgent questions of blackness and antiblackness have been explored in prose writings by Chaucerian authors of color around the globe including Karen King-Aribisala (Nigerian born in Guyana), Gloria Naylor (African American), and Ana Lydia Vega (Puerto Rican), to name a few.[9] This chapter explores how Chaucerian authors grapple with the consequences of claiming or disclaiming racialized literary personas through poetry. I explore how these poets—wherever in the globe they are positioned—explore the mobility of racial identities, experiment with the craft of fictive voicing, and reflect on the complex ethics of speaking for others.

Reverse Migrations: Transatlantic and Hemispheric

Chaucer's pilgrimage narrative is famously incomplete. The original plan was for each pilgrim to tell two stories en route to Canterbury and two during the return—but the pilgrims don't even reach their destination, and some pilgrims never tell a story, and the text ends before any return journey. I begin by considering poets throughout African diaspora contexts (Afro-Caribbean and African American backgrounds) who use the openness of the Chaucerian pilgrimage and its lack of a "return" to their advantage, repurposing Chaucerian allusions to experiment with rhetorics of "reverse" colonization and to address the thwarted possibilities of "return" in migration stories.

Reading Caribbean poetry in English requires a fundamental rethinking of the relationship between language and geographical space, as well as the intertwined histories

---

6 Chu, *Where I Have Never Been*, 21.

7 Ty, *Unfastened*, xxix–xxx.

8 Whitaker, *Black Metaphors*, 11.

9 See this book's Further Readings and Resources, "Creative Works by People of Color."

of language and race. Lalla has observed that "Caribbean experience differs markedly from that of medieval England," with "one glaring distinction" of how "race and ethnicity are implicated in Caribbean postcoloniality" through a "massive translocation of peoples of varied races."[10] Kofi Omoniyi Sylvanus Campbell shows how anglophone Caribbean writers have drawn from medieval literary traditions "to create new, hybridized identities capable of surviving in the face of centuries-old racisms,"[11] and the "literary emergence of English as a literary vernacular" in Chaucer's day was the "birth and growth" of a "nation language" that emerged as an expression of "independence from a recent history of French literary and cultural domination" after the Norman Conquest.[12] This term "nation language" derives from an influential lecture by Barbadian poet and intellectual Kamau Brathwaite, who discerns in the anglophone Caribbean a "nation language" that is not Chaucer's Middle English but rather a "kind of English spoken by the people who were brought to the Caribbean" and it is "not the official English now, but the language and slaves and labourers, the servants who were brought in by the conquistadors."[13]

In contrast to an official form of "English, which is the imposed language on much of the archipelago" by British colonialism,[14] Braithwaite defines "nation language" as "the submerged language" of enslaved Black Caribbean people, "that underground language … constantly transforming itself into new forms," incorporating African structures and "adapted to the new environment" in a "very complex process … now beginning to surface in our literature."[15] Brathwaite pointedly rejects the iambic pentameter long associated with Chaucer[16] for a local Black Caribbean "syllabic intelligence" and calypso rhythms that can "describe the hurricane, which is our own experience," rather than white Eurocentric forms that "describe the imported alien experience of the snowfall."[17] Brathwaite's rhetoric of imposition, importation, and "alien experience" does not just refer to movements of language and cultural values from medieval Britain across the Atlantic; his story about "nation language" also names the harms of racial hierarchies and the dehumanizing legacies of forced migration, enslavement, and colonization throughout what Paul Gilroy and Campbell would later call the Black Atlantic.[18]

Jamaican poet Louise Bennett anticipates Brathwaite's principles of "nation language" in her own works that employ a decidedly local vernacular, rhyme, and rhythm. Bennett's "Bans O'Killing" (1944), which roughly means "lots of killing," uses poetry to name the historical mechanisms of power and violence that result in one prestigious London-based form of English claiming its status as the "standard" and being positioned

---

10 Lalla, *Postcolonialisms*, 28.

11 Campbell, *Black Atlantic*, 1.

12 Ibid., 12.

13 Brathwaite, "Nation Language," 459.

14 Ibid.

15 Ibid., 461.

16 Ibid., 463.

17 Ibid., 462. See also Warren, "Chaucer in Caribbean," 83.

18 Gilroy, *Black Atlantic*; Campbell, *Black Atlantic*.

over time as superior to other varieties around the world. Speaking to "Mass Charlie" (white Master Charlie) who wants to eliminate nonstandard dialects, the poetic speaker asks: "Yuh gwine kill all English dialect / Or jus Jamaica one?"[19] Prestigious forms of English poetry, the poetic speaker argues, were themselves "dialects" to begin with, springing from earlier vernacular traditions dating back to the fourteenth century: "Dah language we yuh proud o' ... it spring from dialect!"[20] and it was initially crafted when "dem start fe try tun language, / From the fourteen century."[21] To eradicate nonstandard Englishes now would mean killing off existing regional variations within Britain[22] and also ripping out texts by Chaucer and other historical authors from *The Oxford Book of English Verse*: "Yuh wi haffee get the Oxford book / O' English verse, and tear / Out Chaucer, Burns ... An plenty o' Shakespeare!"[23] In what might very well be a submerged allusion to Chaucer's bold Wife of Bath, who rips pages out of a misogynist anthology or "book of wikked wives"[24] compiled by her husband who "somtime was a clerk of Oxenford,"[25] Bennett rhetorically imagines violence against an "Oxford book" that embodies an oppressive system.

Bennett's Afro-Caribbean voice exposes the myths of purity that underlie the historical process of creating and sustaining white anglophone norms and by extension an ideology of global white supremacy. The prestigious vernacular of "standard" English was not inherently superior to any other language variety and was ultimately based upon a once humble fourteenth-century London "dialect" itself. The construction of one prestigious form of "standard" English that is marked as "superior" and aligned with global white anglophone hegemony was the outcome of a historical process that relied upon social structures such as educational systems and literary anthologies that privilege only certain language varieties. In a recent analysis of racial and linguistic ideologies in the field of anglophone medieval studies, Shyama Rajendran reminds readers of the historical heterogeneity of "multiple Englishes" during the Middle Ages and also critiques longstanding "English raciolinguistic supremacist structures" dating back to nineteenth-century philology.[26] Along similar lines of sociopolitical critique, Bennett's poem reminds readers of a historical multiplicity of Englishes in medieval Britain and also reveals the longstanding systems of violence that suppress all the other forms of language that are deemed inferior by comparison to some "standard" prestigious variety of English.

Bennett's later and more well-known poem "Colonization in Reverse" (1966) uses a complex form of Chaucerian irony to characterize mass migration from Jamaica to

19 Louise Bennett, "Bans O'Killing" (1944), in *Rotten English*, ed. Ahmad, 40–41, at 40.
20 Ibid.
21 Ibid, 41.
22 Ibid.
23 Ibid.
24 Chaucer, *Canterbury Tales*, "Wife of Bath's Prologue," line 685.
25 Ibid., line 527.
26 Rajendran, "Raciolinguistic Supremacy," 2.

Britain as a "reverse" migration across the Black Atlantic.[27] The seemingly naive poetic speaker, addressing "Miss Mattie" and other women, brings "joyful news" that makes her "feel like me heart gwine burs."[28] She observes that Jamaicans are departing from their island of birth to settle in England, a process of "Jamaica people colonizin / Englan in reverse."[29] Jamaicans by "de hundred" and by "de tousan"[30] depart on ships and planes to "settle in de mother lan"[31] with an aim to "immigrate an populate / De seat a de Empire."[32] In this inversion of forced migration across the Atlantic, Black Caribbean migrants "reverse" the direction of settler colonialism, willingly traversing a modern Black Atlantic to populate and settle in the former imperial center. Bennett uses a nuanced Black Caribbean poetic voice to ironize discourses of transplanting and "settling" and creates a comic geographical ambiguity in the process: "What an islan! What a people!"[33] could refer either to Jamaica or to a disoriented Britain.

While this phenomenon of "colonizin in reverse" might seem like poetic justice, the tone of the poem is not entirely celebratory. Many Black Caribbean women seeking employment and social advancement in Britain will in the end find their goals and ambitions thwarted: "Some will settle down to work / An some will settle fe de dole."[34] The verb "settle" assumes another valence beyond putting down roots; it now refers to "settling" for lower expectations. Ominously, the poet ends by remarking that the English have faced "war and brave de worse" and might not respond well to a continuing influx of immigrants: "But me wonderin how dem gwine stan / Colonizin in reverse."[35] Bennett's poem ends with an admonition: racism, xenophobia, nativism, and sexism all loom as threats for Black Caribbean immigrants upon their arrival in, or colonial "return," to Britain.

A more lighthearted instance of "transplanting" Black Caribbean English into a London setting is a poem by Jamaican poet Jean "Binta" Breeze. "The Wife of Bath speaks in Brixton Market," first published in *The Arrival of Brighteye* (2000), offers a line-by-line translation (or adaptation) into Jamaican Patois of the opening portion of Chaucer's "Wife of Bath's Prologue." Here are the opening lines of each text compared:

Experience, thogh noon auctoritee	My life is my own bible
Were in this world, is right inough for me	wen it come to all de woes
To speke of wo that is in mariage.	in married life
For, lordinges, sith I twelve yeer was of age,	fah since I reach twelve,
Thonked be God that is eterne on live,	Tanks to Eternal Gawd,

---

27 Bennett, "Colonization in Reverse" (1966), in *Rotten English*, ed. Ahmad, 38–39.

28 Ibid., 38.

29 Ibid.

30 Ibid.

31 Ibid.

32 Ibid., 39.

33 Ibid., 38.

34 Ibid., 39.

35 Ibid.

| Housbondes at chirche-dore I have had five— | is five husban I have |
| If I so ofte mighte han wedded be ...[36] | (if dat is passible)[37] |

Breeze's practice of translation—or perhaps linguistic transplantation—asserts the vitality of a Black Caribbean "nation language" against the historical vernacular aligned with the predominantly white norms of Standard English. In this poem, Breeze rejects Chaucer's use of iambic pentameter (i.e., she eliminates the use of rhyme and reduces the length of each poetic line); she simplifies Chaucer's Latinate vocabulary by swapping in short words ("experience" and "auctoritee" become "my own bible"); and the spelling reflects the sounds of Jamaican Patois ("wen," "de," "fah," and "Tanks" instead of *when, the, for,* and *Thanks*) as well as its grammar ("is five husban I have").[38] Chaucer's fictive Wife of Bath has been dislocated in place and time from the medieval Canterbury pilgrimage to the contemporary Brixton Market, a location in south London that became the locus of Black Caribbean immigration and settlement in the mid-twentieth century.[39] Breeze's linguistic transplantation enacts Bennett's "colonizin in reverse" by moving Black Caribbean sounds into a Black British space.

In Breeze's poem, place and race are richly entwined. By writing a poem with a distinctively Black Caribbean female voice and situating the fictive setting as Brixton Market, Breeze reclaims Chaucerian "universality" through a particular cultural location often called the "soul of Black Britain."[40] The reclaiming of space through poetic performance is particularly clear in Breeze's recorded audiovisual reenactment of this same poem, filmed on-site in 2006 with the poet herself walking throughout the covered market of Granville Arcade in Brixton Market, recently rebranded as "Brixton Village."[41] In this videorecording, Breeze embodies the fictive female speaker in this poem, dressed in a white headwrap signaling Black Caribbean heritage.[42] Composed entirely of footage of Breeze speaking directly to the camera, the recording creates a vivid sense of immediacy; colorful storefronts, restaurants, and grocery shoppers are in view in the background of the rapidly interspliced camera shots with passersby at times reacting with confusion, amusement, or disapproval of the poet's disruptive performance.[43]

---

36 Chaucer, *Canterbury Tales*, "Wife of Bath's Prologue," lines 1–7.

37 Breeze, *Arrival of Brighteye*, 62–64, at 62.

38 Breeze's project of resituating Chaucerian English becomes even clearer through the act of translation. "God bad us for to wexe and multiplye" (Chaucer, "Wife of Bath's Prologue," line 28)—the Wife of Bath's translation of the "gentil text" (line 29) of Genesis stating *crescite et multiplicamini*, meaning "increase and multiply"—becomes "Im order we [i.e., He ordered us] to sex an multiply" (Breeze, *Arrival of Brighteye*, 62).

39 Gbadamosi, "Road to Brixton Market."

40 Ibid.

41 Breeze, *Wife of Bath in Brixton Market.*

42 Elizabeth, "A Short History of African Headwrap."

43 At one moment, the poetic narrator says "de man mus lef im madda an im fadda / an cling to me" and Breeze clings her breasts with her hands; a pedestrian in the background shoots a look in her direction and then resumes walking (Breeze, *Wife of Bath in Brixton Market*, 1:01–1:04). See also Hsy, "Teaching the Wife of Bath through Adaptation."

Figure 12: Multicultural storefront in an arcade in Brixton Market, in south London, also known as the "Soul of Black Britain." In 2006, Jean "Binta" Breeze recorded her "Wife of Bath speaks in Brixton Market" while walking through this arcade. London, March 2014. Photo by the author.

In performing Chaucer's distinctive and bold Wife of Bath in this Black British space, Breeze's body in motion artfully disrupts perceived social scripts. In "reclaiming" (or reincarnating) Chaucer's Wife of Bath as a Black British woman, Breeze demonstrates how a contemporary "nation language" of Jamaican English rivals the claims to legitimacy, complexity, and rootedness that Chaucer's Middle English enjoys.

Marilyn Nelson, Poet Laureate of Connecticut from 2001 to 2006, relocates the Chaucerian pilgrimage not in terms of "colonizin in reverse" or transatlantic trajectories but a hemispheric American context in her verse novel *The Cachoeira Tales* (2005). Nelson's first-person narrative relates a journey of African Americans that is initially envisioned as "a reverse diaspora ... a pilgrimage to Africa" or "some place sanctified by the Negro soul,"[44] but it is instead rerouted to the predominantly Black state of Bahia in Brazil. It culminates with the group's arrival at "A Igreja do Nostra Senhor do Bonfim" [The Church of Our Lord of the Good End] in the city of Salvador, the capital of Bahia.[45] Composed in iambic pentameter couplets (with occasional slant rhyme), *The Cachoeira Tales* explores the socioeconomic, religious, and linguistic heterogeneity of Black diaspora

---

44 Nelson, *Cachoeira Tales*, 11.

45 Ibid., 52.

communities. The word "fellowship" first refers to the prestigious Guggenheim grant that financed the trip: "I'd have to modify the plan I had / concocted on the fellowship application, / but at least we'd have a wonderful vacation."[46] New meanings of "fellowship" (community) emerge as the group travels. Nelson's "General Prologue" introduces a Director of a Black theater, a Jazz Musician who "improvised Portuguese / as he had French, Spanish, and Japanese,"[47] a retired Pilot, and an Activist with prior experience in the Peace Corps—with additional African American travelers Harmonia and Moreen joining the group by chance in Brazil.

The verse novel interweaves shared diasporic experiences and (at times) comic intercultural perceptions among Black Americans and Africans across the Atlantic. The Jazz Musician invents a nonsense language "Creole Swahili" during a visit to Zimbabwe to compensate for his complete lack of knowledge of local languages.[48] The Jazz Musician's account of his comic "return" to Africa demonstrates his improvisational performance skills, and the phrase "Creole Swahili" playfully denotes at least two different historical Black diaspora contact zones. "Swahili" could refer to Waswahili, a cultural and ethnic group in eastern Africa, or to Kiswahili, a lingua franca in the Bantu family of languages, with considerable influence from Arabic, spoken throughout eastern and southern Africa; "Creole" can ambiguously refer to a number of Black Caribbean cultural and linguistic contexts including francophone Louisiana.

Ultimately it is Brazil's vivid syncretism that fully juxtaposes colonial European and diasporic African frameworks in Nelson's novel: "I wondered what the statues really meant: / Was it Mary, or was it Yemanja / in the chapel ... or was it the Orixa of the sea?"[49] The destination of the rerouted pilgrimage is not a "return" to origins in Africa, nor a "reverse" colonization of the imperial center by arriving at Brixton Market or Westminster Abbey or the shrine of Thomas Becket in Canterbury. Rather, this mixed group of African Americans arrive at a site of religious and cultural fusion and cultural hybridity in Latin America: a Chaucerian nod to a pilgrimage that has reached a *bonfim* or "good end."

Urban Spaces: Multiethnic and Multiracial

Contemporary authors of color use Chaucerian poetics to navigate questions of race and place. This section addresses two poets who transport the mixed Canterbury storytelling collective to contemporary multiethnic cities: Patience Agbabi, whose poetic anthology *Telling Tales* (2014) features a fictive multiracial cast of characters in present-day London;[50] and Frank Mundo, whose verse novel *The Brubury Tales* (2010) features a multiracial group of storytellers in Los Angeles soon after the race riots of the 1990s.[51] Both

---

46 Ibid., 12.

47 Ibid., 14.

48 Ibid., 28.

49 Ibid., 50. See also Barrington and Hsy, "Afterlives," 15.

50 Agbabi, *Telling Tales.*

51 Mundo, *Brubury Tales* (2010).

poets create space for a fictive multiracial ensemble of storytellers while also addressing harmful legacies of racial violence in the past and their implications for systemic
racism and social conflict today. Each poet uses the Chaucerian pilgrimage and storytelling game structure to explore interpersonal and sociopolitical dimensions of urban
spaces and to navigate shifting social positions across ever-changing environments.

Nigerian British poet Patience Agbabi's *Telling Tales* (2014) brings Chaucer's tales
into a multiracial and multiethnic London. Spoken-word performing artist and 2009
Poet Laureate for Canterbury, Agbabi was born in London to Nigerian parents and raised
by a white English family in Sussex and later in Wales, and she brings a transnational and
multicultural sensibility to her poetic exploration of motion across spaces and communities.[52] *Telling Tales* presents itself as if it were a poetic anthology, with fictive "Author
Biographies" for the narrators contributing to a thickly layered representation of the
multicultural milieu of modern London; these author-narrators compose in a variety of
verse structures including iambic pentameter couplets, sonnets, free verse, sestina, and
modern forms derived from contemporary popular culture (such as grime, spoken-word
poetry, 144-character tweets, and ransom notes).[53]

One poem in *Telling Tales* that explicitly addresses contemporary anti-Black racism
in Britain as well as harmful legacies of the medieval past is "Sharps an Flats" (Agbabi's
remix of Chaucer's "Prioress's Tale").[54] In the medieval version of the story, Chaucer's
French-speaking Prioress who acts as the narrator styles herself as "Madame Eglentine"
but she has never traveled extensively beyond London;[55] her antisemitic story takes place
within a multiethnic city in Asia inhabited by Christians and Jews ("Ther was in Asie, in
a greet citee, / Amonges Cristen folk, a Jewerye")[56] and she recounts the martyrdom of a
young Christian boy, with the entire performance presented as if it is an extended prayer
to the Virgin Mary.[57] "Sharps an Flats" is assigned, by contrast, to a contemporary Afro-
Caribbean social justice activist named "Missy Eglantine" who is originally from St. Lucia,[58]
and her spoken-word poetry testifies to Black victims of violence in modern London.[59]

The posthumous narrator of "Sharps an Flats" uses a distinctive form of "nonstandard" English (in terms of spelling, sounds, and vocabulary) to tell the story of a Black
British schoolboy murdered on the streets of southeast London. In a rap letter (or song)
to his mother, the posthumous narrator who enigmatically identifies himself only as
"your son, J, chattin on a mix made / in Heaven," tells the story of how he was suddenly

52 Agbabi, "Stories in Stanza'd English," 1–3.

53 Agbabi, *Telling Tales*, 115–20.

54 Ibid., 81–82.

55 "Frenssh she spak ful faire and fetisly, / After the scole of Stratford-atte-Bowe, / For Frenssh of
Paris was to hire unknowe" (Chaucer, *Canterbury Tales*, "General Prologue," lines 124–26).

56 Chaucer, *Canterbury Tales*, "Prioress's Tale," lines 488–89.

57 Ibid., "Prioress's Prologue," lines 453–87.

58 Agbabi, *Telling Tales*, 116.

59 Ibid. The author biography of "Missy Eglantine" evokes a compressed Twitter bio: "born St
Lucia / raised in Lewisham / R&B singer-rapper-poet [...] studied French UEL Stratford [...] Love
Peace & Justice" (slash marks in original).

"cut off by a switchblade"[60] or "stabbed with a sharp" by "2 boys from the back flats" resulting in his untimely death.[61] This poem is thick with allusions to Chaucer's narrative of a schoolboy who sings the Marian hymn *Alma redemptoris mater* ["Loving Mother of Our Savior"] in the Jewish neighborhood of a medieval city and miraculously keeps singing even after his throat is cut.

Agbabi's posthumous narrator states to his mother: "*Mater?* Made a martyr 4 backchattin in Latin / sharps and flats, I had no idea what I woz chattin … Do Re Mi Fa, with my spa [i.e., buddy, pal, mate], Damilola."[62] The name "Damilola" (here used as a rhyme word) evokes the tragic murder of Damilola Taylor, a schoolboy originally from Nigeria whose killing on November 27, 2000 exposed the lack of visibility for Black and immigrant victims of violence and the slow process of bringing justice to their communities. Damilola Taylor, described in public discourse as "a good boy who never would have joined a gang,"[63] was on his way home from the library when he was stabbed with shards of glass and bled to death, and numerous failures during a six-year trial process delayed the arrival of justice for his murder.[64]

As Agbabi herself has noted, the story of urban violence against a Black British boy in "Sharps an Flats" provides an eerily modern intertext for the Prioress's own invocation of Hugh of Lincoln, the medieval English schoolboy allegedly murdered and thrown into a privy by Jews.[65] Chaucer's disturbing tale of antisemitism and martyrdom becomes a venue for Agbabi to question social attitudes towards Black vulnerability in contemporary Britain—with her text repeatedly asserting the boy's innocence by aligning him with an angelic "chorus / in God's gang."[66] Meanwhile, the "boys in blue" (i.e., police and authorities associated with the legal system) fail to bring solace to the victim's family.[67]

Whether it is Agbabi or Missy Eglantine or the dead boy himself whose voice is "really" recorded in this work, "Sharps an Flats" prompts the audience to consider who gets to be recognized—and mourned—as an "innocent" victim of violence. Racist public discourses of violent youth crime of the kind emerging in Britain after Damilola Taylor's death persist to the present day, and a politicized rhetoric of "black on black" violence perpetuates harmful stereotypes that align blackness with criminality and contribute to a pervasive and deadly policing of Black communities in predominately white societies.[68] "Sharps an

---

60 Ibid., 81.

61 Ibid., 82.

62 Ibid.

63 "Damilola Taylor: Killing."

64 "Damilola Taylor: Timeline."

65 On Damilola Taylor as modern Black "mirroring" of Hugh of Lincoln, see Patience Agbabi's Twitter thread from January 22, 2015. https://twitter.com/PatienceAgbabi/status/558312910074953729.

66 Agbabi, *Telling Tales*, 81.

67 Ibid., 82.

68 Headley, "'Black on Black' Crime: The Myth and the Reality"; Braga and Brunson, "Police and Public Discourse."

Flats" forces the audience to confront the pervasive harms that Black people face on a daily basis in societies structured by white supremacy, and to ask which lives matter.[69]

Agbabi deliberately leaves the racial identities of the Black British boy's assailants unspecified in "Sharps an Flats,"[70] but her allusion to the murder of Damilola Taylor suggests an awareness of failure of the legal system to bring justice to, or create safety for, Black communities. Black Lives Matter, the global movement founded in the US in 2013 by radical Black organizers Alicia Garza, Patrisse Cullors, and Opal Tometi in response to the acquittal of the killer of Black teenager Trayvon Martin, drew attention to this high-profile case of anti-Black murder to advocate for systemic change.[71] Agbabi's rap poem published in 2014 testifying to the full humanity of a Black victim of violence in Britain implicitly resonates with the current international aims of Black Lives Matter as "an ideological and political intervention in a world where Black lives are systematically and intentionally targeted for demise,"[72] regardless of the particular racial identities of those who commit lethal acts of anti-Black violence.

Frank Mundo's verse novel *The Brubury Tales* (2010), set in contemporary Los Angeles in the 1990s, grapples with questions of systemic anti-Blackness and models a process of self-reflection on racial stereotyping.[73] Mundo's fictive storytellers are hotel security guards passing away the time on the graveyard shift. The text's "General Prologue" is composed in rhyming iambic pentameter couplets and attributed to a first-person narrator named J. T. Glass, who introduces to the audience a range of fictive storytellers from varied ethnic, racial, and national backgrounds: Leo Kapitanski ("a Russian Jew"), Alex Loma (race or ethnicity not immediately specified), John Shamburger (Black American), Joseph Dator (Filipino immigrant born near Manila), Rolla Amin (female student from Iraq), and Darrin Arita ("unsuccessfully Japanese") are all described in turn.[74] The narrator's erratic use of ethnic and racial descriptors across these portraits invites the reader to ask how "relevant" an externally perceived racial or ethnic identity is to the particular "content" of the story that a person tells.

John Shamburger, who is well aware of systems of racial oppression and white settler colonialism, initially emerges as a parody of a Black social justice activist. Ventriloquizing Shamburger's discourse, the narrator states: "Shamburger, he said, was a slave name / Imposed upon his shackled ancestors" by white capitalists or "white American Dream investors / Who killed the Natives and enslaved the blacks" and "built this country upon their backs."[75] J. T. Glass—who cryptically remains "unmarked" in terms of his

---

69 Cachia, "Damilola Taylor's father [and] Black Lives Matter." Agbabi critiques racist police brutality as well as homophobic violence in "The Black The White and The Blue," *R.A.W.*, 26–27; see Goddard, *Staging Black Feminisms*, 168–72. On Agbabi and intersectional Black feminist and queer diaspora approaches, see Hsy and Barrington, "Noir Medievalism."

70 Agbabi, Twitter thread, January 22, 2015 (cited above).

71 Black Lives Matter. "Herstory."

72 Ibid.

73 Mundo, *Brubury Tales: Illustrated Edition* (2014).

74 Ibid., 2–9. Alex Loma is later revealed to be originally from Mexico (ibid., 287).

75 Ibid., 3.

own race or ethnicity—suggests that he doesn't fully share Shamburger's worldviews, characterizing Shamburger as always "pull[ing] the race card" in order to win arguments.[76] Nonetheless, the narrator respects Shamburger's activism and deep commitments to his community: "But, I must admit, I admired him. / The fire that inspired him / Made him always look outside of the box," and Shamburger is "one of the best men I ever knew … a volunteer mentor in the hood."[77] This same narrator acknowledges his changed perceptions of Shamburger after hearing his story relating among other things his father's traumatic experience as a soldier in the Korean War and offering a tender, nuanced model of Black masculinity.[78] The narrator declares Shamburger the winner of the storytelling contest for his "heartfelt tale" with a "story … so untypically male," a performance that is simultaneously "instructional and entertaining."[79] By layering the text through Shamburger's performance and J. T. Glass's response, Mundo gradually disassociates Blackness from harmful notions of militant or toxic masculinity.

Although the fictive narrator's own engagements with antiracist theory and activism aren't entirely clear, the evasive figure of the "sup" (supervisor) named "Frank Mundo" who is "hard to label" and "doesn't fit neatly in a table / Of beliefs, politics or even race" is even more difficult to pin down: "He has like a permanent poker face / That's somehow both eager and resistant / To being stable and inconsistent."[80] A perpetual resistance to tidy racial and political categories is consistent with the first-person writings of Frank Mundo *in propria persona*, when the author writes about his own complex social positionings as a Mexican American. "How I Became a Mexican" (2012), published after the first edition of *The Brubury Tales*, exposes the absurdity of essentialized racial formations. Mundo begins by stating: "When I was eleven years old, I became a Mexican."[81] Born to a brown Mexican father and blonde American mother and raised in Maryland as "the 'brown' white kid of an interracial marriage gone bad,"[82] he had "never identified with a single race" and it was only once he "moved to California [that] I became a Mexican."[83] Soon after his move to California, he encounters an efficient "variation on the old shirts-and-skins theme" called "Whites versus Mexicans,"[84] the method of forming teams on the basketball court at recess. "Everyone with brown skin was on one team, and everyone with white skin was on the other,"[85] and Mundo finds himself grouped with "seven brown-skinned kids like me."[86] This reductive sorting into teams based on

---

76 Ibid.

77 Ibid., 4.

78 Ibid., 155–85.

79 Ibid., 283.

80 Ibid., 194.

81 Mundo, "How I Became a Mexican," 1.

82 Ibid., 4.

83 Ibid., 3.

84 Ibid., 1.

85 Ibid., 1–2.

86 Ibid., 2.

physical appearance robs Mundo of any say in how he might identify. "It's not like I even had a choice of what to call myself," Mundo recalls, and his complex bicultural identity is reduced to the external matter of skin color alone.[87]

Mundo resists essentialized categorizations that white anglophone American culture imposes, and he also critiques narrow notions of authenticity that Mexican American communities can reinforce on the basis of Spanish fluency. The "young Mexican girls and Mexican women" first called him "pocho" (a derogatory term for an "Americanized" person of Mexican descent) due to his limited Spanish skills, and eventually he is "downgraded" to "gringo" (usually referring to a white American with a negative connotation depending on context) or "guero" (referring to a person with lighter skin) once it becomes apparent that "I would never learn to speak their language."[88] Mundo reveals a contingent and context-specific alignment of language and racial identity, navigating ambivalent and complex claims to "Mexican" identity due to his lopsided language skills as well as his biracial background.

One opportunity to evade binary thinking emerges when Mundo recognizes "brown" as a capacious sociopolitical category that unwittingly groups disparate ethnic and racial groups together. The "Mexican" team includes a number of "browned-skinned ballers" who were "not Mexican or even Latino," including an Iranian immigrant as well as a friend of Italian ancestry who happens to have a Portuguese surname.[89] The heterogeneous meanings of Mundo's "brown" suggests a localized manifestation of what Kelly Lytle Hernández calls "Mexican Brown," a pervasive rhetorical tool of social profiling on the basis of class, color, and perceived immigration status,[90] as well as what Nitasha Tamar Sharma calls the "always-under-construction lines" of "brown" as a racial designation or identity category that encompasses individuals with actual or perceived origins in the Middle East, South Asia, and Latin America.[91] Mundo likens himself and peers who thwart binary categories of classification to "'liminal' characters ... mystical sort of beings or creatures (monsters even) ... that [live] 'in the threshold' between two distinct realms or realities."[92] Observing that "I was brown and my last name ... Mundo meant 'world' in Spanish,"[93] Mundo acknowledges the fraught conditions of "brown" identity on a global scale and suggests worlds of possibility for hybrid identities in literature and theory.[94]

Mundo's context-specific understanding of cultural and racial identities implicitly evokes Chicana lesbian feminist Gloria Anzaldúa's rhetoric of a *mestiza* subjectivity that

---

87 Ibid., 4.

88 Ibid., 3.

89 Ibid., 4.

90 Hernández, *History of U.S. Border Patrol*.

91 Sharma, "Brown," 19.

92 Mundo, "How I Became a Mexican," 5.

93 Ibid., 3.

94 On "brown" as a framework that creates political solidarity as well as constructing new literary archives, see Chander, *Brown Romantics*; Hsy, "Brown Faces." On a different Mexican American's "feelings of nonbelonging" in California, see Muñoz, "Feeling Brown," 679.

navigates multiple linguistic and cultural identities (in her case anglophone American, Indigenous, and Chicano Spanish); Anzaldúa states that "to be an Indian in Mexican culture [and] to be Mexican from an Anglo point of view" entails "a tolerance for ambiguity" and living "in a pluralistic mode," and her text abounds with imagery of mythic hybrid creatures and first-person reflections on navigating positions that are always in flux and socially situated.[95] The character of "Frank Mundo" who evades fixed categories and the (racially unmarked) first-person narrator of J. T. Glass in *Brubury Tales* embody poetic counterparts to the flexible sociopolitical positionings in Mundo's autoethnographic writing. Nonetheless, claims of identity that seek to break free from, or somehow remain innocent of, external social categories or perceptions of race can never fully prevent an individual from navigating the sociopolitical realities of racialization in everyday life.

Crossing Waters: Mediterranean and Pacific Mobilities

The final section of this chapter examines the sociopolitical dimensions of two Chaucerian projects from disparate parts of the globe: *The Refugee Tales* (2015 to the present), an ongoing collaborative effort, drawing upon an ethos of Chaucerian storytelling, that seeks to end indefinite immigrant detention in the UK; and Ouyang Yu's *The Kingsbury Tales* (2008), a verse novel set near Melbourne, Australia, that addresses complexities of migration, xenophobia, racial belonging, and mobility in a contemporary Asia-Pacific context.

The Refugee Tales, organized by Gatwick Detainees Welfare Group in collaboration with Kent Refugee Help, was originally entitled "A Walk in Solidarity with Refugees, Asylum Seekers and Detainees (from Dover to Crawley via Canterbury)," and the annual walk and its associated events stage collaborations between an "established writer" and an "asylum seeker, former immigration detainee or refugee" whose story is told with the aim to put "an immediate end to indefinite immigration detention in the UK."[96] Inspired by *The Canterbury Tales*, the project creates "a charged sense of place," foregrounding "the visible fact of human movement" and offering "an exchange of information in the act of telling stories."[97] Three literary anthologies have appeared associated with the project, each collection grappling with the ethics of speaking for and with others in pursuit of social justice. Sierra Lomuto states that the *"Refugee Tales* transforms the imperial power of English into a tool of resistance precisely by speaking through Chaucer," who is "a looming, masculine figure of the English canon" yet also composes in a poetic language that holds "the potential for 'welcome'" in the present day.[98]

The first anthology of works published by *The Refugee Tales* project was entitled *Refugee Tales* (2016) and it includes a poem by Patience Agbabi; entitled "The Refugee's Tale," her poem relates the first-person narrative of a woman named "Farida" who fled religious violence in her homeland before relocating to Britain. Composed as

---

95 Anzaldúa, *Borderlands / La Frontera: The New Mestiza*, 101.

96 Herd and Pincus, eds., *Refugee Tales*, "Afterword," 133.

97 Ibid.

98 Lomuto, "Chaucer and Humanitarian Activism."

a sequence of sonnets, Agbabi's poem offers some traces of a collaboration with the woman whose story she narrates: "I make a very good falafel, / you must try. Are you recording?"[99] Farida reveals she is a Coptic Christian, raised in Egypt, of Sudanese birth: "though my parents are Egyptian, / I am born in Sudan, Sudan is in my blood."[100] She invokes a strong sense of belonging across multiple homelands, invoking tender Christian/Muslim coexistence "back home"[101] in Egypt before religious violence began as well as her affective ties to Sudan: "Christians and Muslims break the same bread / before the change ... Though I am always a Christian ... I loved Muslims as I love the Nuba" [i.e., Nuba Mountains in Sudan], referring to the land of her birth.[102] Her story is charged with motifs of motion, and waterways act both as boundaries and pathways. "How can we be at war / when the Nile flows through our twin faiths?"[103] Farida asks in reference to Christianity and Islam and also (more obliquely) to her "twin" homelands of Egypt and Sudan, through which the Nile also flows. When Farida survives religious violence due to the protective shell of her car, she sees "waving fists part like the Red Sea" and "I still think it's a miracle I find myself free": an allusion to a biblical exodus from Egypt that anticipates her own departure.[104] When her mother dies, "my whole body drowned with grieving / in this room, with the ribbed roof ... heavy as Jonah," a rich evocation of environmental space that evokes a prophet's biblical transit across the Mediterranean.[105]

The Refugee Tales (in all its iterations) maintains that a Chaucerian voicing of others might enable world transformation and social justice if only anglophone readers can empathize with migrants who are so often dehumanized in public discourse. A woman with a rich cultural background, life experience, and faith tradition can so often find herself reduced to the signifier *refugee*: "'Refugee' is in your head when you call me Farida."[106] Agbabi uses the formal structure of a crown of sonnets, a recursive form in which the final line of each sonnet becomes the first line of the next; the final line of the final sonnet echoes the entire text's opening line: "Maybe the real story begins here."[107] By bringing the end of the story back to its beginning, Agbabi builds empathy with Farida and conveys some of the feelings of stagnation and perpetual "new beginnings" that legal structures can create.[108] An unjust immigration system or unwelcoming environment for

---

99 Patience Agbabi, "The Refugee's Tale," in *Refugee Tales*, ed. Herd and Pincus, 125–32, at 125.

100 Ibid., 126.

101 Ibid., 125.

102 Ibid., 126. On Sudanese and Nubian diasporic identities in relation to Arab Egyptian culture in a different literary context, see Abbas, "Nubian Diasporic Identity," 149–50.

103 Ibid., 128.

104 Ibid.

105 Ibid., 132.

106 Ibid., 125. "Farida" means "unique or precious" in Arabic.

107 Ibid., 132 and 125.

108 Agbabi uses this same poetic form in "Joined-up Writing" (her retelling of Chaucer's "Man of Law's Tale"), which relates the story of an African immigrant through the first-person voice of her racist northern British mother-in-law (Agbabi, *Telling Tales*, 21–27). See also Agbabi, "Stories in Stanza'd English."

refugees can result in an extended limbo: a state of suspended animation and thwarted motion.

Agbabi's literary voicing of the story of "Farida," and the poet's critique of how her entire identity and life experience can get reduced to the legal or social designation of "refugee," potentially aligns with some of the activist approaches currently employed in the interdisciplinary field of critical refugee studies. This field of study, as announced and outlined by Yến Lê Espiritu, examines how "the refugee, who inhabits a condition of statelessness, radically calls into question the established principles of the nation-state" as well as an "idealized goal of inclusion and recognition within it."[109] The field of critical refugee studies attends to "the displaced refugee, rather than the rooted citizen," as a "social actor whose life, when traced, illuminates the interconnections of colonization, war, and global social change."[110] Poetry that centers the perspectives of dehumanized migrants and displaced individuals can not only make the case for the full inclusion of marginalized people as citizens within the existing legal structures of nation-states, but such storytelling can also critique the ubiquitous forms of violence and border policing that these same nation-states enact.[111]

Across the globe, Ouyang Yu (Chinese-born Australian poet, novelist, and translator publishing works in English and in Chinese) offers disparate individual stories of migration, but through the experiences of many travelers over time. Ouyang's verse novel *The Kingsbury Tales* (2008) focuses primarily on Kingsbury, a suburb of the city of Melbourne where Australia's oldest Chinatown is located.[112] Founded during the Gold Rush of the 1850s, Melbourne's Chinatown is an "iconic enclave" that is arguably the oldest continuously inhabited Chinatown in the so-called Western world.[113] Ouyang's multi-voiced novel incorporates a variety of verse forms (none of which are rhyming couplets nor iambic pentameter), telling discontinuous stories of Chinese migrants and people born in Australia over the centuries—as well as charting his own movements throughout Singapore, Malaysia, and Chinese diaspora communities across Australasia.

Ouyang's verse novel opens with a prologue-poem "A Novel, Tentatively" that acknowledges the complexity of speaking for others across time: "The Kingsbury Tales are no match / For The Canterbury Tales ... A novel, tentatively ... in a jagged form / A crap old / Format / That treats other's histories as / If they were my own."[114] In these lines, Ouyang evokes Chaucer's comments that "[w]hoso shal telle a tale after a man ... moot reherce as neigh as evere he kan ... or finde wordes newe" [whoever wants to repeat a story from somebody else must repeat it as closely as he can or find new words].[115] Ouyang offers "[a] novel written, to be written / In a novel form / For novel

109 Espiritu, *Body Counts*, 10.

110 Ibid, 11.

111 Ng, "Detention Islands."

112 Ouyang, *Kingsbury Tales*.

113 Chau, Dupre, and Xu, "Melbourne Chinatown as Iconic Enclave."

114 Ouyang, *Kingsbury Tales*, 15.

115 Chaucer, *Canterbury Tales*, "General Prologue," lines 731–36.

readers."[116] In the context of Ouyang's work as an announced adaptation of Chaucer, the double meanings of "novel" (as a noun and as an adjective) transform the Canterbury pilgrimage from an anthology of stories in motion into a multivoiced historical novel in verse. Ouyang transforms the conventions of Chaucerian storytelling to craft a new community of voices in transit across time and to tell divergent stories of individual inhabitants of, or travelers through, a particular place.

"The Aussie's Tale" opens with a seemingly typical male Aussie narrator: "I take a lot of pride in being an Aussie / I go to the footy / If you are an Aussie that's what you do."[117] Race and gender norms set the conventions of the presumed "default" of white Australian masculinity. It is the sudden reality of a Chinese face that disrupts the speaker's perceived belonging: "You think I look like an Aussie? / Of mixed blood? / I am as Chinese as you guys."[118] These rhetorical questions provisionally mark the silently unmarked whiteness that underlies the term "Aussie." Ouyang's verse novel toys with acts of racial disclosure and uses a mobile first-person voice to explore Australia's own history of Chinese exclusion through its own "Yellow Peril" era genres of anti-Asian "Invasion Literature" and its "White Australia" immigration policy,[119] and Ouyang reflects on histories of displacement of Aboriginal Australians through ongoing settler colonialism as well.[120] Throughout these poems, Ouyang creates new spaces for a Chinese face or voice in Australia, and he asks how Chaucerian personas might change social perceptions of who is "authentically" Australian.[121]

Ouyang primarily writes in "standard" English, but he occasionally uses a Chaucerian middling vernacular to reflect uneasy positionings across Chinese and Australian and "Chinese Australian" identities. "New Accents" uses the words "Anguish" and "English" as near-homonyms: "In Kingsbury, in the late 1990s" he hears many "new accents," and upon his arrival in Australia people "tried to fool me around because I couldn't / Speak 'Anguish.'"[122] "Place Names, A Tale of Chinese Invasion" offers literal translations (phonetic transliterations) of Australian place names. The poetic speaker observes that politicians "are so concerned with Asian read non-white immigration / Into Australia" but the "Chinese have sinicized Australia / Without your knowledge, graphically."[123] Chinese sounds and phrases replace English and Aboriginal place names: "xueli (Snow Pear) is their name for Sydney / moerben (Ink That Book) is theirs for Melbourne /

---

116 Ouyang, *Kingsbury Tales*, 15.

117 Ibid., 64.

118 Ibid.

119 Ibid., "Sir Wong Hung Foo's Tale," 22–23.

120 Ibid., "An Aboriginal Tale," 21–22.

121 On the myth of the "monochrome Middle Ages" and "the Whiteness of the imagined world" in medieval-inspired fictions, see Young, *Habits of Whiteness*, 72–76, regarding an online discussion about the lack of Asian and Indigenous Australian influences in George R. R. Martin's novels and the *Game of Thrones* franchise.

122 Ouyang, *Kingsbury Tales*, 46.

123 Ibid., 59.

wulongang (Five Dragon Ridge) theirs for Wollongong."[124] Enacting a linguistic form of displacement (which white settler colonialism has previously enacted against Aboriginal Australians), Chinese migrants move across the Pacific to settle in white anglophone spaces and proliferate new place names. "Speaking English in Chinese" reflects on how Chinese and English intermingle in Singapore: "'Here we are la,' our Malay driver says ... 'Is this [word 'la'] something like the English 'Isn't it'?"[125] Simultaneously a form of making and breaking, Singlish "can create things like 'break English,' not 'broken English.'"[126]

In "English Language, My Colony," Ouyang layers his critique of white settler colonialism in Australia with histories of Chinese migrant labor in the Australian gold mines. Just as white settlers used names such as "Sin Fat" or "heathen Chinee" to assert their dominance over "the early dinkum Chinaman diggers," so does Ouyang struggle to control "the bastardly colony, the English Language ... I have much to do to establish, to destroy, in this colony of mine ... this derelict mine of words."[127] Attentive to intricacies of vernacular speech and an unsettled English language, Ouyang's modern Chaucerian poetry traces forms of racial unbelonging across Australia and the Pacific—breaking down conventions in order to create something new.

Fellow Travelers and New Solidarities

Anticipating some of the sociopolitical critiques currently explored in the field of critical refugee studies, Ouyang crafts a markedly Asian voice inscribing a multifaceted and multiracial history of migrants, travelers, and settlers inhabiting a local Australian environment. Ouyang's poetic craft develops a "novel voice" that not only accommodates a plurality of unrooted or displaced experiences throughout Australasia but also critiques the historical and ongoing harms of white supremacy and settler colonialism—as well as the ongoing violence of xenophobia and border policing that so often vilifies migrants throughout the so-called Global North.

The Chaucerian poets of color discussed in this chapter all come from distinct geocultural and sociopolitical environments, and their positions on antiracism and activism diverge, with some writers more deeply aligned with particular histories of antiracist theory and practice and others expressing more informal experience, or even some rhetorical distance, from such approaches. Poets of color are not a monolith, but all of these writers invite readers to think carefully about our own social and racial positionings and our own complicity (in whatever communities we find ourselves) in ongoing structures of oppression and exclusion. We can also, just as crucially, continue to create and sustain spaces for people of color and historically marginalized voices—and work to dismantle unjust structures as we collectively construct a more just world.

---

124 Ibid.
125 Ibid., 78.
126 Ibid., 79.
127 Ibid., 94.

FURTHER READINGS AND RESOURCES

Antiracism

Ahmed, Sara. *On Being Included: Racism and Diversity in Institutional Life*. Durham: Duke University Press, 2012.

Black Women Radicals and the Asian American Feminist Collective. "Black and Asian-American Feminist Solidarities: A Reading List." *Black Women Radicals*, May 2020. https://www.blackwomenradicals.com/ blog-feed/ black-and-asian-feminist-solidarities-a-reading-list.

Coalition for Diversity & Inclusion in Scholarly Communications. *Toolkits for Equity: Transforming Scholarly Publishing Communities* (three-part series for Allies, BIPOC, and Organizations). https://c4disc.org/toolkits-for-equity/.

Dismantling Racism Works (dRworks). Web Workbook. Updated June 2020. http://www.dismantlingracism.org.

Eddo-Lodge, Reni. *Why I'm No Longer Talking to White People About Race*. London: Bloomsbury, 2019.

Kendi, Ibram X. *How to Be an Antiracist*. New York: One World, 2019.

Lopez Bunyasi, Tehama, and Candis Watts Smith. *Stay Woke: A People's Guide to Making All Black Lives Matter*. New York: New York University Press, 2019.

Multiculturalism, Race and Ethnicity Classics Consortium (MRECC). "Principles of Antiracist Teaching & Reflection." June 2020. https:// multiculturalclassics.wordpress.com/ teaching-resources-for-all-levels/.

National Museum of African American History and Culture, Smithsonian Institution, Washington, DC. *Talking About Race*. May 31, 2020. https://nmaahc.si.edu/learn/talking-about-race.

Oluo, Ijeoma. *So You Want to Talk About Race*. New York: Hachette, 2019.

ong, christina, and Amy Zhang. *Research Report & Resources for Disentangling Anti-Asian Violence*. The AAPI COVID-19 Project, March 24, 2021. Link available at www.aapicovid19.org.

Wekker, Gloria. *White Innocence: Paradoxes of Colonialism and Race*. Durham: Duke University Press, 2016.

Bibliographies and Resources

Arizona Center for Medieval and Renaissance Studies (organizer: Ayanna Thompson). "To Protect and Serve: A RaceB4Race Roundtable." Arizona State University, July 23, 2020. https://youtu.be/AYnmcBu0b-8

Daddabhoy, Ambereen, and Nedda Mehdizadeh. "Critical Race Conversations: Cultivating an Anti-Racist Pedagogy." Folger Institute, July 9, 2020. https://youtu.be/_4oCWst1cPc

Ehrenberg, Hannah, with Kim F. Hall and Peter Erikson. "Early Modern Race/Ethnic/Indigenous Studies: A (crowdsourced) Annotated Bibliography." https://t.co/nvNMhKkkmF?amp=1

Folger Institute and Arizona Center for Medieval & Renaissance Studies (co-sponsors). "Race and Periodization: Opening Lectures from the RaceB4Race Symposium." Folger Shakespeare Library, Washington, DC. September 2019. https:// www.folger.edu/ institute/ scholarly-programs/race-periodization.

Hsy, Jonathan, and Julie Orlemanski. "Race and Medieval Studies: A Partial Bibliography." *postmedieval* 8, no. 4 (December 2017): 500–531. https://doi.org/10.1057/s41280-017-0072-0.

McCannon, Afrodesia, and Geraldine Heng (organizers), on behalf of the Medieval Academy of America. "Race, Racism, and Teaching in the Middle Ages." Webinar, July 20, 2020. https://youtu.be/LOxc9KTauT8.

Medievalists of Color. "Resources." https://medievalistsofcolor.com/resources/

Modern Language Association, "Community Submitted Resources." *Antiracist Resources for Your 2020–2021 Teaching.* Compiled June 2020. https://antiracistresources.hcommons.org/community-submitted-resources/

Rambaran-Olm, Mary, and Erik Wade. "Race 101 for Early Medieval Studies: Selected Readings." *Medium,* July 18, 2020. https:// / medium.com/ @mrambaranolm/ race-101-for-early-medieval-studies-selected-readings-77be815f8d0f.

SAA (Shakespeare Association of America) Diversity Committee, "Antiracist Resources" (including resources relating to pedagogy and academia in general). https://shakespeareassociation.org/resources/antiracist-resources/.

Creative Works by People of Color (not discussed in this book)

Ahmed, Saladin. *Throne of the Crescent Moon.* New York: DAW, 2012.

Anzaldúa, Gloria. *Borderlands* / La Frontera: *The New Mestiza.* 4th ed. (25th anniversary of orig. ed., 1987). San Francisco: Aunt Lute, 2012.

Brolaski, Julian Talamantez. *Advice for Lovers.* San Francisco: City Lights, 2012.

Bruchac, Joseph. *The Ice-Hearts.* Austin: Cold Mountain, 1979.

Cha, Theresa Hak Kyung. *Dictee.* 2nd ed. Berkeley: University of California Press, 2009.

Chesnutt, Charles W. *The House Behind the Cedars.* Boston: Houghton Mifflin, 1900.

Du Bois, W. E. B. *Dark Princess: A Romance.* New York: Harcourt Brace, 1928.

——. *Darkwater: Voices from Within the Veil.* New York: Harcourt Brace, 1920.

Global Chaucers (crowdsourced bibliography, organizers: Candace Barrington and Jonathan Hsy). "Translations and Adaptations, listed by country." Note the range of Chaucerian adaptations beyond Anglophone countries and throughout the Global South. https://globalchaucers.wordpress.com/resources/translations-and-adaptations-listed-by-country/.

Hwang, David Henry. *FOB and Other Plays.* New York: Plume, 1990.

Ishiguro, Kazuo. *The Buried Giant.* London: Faber and Faber, 2015.

Kenan, Randall. *A Visitation of Spirits.* New York: Anchor, 1989.

King-Aribisala, Karen. *Kicking Tongues.* Portsmouth: Heinemann, 1998.

Kingston, Maxine Hong. *The Woman Warrior: Memoirs of a Girlhood Among Ghosts.* New York: Knopf, 1976.

Naylor, Gloria. *Bailey's Café.* New York: Harcourt Brace, 1992.

Overo-Tarimo, Ufuoma. *The Miller's Tale: Wahala Dey O! A Nigerian Play Adaptation of Chaucer's Canterbury Tale.* Edited by Jessica Lockhart, with Alaheh Amini, Mussie Berhane, Mahera Islam, and Justin Phillips. Toronto: University of Toronto–Mississauga, 2018.

Smith, Zadie (playwright). *The Wife of Willisden.* London: Kiln Theatre, 2020.

Tan, Amy. *Saving Fish from Drowning.* New York: Putnam's, 2005.

Vega, Ana Lydia. *Falsas Crónicas del Sur.* San Juan: Editorial Universidad de Puerto Rico, 1991. Translated by Andrew Hurley as *True and False Romances: Stories and a Novella.* New York: Serpent's Tail, 1994 (esp. "Cuento en Camino" translated as "Eye-Openers").

Yang, Gene Luen. *Boxers & Saints.* New York: First Second, 2013.

BIBLIOGRAPHY

Abbas, Fatin. "Egypt, Arab Nationalism, and Nubian Diasporic Identity in Idris Ali's *Dongola: A Novel of Nubia*." *Research in African Literatures* 45, no. 3 (Fall 2014): 147–66.

Aberth, John. *The Black Death: The Great Mortality of 1348–1350. A Brief History with Documents*. New York: Palgrave, 2005.

Abrams, Annie. "'The Miserable Slaves, the Degraded Serfs': Frederick Douglass, Anglo-Saxonism, and the Mexican War." *postmedieval* 10, no. 2 (June 2019): 151–61.

Achi, Andrea Myers, and Seeta Chaganti. "'Semper Novi Quid ex Africa': Redrawing the Borders of Medieval African Art and Considering Its Implications for Medieval Studies." In *Disturbing Times: Medieval Pasts, Reimagined Futures*, edited by Catherine E. Karkov, Anna Kłosowska, and Vincent W. J. van Gerven Oei, 73–106. Brooklyn: punctum, 2020.

Adams, William Edwin. *Our American Cousins: Being Personal Impressions of the People and Institutions of the United States*. London: Scott, 1883.

Agbabi, Patience. "The Prioress' Tale"—Petersfield Write Angle—July 2013. Uploaded August 13, 2013. https://www.youtube.com/watch?v=2xqadqIU0CY.

———. *R.A.W.* London: Izon Amazon / Gekko, 1995.

———. "Stories in Stanza'd English: A Cross-cultural *Canterbury Tales*." *Literature Compass* 15, no. 6 (2018): 1–8. https://doi.org/10.1111/lic3.12455.

———. *Telling Tales*. Edinburgh: Canongate, 2014.

Ahmed, Sara. *Living a Feminist Life*. Durham: Duke University Press, 2017.

———. *On Being Included: Racism and Diversity in Institutional Life*. Durham: Duke University Press, 2012.

Akbari, Suzanne Conklin. *Idols in the East: European Representations of Islam and the Orient, 1100–1450*. Ithaca: Cornell University Press, 2009.

Al Maleh, Layla. "The Literary Parentage of *The Book of Khalid*." In *The Book of Khalid: A Critical Edition*, edited by Todd Fine, 311–37. Syracuse: Syracuse University Press, 2016.

Andaya, Barbara Watson. "Rivers, Oceans, and Spirits: Water Cosmologies, Gender, and Religious Change in Southeast Asia." *TRaNS: Regional and National Studies of Southeast Asia* 4, no. 2 (July 2016): 239–63.

Angel Island Immigration Station Foundation, "Chinese Poetry of the Detention Barracks." https://www.aiisf.org/poems-and-inscriptions.

———. "History of Angel Island Immigration Station." https://www.aiisf.org/history.

Anon. *The Book of John Mandeville, with Related Texts*. Edited and translated by Iain Macleod Higgins. Indianapolis: Hackett, 2011.

Anzaldúa, Gloria. *Borderlands* / La Frontera: *The New Mestiza*. 3rd ed. San Francisco: Aunt Lute, 2007.

APM [American Public Media] Research Lab Staff, "The Color of Coronavirus: COVID-19 Deaths by Race and Ethnicity in the U.S." July 8, 2020. https://www.apmresearchlab.org/covid/deaths-by-race.

Appiah, Kwame Anthony. "Thick Translation" (1993). In *The Translation Studies Reader*, edited by Lawrence Venuti, 417–29. London: Routledge, 2000.

Arvas, Abdulhamit, Afrodesia McCannon, and Kris Trujillo, ed. "Critical Confessions Now." Special issue, *postmedieval* 11, nos. 2–3 (August 2020).

Asian Americans Advancing Justice—AAJC. Testimony to the US Commission on Civil Rights on "Immigration Detention Centers and Treatment of Immigrants." April 12, 2019. https:/

/ www.advancingjustice-aajc.org/ publication/ testimony-us-commission-civil-rights-immigration-detention-centers-and-treatment.

Bae, Minju, and Mark Tseng-Putterman. "Reviving the History of Radical Black-Asian Internationalism." *ROAR Magazine*, July 21, 2020. https://roarmag.org/essays/reviving-the-history-of-radical-black-asian-internationalism.

Bailey, Moya, and Trudy (aka @thetrudz). "On Misogynoir: Citation, Erasure, and Plagiarism." *Feminist Media Studies* 18, no. 4 (2018): 762–68.

Barnard, Phillip. "Les Cenelles." In *The Concise Oxford Companion to African American Literature*, edited by William L. Andrews, Frances Smith Foster, and Trudier Harris, 67–68. Oxford: Oxford University Press, 2001.

Barrington, Candace. *American Chaucers.* New York: Palgrave, 2007.

———. "Dark Whiteness: Benjamin Brawley and Chaucer." In *Dark Chaucer: An Assortment*, edited by Myra Seaman, Eileen Joy, and Nicola Masciandaro, 1–12. Brooklyn: punctum, 2012.

———. "Editors' Introduction: Chaucer's Global Orbits and Global Communities." *Literature Compass* 15, no. 6 (June 2018): 1–12. https://doi.org/10.1111/lic3.12457.

———. "Global Medievalism and Translation." In *Cambridge Companion to Medievalism*, edited by Louise D'Arcens, 180–95. Cambridge: Cambridge University Press, 2016.

———. and Jonathan Hsy. "Afterlives." In *A New Companion to Chaucer*, edited by Peter Brown, 7–19. Chichester: Wiley, 2019.

Bashford, Alison, Peter Hobbins, Anne Clarke, and Ursula K. Frederick. "Geographies of Commemoration: Angel Island, San Francisco and North Head, Sydney." *Journal of Historical Geography* 52 (2016): 16–25.

Basu, Tanya. "Asian Americans are Using Slack Groups to Explain Racism to their Parents." *MIT Technology Review*, June 22, 2020. https:///www.technologyreview.com/2020/06/22/1004312/asian-americans-are-using-slack-groups-to-explain-racism-to-their.parents.

Betancourt, Roland. *Byzantine Intersectionality: Sexuality, Gender, and Race in the Middle Ages.* Princeton: Princeton University Press, 2020.

Black Lives Matter, "Herstory—Black Lives Matter." *Black Lives Matter.* https://blacklivesmatter.com/herstory.

Blackshear, Edward L. "The Negro as Passive Factor in American History." *AME Church Review* 20 (1901): 62–63.

Blain, Keisha N. "The Deep Roots of Afro-Asia." *Black Perspectives*, January 30, 2015. https://www.aaihs.org/the-deep-roots-of-afro-asia.

Braga, Anthony A., and Rod K. Brunson. "The Police and Public Discourse on 'Black-on-Black Violence." *New Perspectives on Policing* (May 2015): 1–21.

Brathwaite, Kamau. "History of the Voice: The Development of Nation Language in the Anglophone Caribbean" (1984). In *Rotten English: A Literary Anthology*, edited by Dohra Ahmad, 459–68. New York: Norton, 2007.

Breeze, Jean "Binta." *The Arrival of Brighteye and Other Poems.* Newcastle: Bloodaxe, 2000.

———. *The Wife of Bath in Brixton Market (Poetry)*, November 30, 2009. https://www.youtube.com/watch?v=MiyKat1QzbQ0.

Briggs, John C. "The Exorcism of Macbeth: Frederick Douglass's Appropriation of Shakespeare." In *Weyward Macbeth: Intersections of Race and Performance*, edited by Scott L. Newstok and Ayanna Thompson, 35–43. New York: Palgrave, 2010.

Bright, Martin. "Damilola police 'missed gay link." *The Guardian*, January 11, 2003. https://www.theguardian.com/uk/2003/jan/12/gayrights.ukcrime.

Brogan, T. V. F., and D. A. Colón. "Abecedarius (abecedarian)." In *The Princeton Encyclopedia of Poetry and Poetics: Fourth Edition*, edited by Roland Greene, Steven Cushman, Clare Cavanagh, Jahan Ramazani, and Paul Rouzer, 1. Princeton: Princeton University Press, 2012.

Brolaski, Julian Talamantez. *Of Mongrelitude*. Seattle: Wave, 2017.

Brooks, Rodney A. "African Americans Struggle with Disproportionate COVID Death Toll." *National Geographic*, April 24, 2020. https:/ / www.nationalgeographic.com/ history/ 2020/04/coronavirus-disproportionately-impacts-african-americans.

Brown, Sterling A. "Negro Character as Seen by White Authors." *The Journal of Negro Education* 2, no. 2 (April 1933): 179–203.

Bunch, Lonnie G., III. "Recovery and Resilience." *Smithsonian* 51, no. 4 (July–August 2020): 6.

Burger, Glenn D., and Holly A. Crocker, eds. *Medieval Affect, Feeling, and Emotion*. Cambridge: Cambridge University Press, 2019.

Bushrui, Suheil B. "The First Arab Novel in English: *The Book of Khalid*." *Odisea* 14 (2013): 27–36.

Cachia, Alice. "Damilola Taylor's Father Hails his Son's School Friend Hollywood Actor John Boyega a 'Hero' after Impassioned Speech at Black Lives Matter Protest." *Daily Mail Online*, June 6, 2020. https:/ / www.dailymail.co.uk/ news/ article-8395685/ Damilola-Taylors-father-hails-John-Boyega-hero.html.

Campbell, Kofi Omoniyi Sylvanus. *Literature and Culture in the Black Atlantic: From Pre- to Postcolonial*. New York: Palgrave, 2006.

Cather, Willa. "The Conversion of Sum Loo." *Library* (1900). In *Mrs. Spring Fragrance: Edith Maude Eaton/Sui Sin Far*. Edited by Husan L. Hsu, 261–69. Peterborough: Broadview, 2011.

Cecire, Maria Sachiko. *Re-Enchanted: The Rise of Children's Fantasy Literature in the Twentieth Century*. Minneapolis: University of Minnesota Press, 2019.

Chaganti, Seeta. "B-Sides: Chaucer's 'The House of Fame.'" *Public Books*, February 14, 2019. https://www.publicbooks.org/b-sides-chaucers-the-house-of-fame.

———. "Confederate Monuments and the *Cura pastoralis*." *In the Middle*, February 27, 2017. http:/ / www.inthemedievalmiddle.com/ 2018/ 02/ confederate-monuments-and-cura. html.

———. "Statement Regarding ICMS Kalamazoo." *Medievalists of Color*, July 9, 2018. https:// medievalistsofcolor.com/race-in-the-profession/statement-regarding-icms-kalamazoo.

Chan, J. Clara. "Medievalists, Recoiling from White Supremacy, Try to Diversify the Field." *Chronicle of Higher Education*, July 16, 2017. https://www.chronicle.com/article/ Medievalists-Recoiling-From/240666.

Chander, Manu Samriti. *Brown Romantics: Poetry and Nationalism in the Global Nineteenth Century*. Lewisburg: Bucknell University Press, 2019.

Chang, Jennifer. "Contemporary Voices in Asian American Lyric Poetry." In *The Oxford Encyclopedia of Asian American Literature and Culture*, edited by Josephine Lee. New York: Oxford University Press, 2020.

———. *The History of Anonymity*. Athens: University of Georgia Press, 2008.

———. "Pastoral and the Problem of Place in Claude McKay's *Harlem Shadows*." In *A Companion to the Harlem Renaissance*, edited by Cherene Sherrard-Johnson, 187–202. Chichester: Wiley, 2015.

———. *Some Say the Lark*. Farmington: Alice James, 2017.

Chang, Yoonmee. *Writing the Ghetto: Class, Authorship, and the Asian American Ethnic Enclave*. New Brunswick: Rutgers University Press, 2010.

Chao-Fong, Léonie. "'My Dad Doesn't Feel Safe': Anti-Chinese Abuse Skyrockets During Coronavirus Outbreak." *Huffington Post UK*, July 5, 2020. https://www.huffingtonpost.co.uk/entry/coronavirus-chinese-heritage-racism_uk_5eb33422c5b6526942a1620d.

Chapman, Mary, ed. *Becoming Sui Sin Far: Early Fiction, Journalism, and Travel Writing by Edith Maude Eaton.* Montreal: McGill–Queen's University Press, 2016.

Chau, Hing-wah, Karine Dupre, and Bixia Xu. "Melbourne Chinatown as an Iconic Enclave." *Proceedings of the 13th Australasian Urban History Planning History Conference 2016*, edited by Caryl Bosman and Aysin Dedekortut-Howes, 39-51. Gold Coast: Griffith University, 2016.

Chaucer, Geoffrey. *The Canterbury Tales.* Edited by Jill Mann. New York: Penguin, 2005.

Chen, Mel Y. *Animacies: Biopolitics, Racial Mattering, and Queer Affect.* Durham: Duke University Press, 2012.

Cheung, Floyd. "Early Chinese American Autobiography: Reconsidering the Works of Yan Phou Lee and Yung Wing." *a/b: Auto/Biography Studies* 18, no. 1 (2003): 45–61.

———. "*Les Cenelles* and Quadroon Balls: 'Hidden Transcripts' of Resistance and Domination in New Orleans, 1803–1845." *The Southern Literary Journal* 29, no. 2 (Spring 1997): 5–16.

Chin, Frank. "Come All Ye Asian American Writers of the Real and the Fake." In *The Big Aiiieeeee! An Anthology of Chinese American and Japanese American Literature*, edited by Jeffrey Paul Chan, Frank Chin, Lawson Fusao Inada, and Shawn Wong, 1–92. New York: Meridian, 1991.

"Chinatown Is a Menace to Health!," *The San Francisco Call*, November 23, 1901: 3. *Chronicling America: Historic American Newspapers*, Library of Congress; https://chroniclingamerica.loc.gov/lccn/sn85066387/1901-11-23/ed-1/seq-3/.

Chinese Equal Rights League. *Appeal of the Chinese Equal Rights League to the People of the United States for Equality of Manhood.* New York: Chinese Equal Rights League, 1893.

"A Chinese League." *The San Francisco Call.* May 27, 1897: 6.

Chou, Rosalind S., and Joe R. Feagin. *The Myth of the Model Minority: Asian Americans Facing Racism, Second Edition.* New York: Routledge, 2015.

Chu, Patricia P. *Assimilating Asians: Gendered Strategies of Authorship in Asian America.* Durham: Duke University Press, 2002.

———. *Where I Have Never Been: Migration, Melancholia, and Memory in Asian American Narratives of Return.* Philadelphia: Temple University Press, 2019.

Coleman, Edward Maceo, ed. *Creole Voices: Poems in French by Free Men of Color.* Washington, DC: Associated, 1945.

Coles, Kim, Kim F. Hall, and Ayanna Thompson. "BlacKKKShakespearean: A Call to Action for Medieval and Early Modern Studies." *Profession* (Modern Language Association, November 19, 2019). https://profession.mla.org/blackkkshakespearean-a-call-to-action-for-medieval-and-early-modern-studies.

"The 'Color Line' Excites the Ladies," *San Francisco Examiner*, November 8, 1901: 1.

Crane, Susan. *The Performance of Self: Ritual, Clothing, and Identity During the Hundred Years War.* Philadelphia: University of Pennsylvania Press, 2011.

Crenshaw, Kimberlé Williams. "Mapping the Margins: Intersectionality, Identity Politics, and Violence Against Women of Color." *Stanford Law Review* 42, no. 6 (1991): 1241–99.

"Damilola Taylor: How his Killing Shocked a Nation." *BBC News Magazine*, November 27, 2010. https://www.bbc.com/news/magazine-11848488.

"Damilola Taylor: Timeline." *BBC News*, last updated August 9, 2006. http://news.bbc.co.uk/2/hi/uk_news/4791094.stm.

Dante Alighieri. *Vita Nova: Translation, Introduction, and Notes*. Translated by Andrew Frisardi. Evanston: Northwestern University Press, 2012.

D'Arcens, Louise, ed. *The Cambridge Companion to Medievalism*. Cambridge: Cambridge University Press, 2016.

Das Gupta, Tania. "Teaching Anti-Racist Research in the Academy." *Teaching Sociology* 31, no. 4 (October 2003): 456–68.

Dasgupta, Rohit K. "*Game of Thrones* in India: Of Piracy, Queer Intimacies and Viral Memes." In *Fan Phenomena: Game of Thrones*, edited by Kavita Mudan Finn, 152–62. Chicago: University of Chicago Press, 2017.

Davis, Kathleen, and Nadia Altschul, eds. *Medievalisms in the Postcolonial World: The Idea of "the Middle Ages" Outside Europe*. Baltimore: Johns Hopkins University Press, 2010.

Davison, Mark, and Lauren Meier, in collaboration with the Pacific Great Basin Support Office. *Site History*, vol. 1 of *Cultural Landscape Report for Angel Island Immigration Station*. Brookline: Olmsted Center for Landscape Preservation, National Park Service, December 2002.

Deering, Mabel Craft. "The Firebrand: A Short Story of Old San Francisco." *Sunset Magazine* 19, no. 5 (September 1907): 453–61.

"Denis Kearney." *Chicago Tribune*. July 20, 1883.

Diagne, Souleymane Bachir. "Négritude." *Stanford Encyclopedia of Philosophy*, May 24, 2010, revised May 23, 2018. https://plato.stanford.edu/entries/negritude.

Diaz, Natalie. "Abecedarian Requiring Further Examination of Anglikan Seraphym Subjugation of a Wild Indian Rezervation." In Natalie Diaz, *When My Brother Was an Aztec*, 5. Port Townsend: Copper Canyon, 2012.

Dinshaw, Carolyn. *Getting Medieval: Sexualities and Communities, Pre- and Postmodern.* Durham: Duke University Press, 1999.

——. *How Soon Is Now? Medieval Texts, Amateur Readers, and the Queerness of Time*. Durham: Duke University Press, 2012.

——. "Pale Faces: Race, Religion, and Affect in Chaucer's Texts and Their Readers." *Studies in the Age of Chaucer* 23 (2000): 19–40.

Douglass, Frederick. "I Am a Radical Woman Suffrage Man: An Address Delivered in Boston, Massachusetts, May 28, 1888." In *The Speeches of Frederick Douglass: A Critical Edition*, edited by John R. McKivigan, Julie Husband, and Heather L. Kaufman, 401–13. New Haven: Yale University Press, 2018.

——. "Letter to Francis Jackson, January 29, 1846." Boston Public Library, Boston, MA. https://docsouth.unc.edu/neh/douglass/support6.html.

——. "Letter to William Lloyd Garrison, January 27, 1846." In *The Life and Writings of Frederick Douglass, Vol. 1*, edited by Philip S. Foner, 133. New York: International, 1950. https://glc.yale.edu/letter-william-lloyd-garrison-january-27-1846.

——. *Life and Times of Frederick Douglass, Written by Himself.* Rev. ed. 1881; Hartford: Park, 1892.

——. *My Bondage and My Freedom.* New York: Miller, Orton & Mulligan, 1855.

——. *The Narrative of Frederick Douglass, an American Slave, Written by Himself.* Boston: Anti-Slavery Office, 1845.

——. "Our Composite Nationality: An Address Delivered in Boston, Massachusetts, 7 December 1869." In *The Speeches of Frederick Douglass: A Critical Edition*, edited by John R. McKivigan, Julie Husband, and Heather L. Kaufman, 278–303. New Haven: Yale University Press, 2018.

———. "The Race Problem" (October 21, 1890, Metropolitan AME Church, Washington, DC). In *Great Speeches by Frederick Douglass*. Edited by James Daley, 88–104. Mineola: Dover, 2013.

Du Bois, W. E. B. *The Souls of Black Folk: Essays and Sketches*. Chicago: McClurg, 1903.

Dunbar-Nelson, Alice. *The Goodness of St. Rocque, and Other Stories*. New York: Dodd, Mead, 1899.

———. "The Negro Woman and the Ballot." *Messenger* 9 (April 1927): 111.

———. "People of Color in Louisiana: Part 1." *The Journal of Negro History* 1, no. 4 (October 1916): 361–76.

———. "Stones of the Village." In *The Works of Alice Dunbar-Nelson*. 3 vols. Edited by Akasha Gloria Hull (Gloria T. Hull), 3:3–33. New York: Oxford University Press, 1988.

———. *Violets and Other Tales*. Boston: Monthly Review, 1895.

Dy, Aristotle C., sj. "The Virgin Mary or Guanyin: The Syncretic Nature of Chinese Religion in the Philippines." *Philippine Social Review* 62 (2014): 41–63.

Ebrahimji, Alisha, and Alicia Lee. "Meet the Asian Americans helping to uproot racism in their communities." *CNN*, June 13, 2020. https://www.cnn.com/2020/06/13/us/asian-americans-blm-conversations-trnd/index.html.

Echenberg, Myron. *Plague Ports: The Global Impact of Bubonic Plague, 1894–1901*. New York: New York University Press, 2007.

Elizabeth, Lindsay. "A Short History of African Headwrap." *National Clothing: Africa*, April 3, 2018. http://nationalclothing.org/africa/256-a-short-history-of-african-headwrap.html.

Eng, David L., and Sinhee Han. "A Dialogue on Racial Melancholia." *Psychoanalytic Dialogues* 10, no. 4 (2000): 667–700.

Erdrich, Heid E., ed. *New Poets of Native Nations*. Minneapolis: Graywolf, 2018.

Espiritu, Yến Lê. *Body Counts: The Vietnam War and Militarized Refuge(es)*. Berkeley: University of California Press, 2014.

"Evidences that Chinamen in America are Mentally Broadening and Shaking Off Racial Faults." *New York Tribune Illustrated Supplement*, May 24, 1903: 5–6.

Fauvelle, François-Xavier. *The Golden Rhinoceros: Histories of the African Middle Ages*. Translated by Troy Rice. Princeton: Princeton University Press, 2018.

Feng Xin-ming, trans. "The Ballad of Mulan—Anonymous" (English translation with simplified Chinese characters and pinyin). http://tsoidug.org/Literary/Mulan_Ballad_Simp.pdf.

Ferens, Dominika. *Edith and Winnifred Eaton: Chinatown Missions and Japanese Romances*. Chicago: University of Illinois Press, 2002.

Finn, Kavita Mudan. "Decolonizing Popular Medievalism: The Case of *Game of Thrones*." March 28, 2018. https://kvmfinn.wordpress.com/2018/03/28/decolonizing-popular-medievalism-the-case-of-game-of-thrones.

———. "Introduction." In *Fan Phenomena: Game of Thrones*, edited by Kavita Mudan Finn, 5–17. Chicago: University of Chicago Press, 2017.

———. "Queen of Sad Mischance: Medievalism, 'Realism,' and the Case of Cersei Lannister." In *Queenship and the Women of Westeros: Female Agency and Advice in Game of Thrones and A Song of Ice and Fire*, edited by Zita Eva Rohr and Lisa Benz. 29–52. New York: Palgrave, 2020.

Fong, Grace S. "Engendering the Lyric: Her Image and Voice in Song." In *Voices of the Song Lyric in China*, edited by Pauline Yu, 107–44. Berkeley: University of California Press, 1994.

Forni, Kathleen. *Chaucer's Afterlife: Adaptations in Recent Popular Culture*. Jefferson, NC: McFarland, 2013.

Galvez, Marisa. *Songbook: How Lyrics Became Poetry in Medieval Europe.* Chicago: University of Chicago Press, 2012.

Ganim, John M. *Medievalism and Orientalism: Three Essays on Literature, Architecture, and Cultural Identity.* New York: Palgrave, 2005.

——. "Native Studies: Orientalism and Medievalism." In *The Postcolonial Middle Ages*, edited by Jeffrey Jerome Cohen, 123–34. New York: Palgrave, 2000.

—— and Shayne Aaron Legassie, eds. *Cosmopolitanism and the Middle Ages.* New York: Palgrave, 2013.

Ganz, Shoshannah. *Eastern Encounters: Canadian Women's Writing about the East, 1867–1929.* Taipei: National Taiwan University Press, 2017.

García Román, Gabriel. "About" and "Queer Icons." Artist Website. http://www.gabrielgarciaroman.com.

——. "ALAN: Alán Pelaez Lopez." Artist Website. http:/ / www.gabrielgarciaroman.com/ queer-icons-home#/alan.

Gbadamosi, Gabriel. "The Road to Brixton Market: A Post-colonial Travelogue." In *Travel Writing and Empire: Postcolonial Theory in Transit*, edited by Steve Clark, 185–94. London: Zed, 1999.

Gikandi, Simon. "Response: Africa and the Signs of Medievalism." In *Medievalisms in the Postcolonial World: The Idea of "the Middle Ages" Outside Europe*, edited by Kathleen Davis and Nadia Altschul, 369–82. Baltimore: Johns Hopkins University Press, 2009.

Gilchrist, Tracy E. "What Is Toxic Masculinity?" *The Advocate*, December 11, 2017. https:// www.advocate.com/women/2017/12/11/what-toxic-masculinity.

Gilroy, Paul. *The Black Atlantic: Modernity and Double Consciousness.* Cambridge, MA: Harvard University Press, 1993.

Glasgow, Hamidah. "Q&A: Gabriel García Román." *Strange Fire*, October 27, 2017. http:// www.strangefirecollective.com/qa-gabriel-garcia-roman.

Goddard, Lynette. *Staging Black Feminisms: Identity, Politics, Performance.* Basingstoke: Palgrave Macmillan, 2007.

Godin, Mélisa. "Black and Asian People Are Two to Three Times More Likely to Die of COVID-19, U.K. Study Finds." *Time*, May 6, 2020. https:/ / time.com/ 5832807/ coronavirus-race-analysis-uk.

Goldman, Jennifer. "Exhibitions: Coaching Citizenship." *Verso: The Blog of the Huntington Library, Art Museum, and Botanical Gardens*, November 1, 2013. https://www.huntington. org/verso/2018/08/exhibitions-coaching-citizenship.

Gomez, Andrew, and University of Puget Sound students. "Mapping Anti-Chinese Violence." *The Tacoma Method*, Spring 2017 (revised Spring 2018). https://www.tacomamethod. com/mapping-antichinese-violence.

Gomez, Michael A. *African Dominion: A New History of Empire in Early and Medieval West Africa.* Princeton: Princeton University Press, 2018.

Grady, Constance. "Why the term 'BIPOC' is so complicated, explained by linguists." Vox, June 30, 2020. https:/ / www.vox.com/ 2020/ 6/ 30/ 21300294/ bipoc-what-does-it-mean-critical-race-linguistics-jonathan-rosa-deandra-miles-hercules.

Green, Monica H. "On Learning How to Teach the Black Death." *History of Philosophy of Science and Science Teaching* Note (March 2018): 7–33.

——. "Taking 'Pandemic' Seriously: Making the Black Death Global." *The Medieval Globe* 1 (2014): 27–61.

—— and Jonathan Hsy. "Disability, Disease, and a Global Middle Ages." In *Teaching a Global Middle Ages*, edited by Geraldine Heng. Modern Language Association, forthcoming.

Hall, Kim F. *Things of Darkness: Economies of Race and Gender in Early Modern England.* Ithaca: Cornell University Press, 1995.

Harris, Carissa M. *Obscene Pedagogies: Transgressive Talk and Sexual Education in Late Medieval Britain.* Ithaca, NY: Cornell University Press, 2018.

——. "Pastourelle Fictionalities." *New Literary History* 51, no. 1 (Winter 2020): 239–42.

Harris, Cheryl I. "Whiteness as Property." *Harvard Law Review* 106 (1993): 1707–91.

Hassan, Waïl S. "Orientalism and Cultural Translation in the Work of Ameen Rihani." In *The Book of Khalid: A Critical Edition*, edited by Todd Fine. 369–400. Syracuse: Syracuse University Press, 2016.

Hayoun, Massoud. "Muslim Ban: Japanese and Muslim Americans Join Forces." *Al Jazeera*, February 1, 2017. https://www.aljazeera.com/indepth/features/2017/02/muslim-ban-japanese-muslim-americans-join-forces-170201055155362.html.

Headley, Bernard D. "'Black on Black' Crime: The Myth and the Reality." *Crime and Social Justice* 20 (1983): 50–62.

Heng, Geraldine. "Early Globalities, and Its Questions and Methods: An Inquiry into the State of Theory and Critique." *Exemplaria* 26, nos. 2–3 (Summer/Fall 2014): 234–53.

——. *Empire of Magic: Medieval Romance and the Politics of Cultural Fantasy.* New York: Columbia University Press, 2003.

——. *England and the Jews: How Religion and Violence Created the First Racial State in the West.* Cambridge: Cambridge University Press, 2019.

——. *The Invention of Race in the European Middle Ages.* Cambridge: Cambridge University Press, 2018.

——. "An Ordinary Ship and Its Stories of Early Globalism: World Travel, Mass Production, and Art in the Global Middle Ages." *Journal of Medieval Worlds* 1, no. 1 (2019): 11–54.

Herd, David, and Anna Pincus, eds. *Refugee Tales.* Manchester: Comma, 2016.

Hernández, Kelly Lytle. *Migra!: A History of the U.S. Border Patrol.* Berkeley: University of California Press, 2010.

Ho, Jennifer Ann. *Racial Ambiguity in Asian American Culture.* New Brunswick: Rutgers University Press, 2015.

Hobbs, Allyson. *A Chosen Exile: A History of Racial Passing in American Life.* Cambridge, MA: Harvard University Press, 2014.

Hopkins, Ruth. "America's Legacy of Anti-Indigenous Violence." *Teen Vogue*, November 19, 2019. https:/ / www.teenvogue.com/ story/ sand-creek-massacre-wounded-knee-mass-shootings.

Howard, June. "Sui Sin Far's American Words." *Comparative American Studies* 6, no. 2 (June 2008): 144–60.

Hsu, Hsuan L., ed. *Mrs. Spring Fragrance: Edith Maude Eaton/Sui Sin Far.* Peterborough: Broadview, 2011.

——. *Sitting in Darkness: Mark Twain's Asia and Comparative Racialization.* New York: New York University Press, 2015.

Hsy, Jonathan. "Antiracist Medievalisms: Lessons from Chinese Exclusion." *In the Middle*, February 16, 2018. https:/ / www.inthemedievalmiddle.com/ 2018/ 02/ antiracist-medievalisms-lessons-from.html.

——. "Chaucer's Brown Faces: Race, Interpretation, Adaptation." *Chaucer Review* (forthcoming).

——. "Co-disciplinarity." In *Medievalism: Key Critical Terms*, edited by Elizabeth Emery and Richard Utz, 43–51. Cambridge: Brewer, 2014.

——. "Distemporality: Richard III's Body and the Car Park." *Upstart: A Journal of English Renaissance Studies*, August 12, 2013. https://upstart.sites.clemson.edu/Essays/richard-forum/distemporality.xhtml.

——. "Language Ecologies: Ethics, Community, and Digital Affect." *PMLA* 131, no. 2 (March 2016): 373–80.

——. "Linguistic Entrapment: Interlanguage, Bivernacularity, and Life Across Tongues." *postmedieval* 9, no. 2 (June 2018): 196–208.

——. "Mobile Language-Networks and Medieval Travel Writing." *postmedieval* 4, no. 2 (2013): 177–91.

——. "Racial Dynamics in the Medieval Classroom." *What Is Racial Difference?* Blog created by Cord Whitaker, Wellesley College, January 21, 2016. https://blogs.wellesley.edu/whatisracialdifference/2016/01/21/racial-dynamics-in-the-medieval-literature-classroom.

——. "Teaching the Wife of Bath through Adaptation." *Global Chaucers*, November 21, 2014. https://globalchaucers.wordpress.com/2014/11/21/teaching-the-wife-of-bath-through-adaptation.

——. *Trading Tongues: Merchants, Multilingualism, and Medieval Literature*. Columbus: Ohio State University Press, 2013.

—— and Candace Barrington. "Queer Time, Queer Forms: Noir Medievalism and Patience Agbabi's *Telling Tales*." In *Time Mechanics: Postmodern Poetry and Queer Medievalisms*, edited by David Hadbawnik and Scott Gunem. Kalamazoo: Medieval Institute Publications, forthcoming.

—— and Julie Orlemanski. "Race and Medieval Studies: A Partial Bibliography." *postmedieval* 8, no. 4 (December 2017): 500–531. https://doi.org/10.1057/s41280-017-0072-0.

——, Tory V. Pearman, and Joshua R. Eyler, "Editors' Introduction: Disabilities in Motion." In *A Cultural History of Disability in the Middle Ages*, edited by Hsy, Pearman, and Eyler, 1–18. London: Bloomsbury, 2020.

Huang, Yunte. *Transpacific Imaginations: History, Literature, Counterpoetics*. Cambridge, MA: Harvard University Press, 2008.

Hull, Akasha Gloria (Gloria T. Hull). *Color, Sex, and Poetry: Three Women Writers of the Harlem Renaissance*. Bloomington: University of Indiana Press, 1987.

——, ed. *Give Us Each Day: The Diary of Alice Dunbar-Nelson*. New York: Norton, 1986.

Hurley, Mary Kate, Jonathan Hsy, and A.B. Kraebel, "Editors' Introduction: Thinking Across Tongues." *postmedieval* 8, no. 3 (September 2017): 270–76.

Itagaki, Lynn Mie. *Civil Racism: The 1992 Los Angeles Rebellion and the Crisis of Racial Burnout*. Minneapolis: University of Minnesota Press, 2016.

Jabour, Tania Nicole. "Spectacular Subjects: Race, Rhetoric, and Visuality in American Public Cultures (1870–1900)." PhD diss., University of California, San Diego, 2015.

James, Jennifer C. *A Freedom Bought with Blood: African American War Literature from the Civil War to World War II*. Chapel Hill: University of North Carolina Press, 2007.

—— and Cynthia Wu. "Editors' Introduction: Race, Ethnicity, Disability, and Literature: Intersections and Interventions." *MELUS* 31, no. 3 (Fall 2006): 3–13.

"Julian Talamantez Brolaski: 2019 Fellow-In-Residence." *The Pew Center for Arts & Heritage*, October 19, 2019. https://www.pewcenterarts.org/people/julian-talamantez-brolaski.

Kabir, Ananya Jahanara, and Deanne Williams, eds. *Postcolonial Approaches to the European Middle Ages: Translating Cultures*. Cambridge: Cambridge University Press, 2005.

Kafer, Alison and Eunjung Kim. "Disability and the Edges of Intersectionality." In *Cambridge Companion to Literature and Disability*, edited by Clare Barker and Stuart Murray, 123–38. Cambridge: Cambridge University Press, 2018.

Kambhampaty, Anna Purna, and Haruka Sakaguchi. "'I Will Not Stand Silent.' 10 Asian Americans Reflect on Racism During the Pandemic and the Need for Equality." *Time*, June 25, 2020. https://time.com/5858649/racism-coronavirus.

Kandil, Caitlin Yoshiko. "Muslim-American Manzanar Pilgrimage Finds Parallels Between Internment, Modern Day." *NBC News*, May 4, 2017. https://www.nbcnews.com/news/asian-america/muslim-american-manzanar-pilgrimage-finds-parallels-between-internment-modern-day-n754561.

Kao, Wan-Chuan. "#palefacesmatter?" *In the Middle*, July 26, 2016. https://www.inthemedievalmiddle.com/2016/07/palefacesmatter-wan-chuan-kao.html.

——. "White Attunement." *New Chaucer Society* Blog, November 9, 2018. https://newchaucersociety.org/blog/entry/white-attunement.

——. *White before Whiteness in the Late Middle Ages*. Manchester: Manchester University Press, forthcoming.

Kaufman, Amy S., and Paul B. Sturtevant. *The Devil's Historians: How Modern Extremists Abuse the Medieval Past*. Toronto: University of Toronto Press, 2020.

Kearney, Milo, and Manuel Medrano. *Medieval Culture and the Mexican American Borderlands*. College Station: Texas A&M University Press, 2001.

Keita, Maghan. "Race: What the Bookstore Hid." In *Why the Middle Ages Matter: Medieval Light on Modern Injustice*, edited by Ceila Chazelle, Simon Doubleday, Felice Lifshitz, and Amy G. Remensnyder, 130–40. London: Routledge, 2011.

Khanmohamadi, Shirin A. *In Light of Another's Word: European Ethnography in the Middle Ages*. Philadelphia: University of Pennsylvania Press, 2013.

Kiaer, Jieun, Jennifer Guest, and Xiaofan Amy Li. *Translation and Literature in East Asia: Between Visibility and Invisibility*. London: Routledge, 2019.

Kim, Dorothy. *The Alt-Medieval: Digital Whiteness and Medieval Studies*. Minneapolis: University of Minnesota Press, forthcoming 2021.

——. "The Question of Race in Beowulf." *JSTOR Daily*, September 25, 2019. https://daily.jstor.org/the-question-of-race-in-beowulf.

——. "White Supremacists Have Weaponized an Imaginary Viking Past. It's Time to Reclaim the Real History." *Time*, April 12, 2019. https://time.com/5569399/viking-history-white-nationalists.

Kingston, Maxine Hong. *China Men*. 1977. Reprint, New York: Vintage, 1989.

Kinoshita, Sharon. "Deprovincializing the Middle Ages." In *The Worlding Project: Doing Cultural Studies in the Era of Globalization*, edited by Rob Wilson and Christopher Leigh Connery, 61–75. Berkeley: North Atlantic, 2007.

Komunyakaa, Yusef. *Neon Vernacular: New and Selected Poems*. Middletown: Wesleyan University Press, 1993.

——. "The Ruin." In *The Word Exchange: Anglo-Saxon Poems in Translation*, edited by Greg Delaney and Michael Matto, 298–302. New York: Norton, 2011.

Lai, Him Mark, Genny Lim, and Judy Yung. *Island: Poetry and History of Chinese Immigrants on Angel Island, 1910–1940*. 2nd ed. Seattle: University of Washington Press, 2014.

Lalla, Barbara. *Postcolonialisms: Caribbean Rereading of Medieval English Discourse*. Kingston: University of the West Indies Press, 2008.

Lanusse, Armand. *Les Cenelles: Choix de poesies indigenes*. New Orleans: Lauve, 1845.

Lau, Travis Chi Wing. "On Virality, Corona or Otherwise." *Synapsis*, May 15, 2020. https://medicalhealthhumanities.com/2020/05/15/on-virality-corona-or-otherwise.

Lee, Erika, and Judy Yung, *Angel Island: Immigrant Gateway to America.* Oxford: Oxford University Press, 2010.

Lee, Yan Phou (李恩富). *When I Was a Boy in China.* Boston, MA: Lothrop, Lee & Shepard, 1887.

———. "Why I am Not a Heathen: A Rejoinder to Wong Chin Foo." *The North American Review* 145, no. 370 (September 1887): 306–12.

Lei, Cecilia. "The Little-Known History of Japanese Internment on Angel Island." *KQED News*, May 28, 2020. https://www.kqed.org/news/11821133/the-little-known-history-of-japanese-internment-on-angel-island.

Leong, Jeffrey Thomas. *Wild Geese Sorrow: The Chinese Wall Inscriptions at Angel Island.* Calypso Editions, 2018.

Lew-Williams, Beth. *The Chinese Must Go: Violence, Exclusion, and the Making of the Alien in America.* Cambridge, MA: Harvard University Press, 2018.

Li, H. L. *Chinese Flower Arrangement.* 1956. Reprint, Mineola: Dover, 2002.

Lin, Tsung-Cheng. "Knight-Errantry: Tang Frontier Poems." In *How to Read Chinese Poetry in Context: Poetic Culture from Antiquity Through the Tang*, edited by Zong-Qi Cai, 159–72. New York: Columbia University Press, 2018.

Little, Arthur L., Jr. "Re-Historicizing Race, White Melancholia, and the Shakespearean Property." *Shakespeare Quarterly* 61, no. 1 (Spring 2016): 84–103.

Little, Mary Bernadette, RSM [née C. Dorothy M. Little]. *You Did It Unto Me: The Story of Alpha.* Cincinnati: Beyond the Trees, 2013.

Liu, Haiming. "Kung Pao Kosher: Jewish Americans and Chinese Restaurants in New York." *Journal of Chinese Overseas* 6, no. 1 (2010): 80–101.

Liu, Wan. "Analysis of the Poems Inscribed or Composed at the Angel Island Immigration Station." *Poetry and Inscriptions: Translation and Analysis*, prepared by Charles Egan, Wan Liu, Newton Liu, and Xing Chu Wang for the California Department of Parks and Recreation and Angel Island Immigration Station Foundation (unpublished document). Architectural Resources Group and Daniel Quan Design, 2004.

Lomuto, Sierra. "Chaucer and Humanitarian Activism." *Public Books*, April 24, 2018. https://www.publicbooks.org/chaucer-and-humanitarian-activism.

———. "Public Medievalism and the Rigor of Anti-Racist Critique." *In the Middle*, April 4, 2019. http://www.inthemedievalmiddle.com/2019/04/public-medievalism-and-rigor-of-anti.html.

Looney, Dennis. *Freedom Readers: The African American Reception of Dante Alighieri and the Divine Comedy.* Notre Dame: University of Notre Dame Press, 2011.

López, Ian Henry. *White by Law: The Legal Construction of Race.* Rev. and updated 10th anniversary ed. New York: New York University Press, 2006.

Lowe, Lisa. *The Intimacies of Four Continents.* Durham: Duke University Press, 2015.

Lundquist, Suzanne Evertsen. "Carter Revard as Autoethnographer or *Wa-thi'-gethon*." In *The Salt Companion to Carter Revard*, edited by Ellen L. Arnold, 34–59. Cambridge: Salt, 2007.

Luo, Manling. "Gender, Genre, and Discourse: The Woman Avenger in Medieval Chinese Texts." *Journal of the American Oriental Society* 134, no. 4 (October–December 2014): 579–99.

———. *Literati Storytelling in Late Medieval China.* Seattle: University of Washington Press, 2015.

Ma, Sheng-mei. *Diaspora Literature and Visual Culture: Asia in Flight.* New York: Routledge, 2011.

Madsen, Richard, and Lizhu Fan. "The Catholic Pilgrimage to Sheshan." In *Making Religion, Making the State: The Politics of Religion in Modern China*, edited by Yoshiko Ashiwa and David L. Wank, 74–95. Stanford: Stanford University Press, 2009.

Major, George MacDonald. *Lays of Chinatown and Other Verses*. New York: Ingalls Kimball, 1899.

Malory, Thomas. *Le Morte Darthur: The Winchester Manuscript*. Edited by Helen Cooper. Oxford: Oxford University Press, 1998.

Manuel Cuenca, Carme. "An Angel in the Plantation: The Economics of Slavery and the Politics of Domesticity in Caroline Lee Hentz's 'The Planter's Northern Bride.'" *Mississippi Quarterly* 5, no. 1 (Winter 1997–1998): 87–104.

Medievalists of Color. "On Race and Medieval Studies." August 1, 2017. https://medievalistsofcolor.com/statements/on-race-and-medieval-studies.

———. "Solidarity with Our Jewish Colleagues." September 6, 2017. https://medievalistsofcolor.com/statements/solidarity-with-our-jewish-colleagues.

Mishler, Peter. "Cedar Sigo on Playfulness and Poetry." *Literary Hub*, January 11, 2019. https://lithub.com/cedar-sigo-on-playfulness-and-poetry.

Miyashiro, Adam. "Decolonizing Anglo-Saxon Studies: A Response to ISAS in Honolulu." *In the Middle,* July 29, 2017. http://www.inthemedievalmiddle.com/2017/07/decolonizing-anglo-saxon-studies.html.

———. "Our Deeper Past: Race, Settler Colonialism, and Medieval Heritage Politics." *Literature Compass* 16, nos. 9–10 (September–October 2019): 1–11. https://doi.org/10.1111/lic3.12550.

Momma, Haruko. "Medievalism—Colonialism—Orientalism: Japan's Modern Identity in Natsume Soseki's *Maboroshi no Tate* and *Kairo-ko.*" In *Medievalisms in the Postcolonial World: The Idea of "The Middle Ages" Outside Europe*, edited by Kathleen Davis and Nadia Altschul, 141–73. Baltimore: Johns Hopkins University Press, 2009.

Moreland, Kim. *The Medievalist Impulse in American Literature: Twain, Adams, Fitzgerald, and Hemingway*. Charlottesville: University Press of Virginia, 1996.

Morgan, Murray. *Puget's Sound: A Narrative of Early Tacoma and the Southern Sound*. 1979. Reprint, Seattle: University of Washington Press, 2018.

Morrison, Toni. "Unspeakable Things Unspoken: The Afro-American Presence in American Literature." In Toni Morrison, *The Source of Self-Regard: Selected Essays, Speeches, and Meditations*, 161–97. New York: Knopf, 2019.

Mundo, Frank. *The Brubury Tales*. West Conshohocken: Infinity, 2010.

———. *The Brubury Tales: Illustrated Edition*. Lunatick Trading Company: USA, 2014.

———. "How I Became a Mexican." In ¡*Ban This! The BSP Anthology of Xican@ Literature*, edited by Santino J. Rivera, 1–6. Saint Augustine: Broken Sword, 2012.

Muñoz, José Esteban. *Disidentifications: Queers of Color and the Performance of Politics*. Minneapolis: University of Minnesota Press, 1999.

———. "Feeling Brown: Latina Affect, the Performativity of Race, and the Depressive Position." *Signs* 31, no. 3 (Spring 2006): 675–88.

Nelson, Marilyn. *The Cachoeira Tales and Other Poems*. Baton Rouge: Louisiana State University Press, 2005.

Ng, Su Fang. "Border Walls and Detention Islands in the Viral Age." *The Sundial*, March 31, 2020. https://medium.com/the-sundial-acmrs/border-walls-and-detention-islands-in-the-viral-age-a4bfd7c0c6de.

Niranjana, Tejaswini. *Siting Translation: History, Post-Structuralism, and the Colonial Context*. Berkeley: University of California Press, 1992.

Nirenberg, David. *Communities of Violence: Persecution of Minorities in the Middle Ages*. 1996. Reprint, Princeton: Princeton University Press, 2015.

Nodelman, Blair. "Why Jewish Activists Are on the Front Lines in Mass Protest Against ICE." *Teen Vogue*, July 9, 2019. https://www.teenvogue.com/story/never-again-jewish-activists-national-protests-against-ice.

Noel, Urayoán. "The Queer Migrant Poemics of #Latinx Instagram." *New Literary History* 50, no. 4 (Autumn 2019): 531–57.

NoiseCat, Julian Brave. "Rivers, Lakes and Water Resources." *Indigenous Peoples Atlas of Canada*. Canadian Geographic, September 25, 2018. https://indigenouspeoplesatlasofcanada.ca/article/rivers-lakes-and-water-resources.

Onishi, Yuichiro. *Transpacific Antiracism: Afro-Asian Solidarity in 20th-Century Black America, Japan, and Okinawa*. New York: New York University Press, 2013.

Oppel, Richard A., Jr., Robert Gebeloff, K. K. Rebecca Lai, Will Wright, and Mitch Smith. "The Fullest Look Yet at the Racial Inequity of Coronavirus." *The New York Times*, July 5, 2020. https://www.nytimes.com/interactive/2020/07/05/us/coronavirus-latinos-african-americans-cdc-data.html.

Ossa, Luisa Marcela, and Debbie Lee-DiStefano, eds. *Afro-Asian Connections in Latin America and the Caribbean*. London: Rowman & Littlefield, 2019.

Otaño-Gracia, Nahir. "Lost in Our Field: Racism and the International Congress on Medieval Studies." *Medievalists of Color*, July 24, 2018. https://medievalistsofcolor.com/race-in-the-profession/lost-in-our-field-racism-and-the-international-congress-on-medieval-studies.

———— and Daniel Armenti. "Constructing Prejudice in the Middle Ages and the Repercussions of Racism Today." *Medieval Feminist Forum* 53, no. 1 (2017): 176–201.

Ouyang Yu (歐陽昱). *The Kingsbury Tales: A Novel*. Blackheath: Brandl & Schlesinger, 2008.

Palumbo-DeSimone, Christine. "Race, Womanhood, and Tragic Mulatta: Issues of Ambiguity." In *Multiculturalism: Roots and Realities*, edited by C. James Trotman, 125–36. Bloomington: Indiana University Press, 2002.

Park, Josephine Nock-Hee. "The Poetics of Consolation: Japanese Aesthetics and American Incarceration." *New Literary History* 50, no. 4 (Autumn 2019): 565–80.

Peachey, Paul. "Damilola died 'after bullies taunted his African accent.'" *The Independent*, March 21, 2002. https://www.independent.co.uk/news/uk/crime/damilola-died-after-bullies-taunted-his-african-accent-9159067.html.

Pelaez Lopez, Alán. "About Me." Artist Website. http://www.alanpelaez.com/about-me.

Perlman, Selig. "The Anti-Chinese Agitation in California." In *History of Labour in the United States*. 4 vols., edited by John R. Commons, David J. Saposs, Helen L. Sumner, E. B. Mittelman, H. E. Hoagland, Julia B. Andrews, John B. Andrews, Selig Perlman, 2:252–68. New York: Macmillan, 1918.

Pettinger, Alasdair. *Frederick Douglass and Scotland, 1846: Living an Antislavery Life*. Edinburgh: Edinburgh University Press, 2018.

Poetry Center Digital Archive. "Garrett Caples and Julian Talamantez Brolaski: February 15, 2018." https://diva.sfsu.edu/collections/poetrycenter/bundles/232922.

Prendergast, Thomas A., and Stephanie Trigg. *Affective Medievalism: Love, Abjection, and Discontent*. Manchester: Manchester University Press, 2018.

Quayson, Ato. *Aesthetic Nervousness: Disability and the Crisis of Representation*. New York: Columbia University Press, 2007.

RaceB4Race Executive Board. "It's Time to End the Publishing Gatekeeping!" *The Sundial*, June 11, 2020. https://medium.com/the-sundial-acmrs/its-time-to-end-the-publishing-gatekeeping-75207525f587.

Raimon, Eve Allegra. *The "Tragic Mulatta" Revisited: Race and Nationalism in Nineteenth-Century Antislavery Fiction.* New Brunswick: Rutgers University Press, 2004.

Rajabzadeh, Shokoofeh. "The Depoliticized Saracen and Muslim Erasure." *Literature Compass* 16, nos. 9–10 (September–October 2019): 1–8. https://doi.org/10.1111/lic3.12548.

Rajendran, Shyama. "Undoing 'the Vernacular': Dismantling Structures of Raciolinguistic Supremacy." *Literature Compass* 16, nos. 9–10 (September–October 2019): 1–13. https://doi.org/10.1111/lic3.12544.

Ramazani, Jahan. "Poetry and Race: An Introduction." *New Literary History* 50, no. 4 (Autumn 2019): vii–xxxviii.

Rambaran-Olm, Mary. "'Black Death' Matters: A Modern Take on a Medieval Pandemic." *Medium*, June 5, 2020. https://medium.com/@mrambaranolm/black-death-matters-a-modern-take-on-a-medieval-pandemic-8b1cf4062d9e.

———. "'Black Death' Matters—Mary Rambaran-Olm." *Historian Speaks*, June 5, 2020. https://historianspeaks.org/f/black-death-matters--mary-rambaran-olm.

———. "'Houston, We Have a Problem': Erasing Black Scholars in Old English Literature." *The Sundial*, March 3, 2020. https://medium.com/the-sundial-acmrs/houston-we-have-a-problem-erasing-black-scholars-in-old-english-821121495dc.

———. "Misnaming the Medieval: Rejecting 'Anglo-Saxon' Studies." *History Workshop Online*, November 4, 2019. http://www.historyworkshop.org.uk/misnaming-the-medieval-rejecting-anglo-saxon-studies.

———, M. Breann Leake, and Micah James Goodrich, eds. "Race, Revulsion, and Revolution." *postmedieval* 11, no. 4 (December 2020).

Rampersad, Arnold, and David Roessel, eds. *The Collected Poems of Langston Hughes.* New York: Vintage, 1994.

Rana, Swati. "Brownness: Mixed Identifications in Minority Immigrant Literature, 1900–1960." PhD diss., University of California, Berkeley, 2012.

Randall. "Asian Americans Suffer Higher Death Rate from COVID-19." *AsAmNews*, July 13, 2020. https://asamnews.com/2020/07/13/death-rate-of-asian-americans-in-some-cities-is-3-times-higher-than-general-population.

Raukko, Tanya, and Charis Poon. "Asian American Outlook. A Matter of Survival: Navigating Media During the COVID-19 Pandemic." *InterTrend*, April 5, 2020. https://intertrend.com/news/asian-american-outlook-a-matter-of-survival-navigating-media-during-the-COVID-19-pandemic.

Renshaw, Daniel. "Prejudice and Paranoia: A Comparative Study of Antisemitism and Sinophobia in Turn-of-the-century Britain." *Patterns of Prejudice* 50, no. 1 (2016): 38–60.

Revard, Carter. "Some Riddles in Old English Alliterative Verse." *Florilegium* 18, no. 2 (2001): 1–9.

Rihani, Ameen. *The Book of Khalid: A Critical Edition.* Edited by Todd Fine. Syracuse: Syracuse University Press, 2016.

Risse, Guenter B. *Plague, Fear, and Politics in San Francisco's Chinatown.* Baltimore: Johns Hopkins University Press, 2012.

Roberts, Sir Rev. Oliver Ayer. *The California Pilgrimage of Boston Commandery Knights Templars, August 4–September 4, 1883.* Boston: Mudge, 1884.

Rothman, Lily. "50 Years Ago This Week: Vietnam and the Black Soldier," *Time*, May 22, 2017. https://time.com/4780493/1967-vietnam-race/.

Rubin, Miri. *Gentile Tales: The Narrative Assault on Late Medieval Jews.* Philadelphia: University of Pennsylvania Press, 1999.

Said, Edward W. *Orientalism.* London: Routledge & Kegan Paul, 1978.

Samei, Maija Bell. "Tang Women at the Public/Private Divide." In *How To Read Chinese Poetry in Context: Poetic Culture from Antiquity Through the Tang*, edited by Zong-Qi Cai, 185–204. New York: Columbia University Press, 2018.

Schwartz, Daniel B. *Ghetto: The History of a Word*. Cambridge, MA: Harvard University Press, 2019.

Scott, Emmett J. *Scott's Official History of the American Negro in the World War*. Chicago: Homewood Press, ca. 1919.

"The Scourge of the Century!," *Lincoln County Leader*, Toledo, Lincoln County, OR, May 11, 1900. *Chronicling America: Historic American Newspapers*. Library of Congress; https://chroniclingamerica.loc.gov/lccn/sn85033162/1900-05-11/ed-1/seq-2/.

Seligman, Scott D. *The First Chinese American: The Remarkable Life of Wong Chin Foo*. Hong Kong: Hong Kong University Press, 2013.

——. "The Night New York's Chinese Went Out for Jews: How a 1903 Chinatown Fundraiser for Pogrom Victims United Two Persecuted Peoples." *China Heritage Quarterly* 27 (September 2011): n.p. http://www.chinaheritagequarterly.org/tien-hsia.php?searchterm=027_jews.inc&issue=027.

Sen, Sharmila. *Not Quite Not White: Losing and Finding Race in America*. New York: Penguin, 2018.

Shah, Nayan. *Contagious Divides: Epidemics and Race in San Francisco's Chinatown*. Berkeley: University of California Press, 2001.

Shakespeare, William. *Troilus and Cressida*. Edited by Barbara A. Mowat and Paul Westerine. Washington, DC: Folger Shakespeare Library, 2007.

Sharma, Nitasha Tamar. "Brown." In *Keywords for Asian American Studies*, edited by Cathy J. Schlund-Vials, Linda Trinh Võ, and K. Scott Wong, 18–20. New York: New York University Press, 2015.

Sheshagiri, Urmila. "Modernity's (yellow) perils: Dr. Fu-Manchu and English Race Paranoia." *Cultural Critique* 26 (Winter 2006): 162–94.

Shih, David. "The Seduction of Origins: Sui Sin Far and the Race for Tradition." In *Form and Transformation in Asian American Literature*, edited by Zhou Xiaojing and Samina Najmi, 48–76. Seattle: University of Washington Press, 2005.

Sibara, Jennifer Barager. "Disease, Disability, and the Alien Body in the Literature of Sui Sin Far." *MELUS* 39, no. 1 (Spring 2014): 56–81.

Singh, Maanvi. "Not Your Mother's Catholic Frescoes: Radiant Portraits of Queer People of Color." *Code Switch: NPR (National Public Radio)*, May 28, 2015. https://www.npr.org/sections/codeswitch/2015/05/28/409770203.

"Sir Knights." *Salt Lake Daily Herald*, August 18, 1883: 8.

Skyhorse, Brandon, and Lisa Page, eds. *We Wear the Mask: Fifteen True Stories of Passing in America*. Beacon, MA: Beacon, 2017.

Smith, Laura. "'Don't Be Too Careful of Your Silks and Rags': Domesticity and Race in Nineteenth-Century American Literature." *Literature Compass* 9, no. 5 (2012): 343–56.

Som, Brandon. *The Tribute Horse*. Brooklyn: Nightboat, 2014.

Song Gang (宋剛). "The Many Faces of Our Lady: Chinese Encounters with the Virgin Mary between the Seventh and Seventeenth Centuries." *Monumenta Serica* 66, no. 2 (December 2018): 303–57.

Song, Min Hyoung. "Sentimentalism and Sui Sin Far." *Legacy* 20, nos. 1–2 (2003): 134–52.

——. "The Unknowable and Sui Sin Far: The Epistemological Limits of 'Oriental' Sexuality." In *Q&A: Queer in Asian America*, edited by David L. Eng and Alice Y. Hom, 304–22. Philadelphia: Temple University Press, 1998.

Sui Sin Far (Edith Maude Eaton). "The Chinese Lily." *Out West: A Magazine of the Old Pacific and New* 28 (1908): 508–10.

——. "Leaves from the Mental Portfolio of an Eurasian." *The Independent* (1909).

—— [E. E.]. "A Plea for the Chinaman: A Correspondent's Argument in His Favor." *Montreal Daily Star*, September 21, 1896.

—— [Edith Eaton]. "Away Down in Jamaica." *The Metropolitan* 7, no. 12 (March 19, 1898): 4, 13.

—— [Fire Fly]. "The Departure of the Royal Mail." *Gall's Daily News Letter*, January 21, 1897: 3.

—— [Fire Fly]. "The Girl of the Period: At Alpha College." *Gall's Daily News Letter*, February 2, 1897: 7.

—— [Fire Fly]. "The Girl of the Period: The Theatre." *Gall's Daily News Letter*, January 28, 1897: 1.

—— [Sui Seen Far]. "Sweet Sin: A Chinese-American Story." *Land of Sunshine* 8, no. 5 (April 1898): 223–26.

—— [Unsigned]. "Chinese Religion. Information Given a Lady by Montreal Chinamen." *Montreal Daily Star*, September 21, 1895: 5.

—— [Wing Sing]. "Wing Sing of Los Angeles on His Travels." Part 5. *Los Angeles Express*, February 10, 1904: 6.

—— [Wing Sing]. "Wing Sing of Los Angeles on His Travels." *Los Angeles Express*, February 24, 1904: 6.

Suyemoto, Toyo. *I Call to Remembrance: Toyo Suyemoto's Years of Internment.* Edited by Susan B. Richardson. New Brunswick: Rutgers University Press, 2007.

Tanigawa Michio (谷川道雄), trans. Victor Xiong. "Rethinking 'Medieval China.'" *Early Medieval China* 3 (1997): 1–29.

Tapia, Ruby C. *American Pietàs: Visions of Race, Death, and the Maternal.* Minneapolis: University of Minnesota Press, 2011.

Taylor, Keeanga-Yamahtta. "The Black Plague." *The New Yorker*, April 16, 2020. https://www.newyorker.com/news/our-columnists/the-black-plague.

Tchen, John Kuo Wei, and Dylan Yeats, eds. *Yellow Peril! An Archive of Anti-Asian Fear.* London: Verso, 2014.

Teng, Emma Jinhua. *Eurasian: Mixed Identities in the United States, China, and Hong Kong, 1842–1943.* Berkeley: University of California Press, 2013.

Tennyson, Alfred. *Idylls of the King.* London: Edward Moxton, 1859.

Thomas, Ebony Elizabeth. *The Dark Fantastic: Race and the Imagination from Harry Potter to the Hunger Games.* New York: New York University Press, 2019.

Thompson, Shirley Elizabeth. *Exiles at Home: The Struggle to Become American in Creole New Orleans.* Cambridge, MA: Harvard University Press, 2009.

Tian, Xiaofei. "Pentasyllabic *Shi* Poetry: New Topics." In *How to Read Chinese Poetry: A Guided Anthology*, edited by Zong-Qi Cai, 141–60. New York: Columbia University Press, 2018.

Touati, Houari. *Islam and Travel in the Middle Ages.* Translated by Lydia G. Cochrane. Chicago: University of Chicago Press, 2010.

Twain, Mark (Samuel Langhorne Clemens). "Concerning the Jews." *Harper's Magazine*, 99, no. 592 (September 1899): 527–35.

——. *The Innocents Abroad, or The New Pilgrims' Progress.* Hartford: American, 1869.

Ty, Eleanor. *Unfastened: Globality and North Asian American Narratives.* Minneapolis: University of Minnesota Press, 2010.

U'mista Cultural Society, "Potlatch Means 'To Give.'" *Living Tradition: The Kwakwaka'wakw Potlatch on the Northwest Coast.* https://umistapotlatch.ca/potlatch-eng.php.

Untitled. *The Indianapolis Journal.* July 5, 1903: 3.

US National Parks Service, "Collections," *Frederick Douglass National Historic Site*, updated June 11, 2015. https://www.nps.gov/frdo/learn/historyculture/collections.htm.

Valdez Young, Adriana. "Honorary Whiteness." *Asian Ethnicity* 10, no. 2 (June 2009): 177–85.

Vernon, Matthew X. *The Black Middle Ages: Race and the Construction of the Middle Ages*. New York: Palgrave, 2018.

Vishnuvajjala, Usha, and Candace Barrington. "Saints and Sinners: New Orleans's Medievalisms." In *The United States of Medievalism*, edited by Susan Aronstein and Tison Pugh. Toronto: University of Toronto Press, forthcoming.

"The Visiting Knights." *Salt Lake Daily Herald.* August 18, 1883: 8.

Wallace, David. "New Chaucer Topographies." *Studies in the Age of Chaucer* 29 (2007): 3–19.

Warren, Michelle R. *Creole Medievalism: Colonial France and Joseph Bédier's Middle Ages*. Minneapolis: University of Minnesota Press, 2010.

——. "'The Last Syllable of Modernity': Chaucer in the Caribbean." *postmedieval* 6, no. 1 (April 2015): 79–93.

Wekker, Gloria. *White Innocence: Paradoxes of Colonialism and Race*. Durham: Duke University Press, 2016.

Whitaker, Cord J. "B(l)ack home in the Middle Ages: Medievalism in Jessie Redmon Fauset's 'My House and a Glimpse of My Life Therein.'" *postmedieval* 10, no. 2 (June 2019): 162–75.

——. *Black Metaphors: How Modern Racism Emerged from Medieval Race-Thinking*. Philadelphia: University of Pennsylvania Press, 2019.

——. *The Harlem Middle Ages: Color, Time, and Harlem Renaissance Medievalism*, forthcoming.

——, ed. "Making Race Matter in the Middle Ages." *postmedieval* 6, no. 1 (April 2015).

——. "Race-ing the Dragon: The Middle Ages, Race and Trippin' into the Future." *postmedieval* 6, no. 1 (April 2015): 3–11.

—— and Matthew Gabriele, eds. "The Ghosts of the Nineteenth Century and the Future of Medieval Studies." *postmedieval* 10, no. 2 (June 2019): 127–265.

White-Parks, Annette. "We Wear the Mask: Sui Sin Far as One Example of Trickster Authorship." In *Tricksterism in Turn-of-the-Century American Literature: A Multicultural Perspective*, edited by Elizabeth Amons and Annette White-Parks, 1–20. Hanover: University Press of New England, 1994.

Whitman, Albery Allson. *Not a Man, and Yet a Man*. Springfield: Republic, 1877.

Wilhite, David E. "Augustine the African: Post-colonial, Postcolonial, and Post-Postcolonial Readings." *Journal of Postcolonial Theory and Theology* 5, no. 1 (July 2014): 1–34.

Wilson, Charles E., Jr., "Medievalism, Race, and Social Order in Gloria Naylor's *Bailey's Café*." In *Medievalism and the Academy, II: Cultural Studies*, edited by David Metzger, 74–91. Cambridge: Brewer, 2000.

Wilson, Ivy G. *At the Dusk of Dawn: Selected Poetry and Prose of Albery Allson Whitman*. Lebanon: Northeastern University Press, 2009.

Wong, Ao. "Poetry and Literati Friendship: Bai Juyi and Yuan Zhen." In *How to Read Chinese Poetry in Context: Poetic Culture from Antiquity Through the Tang*, edited by Zong-Qi Cai, 240–60. New York: Columbia University Press, 2018.

Wong Chin Foo (王清福; sometimes written as 黃清福). "The Chinese Drama." *Elkhart Daily Review*, August 28, 1883.

——. "The Chinese in New York." *The Cosmopolitan* 5, no. 4 (June 1888): 297–311.

——. "The Chinese Stage." *Texas Siftings*, May 19, 1883.

——. "Poh Yuin Ko, The Serpent-Princess: A Chinese Christmas Story." *The Cosmopolitan* 6, no. 2 (December 1888): 180–90.

——. "To Produce the Chinese Drama." *New York Tribune*, September 2, 1883.

———. "Why Am I a Heathen?" *The North American Review* 145, no. 369 (August 1887): 169–79.

———. *Wu Chih Tien, The Celestial Empress: A Historical Chinese Novel*, serialized in *The Cosmopolitan* 6, no. 4 (February 1889): 327–34; 6, no. 5 (March 1889): 477–85; 6, no. 6 (April 1889): 564–72; 7, no. 1 (May 1889): 65–72; 7, no. 2 (June 1889): 128–32; 7, no. 3 (July 1889): 289–99; 7, no. 4 (August 1889): 361–68; 7, no. 5 (September 1889): 449–59.

Wong, Edlie L. *Racial Reconstruction: Chinese Exclusion, Black Inclusion, and the Fictions of Citizenship*. New York: New York University Press, 2015.

Wong, Edward Hon-Sing. "Sinophobia Won't Save You from the Coronavirus." *Al Jazeera*, February 8, 2020. https://www.aljazeera.com/indepth/opinion/sinophobia-won-save-coronavirus-200208165854849.html.

Wood, Karenne. "Abracadabra, an Abecedarian." In Karenne Wood, *Weaving the Boundary*, 21. Tucson: University of Arizona Press, 2016.

Wu, Judy Tzu-Chun. *Radicals on the Road: Internationalism, Orientalism, and Feminism during the Vietnam Era*. Ithaca: Cornell University Press, 2013.

Yao, Christine "Xine." "Black-Asian Counterintimacies: Reading Sui Sin Far in Jamaica." *J19: Journal of Nineteenth-Century Americanists* 6, no. 1 (Spring 2018): 197–204.

Yao, Steven G. "Transplantation and Modernity: The Chinese/ American Poems of Angel Island." In *Sinographies: Writing China*, edited by Eric Hayot, Haun Saussy, and Steven G. Yao, 300–329. Minneapolis: University of Minnesota Press, 2008.

Yin, Xiao-huang. *Chinese American Literature Since the 1950s*. Chicago: University of Illinois Press, 2000.

Young, Helen. *Race and Popular Fantasy Literature: Habits of Whiteness*. New York: Routledge, 2016.

Yu, Timothy. *100 Chinese Silences*. Los Angeles: Les Figues, 2016.

Yu Danico, Mary. "The Anti-Asian Racism During the COVID-19 Pandemic Has Everything to Do with Black Lives Matter." *Medium*, June 22, 2020. https://medium.com/intertrend/the-anti-asian-racism-during-the-covid-19-pandemic-has-everything-to-do-with-black-lives-matter-732daae222c6.

Yung, Judy. "Poetry and the Politics of Chinese Immigration on Angel Island: Q&A with Judy Yung." University of Washington Press blog, December 10, 2014. https://uwpressblog.com/2014/12/10/poetry-and-the-politics-of-chinese-immigration-on-angel-island-qa-with-judy-yung/.

Yung Wing (容閎). *My Life in China and America*. New York: Holt, 1909.

Zhang Jie (张洁). "Racism Hinders the Fight Against COVID-19." *Language on the Move*, February 25, 2020. https://www.languageonthemove.com/racism-hinders-the-fight-against-covid-19.

INDEX

scenes, 94–96; antisemitism and racism, 25, 83n23, 85, 94, 107, 123; religious syncretism, 95–96, 122; *stella maris* (star of the sea) motif, 85, 96; whiteness, 49n31, 82–83, 95

Martin, Trayvon, 125

masculinities. *See* gendered identities

Mazu (媽祖). *See* Guanyin

medievalisms: affect, xiii, 6, 20–21; antiracist critique, xiii, 7, 17–18; cultural appropriations, 3, 14, 15–18; definitions, xi, 6, 8–9, 19; disidentifications, 4–9, 15, 20, 22, 23, 88–89, 100, 113; toxic, 12, 14

Mediterranean cultures, 41, 129

melancholia (racial), 60

Melbourne, Australia, 128, 130, 131

mestiza identities. *See* hybridity, cultural

Mexican American identities, xv, 15n91, 126–28; Anzaldúa, Gloria, 127–28; Mundo, Frank, 126–28

Mexico/US borderlands and migrants, 30, 32, 71–72, 113n70, 127–28

Middle English (adaptations), 1, 17, 111–13. *See also* Chaucerian adaptations

Middle English language, 22, 111–12, 117–18, 121

migrants, xv, 21, 63–66, 71–73, 113n70, 127, 128–30, 132; border policing, 73, 127, 130, 132. *See also* immigration rights and restrictions; mobilities; refugees

migration. *See* mobilities.

minstrel show (racist performance tradition), 10n58

misogynoir (anti-Black misogyny), 10n58, 26

misogyny, 10n58, 26, 47, 88, 112–13, 118–19; anti-Asian, 47; anti-Black, 10n58, 26, 88, 119; intersections with racism, 112–13, 119; medieval, 118

missionaries, 33, 35–36, 52, 59–60, 92, 94, 96, 108; discourse and ideology, 35–36, 52; missionary gaze, 59–60, 94; settler colonialism, 108; "white savior" tropes, 59, 92–93

mixed-race identities. *See* multiracial identities

Miyashiro, Adam, 3, 100

mobilities (migration and travel), 32, 36, 39, 41, 67, 72, 78, 115–16, 128; migration rights, 32, 128; physical restrictions, 57, 69–73; travel and race, 116; travel restrictions, 78. *See also* immigration rights and restrictions; incarceration; refugees; travel writing

"model minority" myth, 37

monastic communities, 40–41, 113; hermits, 41, 113. *See also* convents

Montreal, 89–90, 91, 92, 96–97

Morrison, Toni, 25–26

Mulan. *See Ballad of Mulan*

multilingual writing. *See* code-switching; translingual writing; triglossia

multiracial identities, 5, 22, 29–30, 56, 58, 79–82, 85, 87, 88–94, 103, 111–13, 126–28; and language, 82, 85, 111–12, 127–28; "Eurasian" identities, 22, 58, 79, 88–93. *See also* Brolaski, Julian Talamantez; Creoles of color; Dunbar-Nelson, Alice; *mestiza* identities; Mundo, Frank; passing; Revard, Carter; Sui Sin Far

Mundo, Frank, 122, 125–28; *The Brubury Tales*, 122, 125–26, 128; "How I Became a Mexican," 126–27

Muñoz, José Esteban, 4, 15, 20, 23, 88, 100, 113, 127n94

Muslim cultures and identities, 3, 5, 39, 40–41, 78n71, 129. *See also* Islamophobia

"nation language." *See* Afro-Caribbean writers

Native American writers. *See* Indigenous writers

Naylor, Gloria, 116

Négritude, 111

Nelson, Marilyn: *The Cachoeira Tales*, 121–22

neologisms, 111–13

New Orleans, LA. *See* Louisiana

New York City, NY, 12–14, 39–40, 49–55, 81; Chinatown, 12–14, 49–55, 81; Little Syria, 39–40; Lower East Side, 52

New York (state), 91

Ng, Su Fang, 45, 77

Wheatley, Phillis, 110

Whitaker, Cord J., 3, 4–5, 15, 16, 37n88, 45, 87n48, 91n76, 116

white supremacy: as ideology, 3, 26, 118; as violent power structure, 3, 7, 26, 83n23, 118; linguistic norms, 117–18; settler colonialism, 3, 21, 30, 77, 100–101, 108–9, 113, 119, 131–32

whiteness: as condition of harm or contagion, 46, 60; as property, 8, 20, 27n32, 101; as unattainable ideal, 5, 60, 81–83, 108; as unmarked norm, 57, 100–101, 116, 125–26, 128, 131; critical whiteness studies, 6; honorary, 36, 55, 61; white innocence, 24, 45, 107, 108–9. *See also* passing; white supremacy

Whitman, Albery Allson: *Not a Man, and Yet a Man*, 29–30

Wong Chin Foo (王清福), 13–14, 21, 23, 33–37, 41, 43, 46, 51–53, 55, 62; autoethnography, 13–14, 50–52, 55, 62; "The Chinese in New York," 13–14, 50–52, 54; "Poh Yuin Kuo, the Serpent-Princess," 14; journalism and essays, 14, 53, 62; "Why Am I a Heathen?" 33–34; *Wu Chih Tien, the Celestial Empress*, 14, 34. *See also* Chinese Equal Rights League

Wong, Edlie L., 16, 32, 33, 37

Wood, Karenne, 109, 113; "Abracadabra, an Abecedarian," 109

Wu, Cynthia, 61

xenophobia, xii, 2, 3, 21, 45–46, 78, 119, 131–32. *See also* antisemitism; refugees; "Yellow Peril"

Yang, Gene Luen, 93n87

Yao, Christine "Xine," 88, 89

Yao, Steven G., 67, 72

Yee of Toishan (台山余題). *See* anonymous Chinese migrant poems

Yee, Tet (Yee Tet Ming), 75, 76n54

yellow (racial term), 88–89

yellow journalism. *See* "Yellow Peril"

"Yellow Peril" (Anti-Asian xenophobia and racism): definition, 43; in Australia, 131–32; in Britain, 46n21; in Canada, 12, 21, 76, 89; in the United States, 13, 21, 43, 45–46, 56, 60–62, 65; journalism, 13, 43–45, 89; medieval European origins, 44–45; "rat libel," 13, 49–52, 81; "yellow journalism," 43–45, 89; "yellow medievalism," 89. *See also* Chinatowns; COVID-19 (coronavirus) pandemic: anti-Asian racism; sinophobia

Yu, Timothy, 105–7, 113; "Chinese Silence No. 85," 106–7

Yung, Judy, 65n4, 70n28, 76

Yung Wing (容閎), 35–36

Zu Di (祖迪), 72